NO LAND AN ISLAND
NO PEOPLE APART

NonViolence THE BETTER WAY

No Land an Island
No People Apart

Foreign Relations • Human Costs • Mediterranean
Horn of Africa crossing Red Sea • Gulfs Aden Arabia Persia Asia

Chronicle of Continued BREAKDOWN

Dr. Carolyn LaDelle Bennett

Author of Same Ole or Something New & BREAKDOWN

This book was printed in the United States of America.

To order additional copies of this book, contact:
Xlibris Corporation
1-888-795-4274
www.Xlibris.com
Orders@Xlibris.com
113472

Contents

Preface

NO LAND AN ISLAND: No People Apart

*I look upon the whole world as my fatherland and every war has
to me the horror of a family-feud. I look upon true patriotism as
the brotherhood of man and the service of all to all.*
—Helen Keller

Idols and images in the United States have created and entrenched a narrow worldview, which is opposite the one I hold. Rising from a sense of society (whole and interdependent, each responsible to and for one another), my worldview says if indeed this land is my land, it is ours/theirs the world over equally to share.

Contrary to this worldview is the attitude across the United States of America that all land belongs to America to use and abuse, to pillage and plunder. There is an attitude abroad in this my native "land of the free and home of the brave" that *our* way is superior to every other people's way. Made by gods we manufacture, a destiny we contrive, we are wonderful; in a far less than perfect union, we are the "greatest." So much so that the world's people not only hunger for "our" way—our form of government, our form of economy, our careless waste and conspicuous consumption—they gladly relinquish their ways, deny their own to serve the self-indulgence of the United States of America.

Not only that but they thank us for driving them to their knees, reversing their progress, enslaving them in a status quo we sustain by lethal force. Those who refuse to fall for our delusion, fail to join our armies against their best interests, we destroy. We destroy their land, their culture, their structures and institutions, their relations near and far. In our breakdown, we create theirs.

NO LAND IS AN ISLAND NO PEOPLE ARE APART—I have thought about a great deal these past few years as a creed and worldview.

What happens in the farthest corner of the world happens to us, affects us. And the model in foreign relations, a model drenched in violence, executed by the U.S. government—our government, its political figures, agents, and corporate collaborators—leaves lasting scars not only on individuals but also on relations among groups of people within and across countries, geographical regions, and continents. Since my 2009 work *BREAKDOWN*, the United States of America has continued its global reckless relations in violence (waging war and invasion, committing assassination and torture, occupying countries with impunity, creating chaos, stoking conflict), deepening fissures, laying bare its own mental, moral, and institutional breakdown in an incessant attack on the life force, which is essential to well-being, to progress, to world society.

In this book are words and images, a case of *continued BREAKDOWN;* and a plea for our embrace of a different worldview:

NO LAND AN ISLAND
NO PEOPLE APART

Introduction

We cannot exist as a little island of well-being in a world where two-thirds of the people go to bed hungry every night.
—Eleanor Roosevelt

PARADIGM OF U.S. FOREIGN RELATIONS IN VIOLENCE CAUSES REGRESS IN GLOBAL SOCIETY

In the public space, government figures, their militaries, media, and other agents weave a continuous web of propaganda; and the people absorb it mindlessly—unquestioningly. Like osmosis or a date with Jonestown, Americans (though not exclusively Americans but my focus is American because I am one) accept and believe the unacceptable, that which is implausible, highly unlikely. The people of the United States en masse accept the ridiculous notion that their government officials kill people (order their deaths) in manufactured wars and conflict (in Afghanistan, Pakistan, Iraq, Libya, Somalia) for "humanitarian" reasons, an idea that is ludicrous on its face. Hegemonic killers killing tyrants, often tyrants with whom they have allied from time to time as suited political expediency, avarice or caprice against the very people—in the course of massacring children, women, and families—they now don a halo as their "savior."

United States foreign relations in violence has waged more than ten years of war on the people of Afghanistan "to save the women" from their fellow citizens known as the Taliban who, in some other incarnation, allied with the United States. The U.S. model of foreign relations wages a remote (drone) war on the people of Afghanistan's neighbor, Pakistan, to supply the continuing war on the Afghan people (and, beyond that, to dominate the land, waterways, and peoples of the region that encompasses eastern Africa, the Middle East, South Central Asia, extending its reach to the north and east). U.S. government figures claim "humanitarian" the air bombing of defenseless people in Libya and Somalia (some already refugees), driving them from their land and farms and homes, creating floods of refugees flowing deep into the countryside, across borders, into the Mediterranean waters, reversing years of movement toward achieving basics in health, food, water, electricity, and facilities. By killing and displacing millions of people, the United States is "saving the world" from U.S.-made "al-Qaeda" or some other conveniently labeled and designated "bad" people: "Taliban," "terrorists," "rebels," "freedom fighters," "militants," "combatants."

In *Before and After: U.S. Foreign Policy and the September 11th Crisis*, Phyllis Bennis writes, "In the context of September 11th, U.S. arrogance takes the form of hypocrisy. The U.S. purports to champion democracy as the linchpin of U.S. foreign policy, while continuing to prop up governments famous for denying any hint of democracy to their own peoples . . . . We may not know for sure the exact motives of the architects of the September [2001] assault. But it is a pretty good bet that the fury of those who cheered them on—in Saudi Arabia, in Indonesia, in Gaza, in Uzbekistan—was fueled not by hatred of American democracy, but at least in part by American support for far-flung governments denying their people the same democracy the U.S. claims to stand for . . . throughout the [Arab Middle East] region." Phyllis Bennis writes, "It is common knowledge that . . . the call for democratization that shapes U.S. policy toward so many other countries is virtually *absent* regarding Saudi Arabia, Kuwait, the United Arab Emirates, and most other Gulf states."

During the seventh year of U.S. violence against Afghanistan, Afghan activist Zoya of the Foreign Committee of the Revolutionary Association of the Women of Afghanistan wrote:

> The U.S. government and its allies were successfully able to legitimize their military invasion on Afghanistan and deceive the people of the U.S. and the world under the banners of "liberating Afghan women," "democracy" and "war on terror." The Taliban's dominance had tormented and oppressed our people and they were filled with hope but soon their dream

of the establishment of security, democracy and freedom was shattered in the most painful manner . . . by the installation of the puppet government of [Afghanistan President Hamid] Karzai, the U.S. reused its creations and continued its deal with the Jehadi criminal warlords.

In a 2009 interview, she said, "The U.S. government has never supported democratic organizations." Zoya concluded her 2009 discussion by urging "all the intellectuals, all the democratic forces and progressive and independence-seeking people" in contravention to U.S. violence and as their duty

> [t]o rise in a constant and decisive struggle for independence and democracy by supporting our wounded people as the independent force against the presence of the U.S. and its allies and the domination of Jehadi and Taliban criminals. Combating the armed and alien forces in the country without being loud-mouthed against the Talibi and Jehadi enemies would mean welcoming the misfortunes of fascism and religious mafia . . . . Struggling against this enemy without fighting the military presence of the U.S., its allies and its puppet government would mean falling before foreign agents.

The pretexts and excuses—saving the women or instituting some form of "democracy"—are all lies. Circular reasoning, contradiction, plain nonsense served up in aid of entrenched opportunism, a military industrial complex, and other private interests that pay government officials *not* to serve the public good, *not* to accurately inform, *not* to properly represent poorly educated, distracted people bamboozled by mass media's round-the-clock-widescreen propaganda packaged powerfully in a concentrated enterprise peddling the latest drugs and toys.

We create war to create war, conflict to create conflict. While U.S. political figures dominating the public space make false charges about international bodies' encroaching upon U.S. sovereignty, the United States repeatedly and with impunity violates other nations' sovereignty. Worst of all, the United States has commandeered a nearly two-hundred-nation body, the United Nations, as instrument of its will—partner in propaganda, violator of law and convention (domestic and international) and universal declaration of human rights—as continuous aggressor (bombs to "peacekeepers") against the world's nations including member states of the United Nations.

In the book I published in 2009, I wrote, "Breakdown domestically is the living reality and consequence of U.S. violence abroad. It is the wounded civil society violated repeatedly. Vital domestic structures, programs and institutions savagely downsized, outsourced, deconstructed at every possible level. Violence is the heart of Breakdown." Through 2010 and 2011, under another executive in the Washington White House, the breakdown continued, and this time I focus exclusively on U.S. hostilities against other peoples of the world, a foreign relations in violence, which insidiously forms an unbroken line, an intersect with U.S. domestic conditions. Whether or not cocooned Americans choose to embrace it, it is a principle I have given a great deal of thought to over the past year; and though a seeming paradox, it rings true for me: No land is an island and no people are apart.

The wind and storms; drought and famine; airborne, inborn, and associative diseases and their complex mutations; rising waters and razed forests and mountains; polluted air; scarcity of food, land, water, and other resources amid plenty among the few; indifference and amorality; cruelty and conflict; corruption and war; plunder and poverty and retribution—all and their consequences redound to us. We are responsible and should feel responsible and act mutually responsibly. Washington's global campaign in foreign affairs has been a deadly crusade in the cause and continuance of what Bennis calls "American-style law of empire."

The Revolutionary Association of the Women of Afghanistan (RAWA), an independent political/social organization of Afghan women fighting for human rights and social justice in Afghanistan, declares, "Freedom, democracy and justice cannot be enforced at gunpoint by a foreign country. Freedom, democracy and justice are values that can be achieved only by our [that is, Afghan] people and democracy-loving forces through a hard, decisive and long struggle. Those who claim to donate these values to the Afghan people through force will only push our country into slavery."

The current state of U.S. foreign relations ignores the principle "No land is an island, no people are apart," preferring instead to perpetuate the status quo, and the problem with the status quo is *regress*. The world naturally moves. As elements in the atmosphere, water on stone, human beings tuned in to and respectful of a shared humanity, the world evolves. The world is in constant change—the status quo is motionless, entrenched, out of step—holding on, it trends backward; promotes regress. Vested interest maintains as against tidal waves, only through force not in compelling ideas or persuasive argument but in raw brutality—threat and propaganda, invasion and occupation—violence.

Pattern of U.S. Foreign Relations in Violence

Create chaos, stoke conflict, then dispatch bombs ("humanitarian" bombs), killing defenseless people to "save the women" (though never the women and children of the Gaza Strip or Occupied Territories) or to protect "U.S. interests" in places where threat has never risen against the United States of America. The pattern is perpetual, the cycle endless and endlessly violent: create chaos and stoke conflict then invade then feign restoration while wasting billions in lives and resources with governmental and nongovernmental agents who, in a well-crafted process of regression, continue to plunder and damage and stir up animosity, making nothing whole (or restored) either in physical infrastructures, hurt, or human relations.

Time and again—all the while lying to the American people and the world—this pattern is acted out by one after another political cabal operating from federal Washington. Violence creating endless violence is the heart and the drive of a U.S. foreign relations paradigm whose essence and consequence, in my view, is a global state of mental, physical, moral, ethical, law-of-nations breakdown.

"In Violence" Instead of "In Blood"

I use the terms "in violence" instead of "in blood" in this book because the U.S. relations paradigm acted out with peoples of the world is not a one-time or even several times' bloodletting. It is an ethos, a character, a constant state of preemption, bullying, and provocation (inherent violence) endlessly far reaching in time, geography, generation, and memory. It destroys families, futures and relations, homes, lives, and livelihoods. It creates and sustains a mind-set, a domestic and global cycle of violence and retaliation in violence. Rooted in a medieval mentality of lord and lesser (i.e., the latter of lower breed, significance, quality or status), the U.S. foreign relations model legitimates its own violation of law. By fiat and brute force, it creates its own laws, enforces and executes with the sweeping impunity of a callous, nuclear-powered, self-justifying tyrant, leaving a trail of consequences ripping apart the fabric, the essential construct, of society and causing endlessly comprehensive breakdown.

This truth is hard but one that we Americans must face without turning away, without escape or denial.

Crisis, Consequences: Rule of Law becomes U.S.-led Global Lawlessness

Online *Pravda* editor David Hoffman in an editorial "America Is Still Dead" (October 3, 2011) alludes to what I believe also expresses the heart and drive of continued breakdown. "Freedom requires people to think for themselves," Hoffman writes, "and to gather facts and information necessary to formulate reasoned judgments or opinions. Freedom also means making difficult, sometimes life-altering decisions, with no guarantee those decisions will reap any positive results [but] . . . fascism favors emotion over reason, appeals to the basest instincts in human nature, and creates omnipotent demagogues who tell the masses what to think and how to think. Freed from the burden of making decisions . . . people can then pretend they are blameless for and powerless to prevent atrocities and injustices committed by the people in power." Hoffman's geography and his knowledge of its history entitle him to know of what he speaks.

> Given the kidnappings, illegal detentions, tortures and murders that have already been committed in the name of the so-called "war on terror," it is frighteningly clear that the American government may be traversing a path of no return. Arrogant, militarily powerful and lacking a viable foe to curb its contempt for international law—the United States government feels 'superior' to every other country in the world. As a result, it has become a lawless, rogue nation operating under the clandestine philosophy that "might makes right" while openly (and hypocritically) cloaking itself in the garments of "freedom," "justice" and "human rights."

Domination, Assassination, War Crime

The United States in 2011, while bombing Afghanistan, Iraq, Pakistan, and Somalia, also attacked Libya and assassinated its head of state. Yet among the heads of state hauled before the International Criminal Court (ICC) in the Hague, none has been a World War II ally or a permanent member state (United States, United Kingdom, France, China, or the Russian Federation) of the UN Security Council.

In light of this status quo, interesting implications could attach to the "war crime" issue raised late last year in the Libya-Qaddafi case. In December 2011, the chief prosecutor of the International Criminal Court (ICC), Luis Moreno-Ocampo, said there "are serious suspicions that the death of Libyan leader Muammar Qaddafi may be a war crime." On October 20, eight months into the revolution that put an end to Qaddafi's forty-two-year rule, "revolutionary fighters found Muammar Qaddafi hiding inside a concrete sewage pipe in his hometown of Sirte." Videos taken at the time show the Libyan leader injured but alive and surrounded by a frenzied crowd. "He is hustled through revolutionaries and beaten to the ground on several occasions." Qaddafi "then disappears in the crush and the crackle of gunfire." On October 25, the senior Qaddafi and his slain son Mu'tassim were buried in a secret location in Libya. What is deeply troubling about this case, as facts revealed at year's end (one example in a pattern of U.S. foreign relations crimes), is its endemic contagion in lawlessness. Nations of "civilized" people without exception operate under the rule of law. The rule of law knits societies as society, global or domestic, each for all, not each according to whim, expediency, or pathology.

The rule of law is a discipline imposed (and should be adhered to) not to deny liberty but to secure liberty for all. Selfish, amoral people fail or refuse to understand that "freedom" is not individual license to do *whatever* a person or political figure wants to do or that discipline is a yoke around the neck of the individual or individualism. Quite the contrary, *discipline frees*. Unchecked, limitless action based on political expediency, brute force, caprice, greed, emotion, ideology—one or more of these as exemplified in the model of U.S. foreign relations—is tyranny, autocracy, cruelty.

When one nation possessing inordinate power backed by enormous weaponry and inordinate transnational corporate influence breaches law with impunity, there is no rule of law. The result is a breakdown in the structures of law, not only within the country holding such power but also throughout the world. The United States' unilateral conduct of a "global war on 'terror'" or "'terrorism'" (depending on convenient usage) opened the door for anybody in the world including within the United States—any powerful (or deranged) person, faction, ruler or warlord, military, intelligence, security agency, or police—to shout "terrorist" or "terrorism" before or after killing or torturing (or both) anybody else. Shouts of "fire in a crowd" may aim to settle old scores. The course and fallout of this U.S. *war on whatever* has slaughtered, wounded, and caused the deaths of countless millions of people and ruined lives for generations.

Some commentators especially those within the United States argue that the violence, the lawlessness in U.S. foreign relations, puts a stain on U.S. "reputation" or "image" in the world, but this critique falls far short of assessing the damage. It sees only a surface, a narrowed frame without context or contribution of history, and falls into the same trap that fuels the United States' individualistic, unilateral, often-coerced bilateral (coalitions of the willing) lawlessness. The foundation, implications, and consequences of U.S. foreign relations are much farther reaching than reputation or image. A superpowered nation in league with select often-secret interests—like toxic assets snaking through international economies and banking systems, like for-hire global militaries but worse, killing for sport, manipulating international conventions, operating beyond check of impartial standards of law; this pervasive unprincipled power is at the heart of continuing breakdown.

NO LAND AN ISLAND
No People Apart

Through the lens of news and current affairs, history, and geography, I look again at U.S. relations this time, more narrowly, with Afghanistan and Pakistan, Iran and Iraq, Libya, and Somalia; the human costs crossing borders and waters; and, again, find a model in violence and its consequence: *continued breakdown.*

Illustrating this *continued BREAKDOWN* are words and pictures of a U.S. foreign relations model in violence and its human costs from the Mediterranean to the Red Sea to Arabia to Persia. I present eight core chapters centered mainly on the South Central Asian countries of Afghanistan and Pakistan, Persia's Iraq and Iran, and North and Eastern

Africa's Libya and Somalia. I have based the content in these chapters on news, current affairs, and commentary sources outside the "CNN-ized" U.S. mass media. Further background material on content and sources follows the summary in the sources and notes and appendix sections directly preceding the index.

This book is unconcerned with political figures per se (or their parties). Certainly not with government, mass media, or any other celebrities or personalities but rather with a malignant system maintained by a parade of tentacled regimes whose official (elected) base of operation begins in the capital of the United States, a system that is seemingly endorsed by the people of the United States. The intent of the book is to further or *differently* inform on the issue of an entrenched, severely damaging ethos and character acted out in U.S. foreign relations; and, linked to it, the nature and faces of some of the suffering and some of the people who suffer.

In *NO LAND AN ISLAND No People Apart*, I challenge us to face the callously immoral, lawless, relentlessly regressive model in U.S. foreign relations and to embrace a true progressivism, an inclusive, collective progressivism imbued with a sense of global society, a sensibility that inspires constructive, continuous forward movement.

I

Heartache and Hotspots

[S]ome people might imagine the silence of guns to be nonviolence but such a silence is merely the dim early enlightenment of anti-violence. To commit oneself to live without arms no matter what happens requires a much deeper pilgrimage—and that pilgrimage is one that many conventional politicians who lecture terrorists have not themselves made.
                                        —Mairead Corrigan Maguire

(U.S. war regions): Arabian/Iranian Basin/Somali Basin/ Persian Gulf (Gulf of Aden/Red Sea/Arabian Sea): Iraq/ Kuwait/ Iran/Bahrain/Yemen/Horn of Africa/Somalia; Arabian Sea: Pakistan/Afghanistan/Iran; Mediterranean Sea gateway to Europe: Libya/Egypt (south)/Palestine (east)

The *BREAKDOWN* I observed in 2009 continued and worsened as the years passed. Young people in 2011 in the United States belatedly offered up mostly self-absorbed protests they called occupy (or an "occupation" movement), an unfortunate usage considering the baggage, history, and connotation of the term—most critically in the Middle East, regionally, and in the Occupied Territories, where U.S. engagement for years has been outrageous.

Occupy and occupation, if we take into account only the most recent sixty-year memory, have been closely, painfully and callously connected with U.S.-partnered Israel in Palestine, its brutal blockade and massacre of people of the Gaza Strip just a few years ago (December 2008-January 2009), and its unchecked, ceaseless taking of lands, the ethnic "cleansing" of a people. Occupy and occupation have long described the United States' brutal presence across landmasses from the Atlantic to the Pacific—besides the Americas; North, West and East Africa; South Central, Middle and Far East Asia—before and after U.S. attacks by cluster bombs, assassination drones, nuclear bombs; and whatever else may fit categories of small, conventional, and otherwise lethal weaponry.

Taken by themselves, "occupy" and "occupation" may be kinder terms for the violent taking of land, the brutal oppression, the annihilation of native and indigenously peoples' right across the globe, from Canada to Southern Africa, South America to the Arctic Circle. However, protest and resistance (even *sit-in*) are more apt and long-honored descriptors the young people (self-described "occupiers") failed to choose (intelligent adults, scholars who knew better smiled and went along), thus putting in bold relief an American *secret* well-known to the outside world: That there is a herd mentality in the United States and a serious defect in U.S. education. U.S. education establishments—from primary school to Princeton and everywhere in between—create tests and test administers, test thieves, and test takers, but fail to instill critical intellect, moral and ethical intuitiveness, facility for independent thought, critical judgment, human sensibility, a worldview of society that is essential for contemporary times. Large numbers of people who enter, stay a while and leave U.S. institutions of learning (some purchase their completion papers) and later attach to private or public enterprises (educational, governmental, nongovernmental, sectarian, mercenary, one or all these)—tend to exude an air of selfish entitlement. They display a boastful arrogance, a careless deliberate ignorance of meaning and history (U.S. history, foreign relations, world cultures) and of the historical contexts in which current affairs and contemporary events play out.

The young U.S. "occupiers" fancied themselves "in solidarity" with (or benefactors of) Egyptian protesters playing on U.S. mass media but less so with a Tunisian immolation that had sparked a revolution before Tahrir Square: a man in protest had set himself on fire. Even so, these are ancient societies, Tunisian and Egyptian, where people have been long aware of their oppression, an oppression often aided and abetted by the West (Western Europe, North America). The peoples of these countries have suffered decades under despots, invaders, and occupiers; and they are fighting (mostly nonviolently) for their lives, for their future, for their country and freedom within it. Americans whine about starter houses and second homes, flexible mortgages, vacant properties, and flipping real estate. Millions of the world's people, from the Middle East's Occupied Territories to the Horn of Africa and points farther west and east, live (if you can call it living) on borders, in camps, on the ground in open air, on dusty roads, running to escape conflict and U.S. bombs.

As the year 2012 dawned in the United States, the U.S. occupiers' sense of history was unclear to me; as was the question of whether they were fighting (nonviolently) for the rights of all: for other peoples' rights and the sovereignty of their countries, for justice under law for all, for the future, for country and freedom within it. To compartmentalize liberty seems criminally ridiculous to me. In contemporary times (the time in which I live), I cannot take seriously a myopic movement focused on issues of domestic class, income, and political tribe and conveniently blind to (or disconnected from) a super-nuclear-powered (bought) government that wields an entrenched violence-prone apparatus, cutting a path of endless death, displacement, and repression through the lives of the world's defenseless peoples.

This is a picture mostly in words of a U.S. foreign relations paradigm in violence acted out and with deadly effect—extensive repression and human misery: displacement, poverty, denial of human rights, constant upheaval, corruption, and rippling conflict—on the lives of peoples of the Middle East Region including South Central Asia and North and East Africa.

At the end of 2011, I counted the countries where there was some form of U.S. aggression and came up with twenty-six. This aggression was endless and took a variety of forms the consequences of which devastated peoples of Afghanistan and Pakistan, Iraq and Iran, Bahrain and Yemen, Somalia, and Libya.

> Abducting foreign nationals (as well as U.S. nationals); engaging in unlawful search, detention and torture; arming all sides; using violent rhetoric in taking sides (any expedient side) in conflict and bankrolling (often manufactured) "rebels" to create domestic and regional pressure; committing direct aggression (invasion, war, long-distance or remote-controlled missile strikes, assassination) and direct/indirect threat/ intimidation; provoking/inciting to protracted violence;

planting and sustaining occupations which effectively displace nations' sovereignty (*creating global migrations and attacking immigrants*); uprooting and displacing thousands of people and destabilizing geopolitical regions; crippling peoples and governments with malicious economic/financial sanctions; failing nations; and failing to negotiate with words or nonviolent diplomacy were continuing forms of U.S. aggression well into 2012.

United States at War with the World's Peoples and Their Countries	
Afghanistan	Bahrain
Cuba	Djibouti
Eritrea	Ethiopia
Haiti	Honduras
Iran	Iraq
Japan (Okinawa)	Kenya
Libya	Mexico
Nigeria	North Korea
Pakistan	Palestine
Russia	Saudi Arabia
Somalia	South Korea
Syria	Turkey
Uganda (dominoes the Sudan, South Sudan, Central African Republic, Republic of the Congo [Brazzaville], Democratic Republic of the Congo [Kinshasa])	Yemen

War never ends when politicians and war makers announce its ending.

Today's Insight News, Saturday, October 22, 2011: War, Conflict Cause Migration, Disease

Violence has far-reaching and long-term consequences. The International Organization for Migration (IOM) along with other organizations pitches in to help when war creates migrants, forcing thousands of people to leave their homes. At the start of the unrest in Libya, IOM began helping with the evacuation of thousands of stranded migrants within Libya and principally at the border with Egypt, Tunisia, and Niger. The chart below shows some of their findings.

Pakistan/Yar Hussain/ Women and children in camps.
Photo UNHCR

IOM cross-border movements map as of October 7, 2011

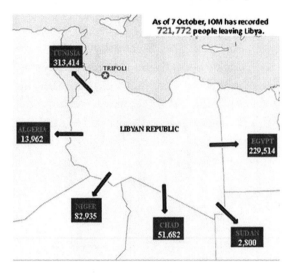

Egypt

Between September 30 and October 6: 2,253 migrants (210 were TCNs) crossed the Egyptian border, bringing the cumulative total of arrivals to 229,514 migrants.

Tunisia

Between September 30 and October 6: 9,287 migrants (335 were TCNs) crossed the border, bringing the cumulative total of arrivals to 313,414 migrants.

Disease, climate, conflict, oppression
Lack of wherewithal for essentials:
Electricity, safe water, facilities

Scabies in Africa

October 11, 2011, Libya/Egypt—in early September, migrants and refugees who had fled Libya and were temporarily at the Salloum transit center awaiting onward transportation complained of skin infections, allergies, and rashes. IOM identified the infection and added health volunteers to reinforce the work of their health team.

Four hundred people had scabies. As a precautionary measure, IOM said they gave treatment to all migrants and refugees (1,400). Their team of specialists, in collaboration with the Egyptian ministry of health and

the UNHCR (United Nations High Commissioner for Refugees), gave scabies infection treatment to one

Kenya/Somali Refugees/Dadaab.
Photo UNHCR/R. Gangale May 2010

thousand migrants and refugees at the Salloum border crossing between Libya and Egypt.

Scabies is an itchy highly contagious skin disease caused by an infestation by the itch mite. It transmits by close personal contact with an infected individual and spreads rapidly. Scabies causes skin rashes and severe relentless itching. Small children and babies are particularly prone to scabies infections.

Cholera, Climate Change, Hunger, Unsafe Water, Conflict in Africa

The World Health Organization has reported an estimated 3 to 5 million cholera cases worldwide annually and 100,000 to 120,000 deaths from the disease whose short incubation period of two hours to five days enhances the potentially explosive pattern of outbreaks.

A 2010 midyear UNICEF report said, for a while, a good performance of rains initiated a process of recovery for drought-affected women and children in Kenya's pastoral and marginal agricultural areas, but the recovery was uneven and diminished by persistently high food prices. The cumulative impact of earlier poor rainy seasons had diminished resilience at the household level. "Levels of acute malnutrition still remain unacceptably high in the Arid and Semi Arid areas," the report said. More than forty-three thousand children under the age of five suffer from severe acute malnutrition. While availability of water had had some recent improvement at the time of the report, "cholera outbreaks continued, despite scaled-up prevention efforts. Rains have also caused localized flooding and landslides in many parts of the country affecting up to 130,000 people, heightening their vulnerability to disease and limiting access to basic services." The study also anticipated an upsurge in cases of malaria because of wet conditions in previous months. "The political environment in Kenya remained fragile, with the potential for inter-communal violence and population displacement triggered by political reform processes.

"Flooding and poor sanitation among displaced people leads to cholera outbreaks and acute watery diarrhea in a number of countries in eastern and southern Africa. Uganda, Kenya, Somalia, and Ethiopia reported cumulatively more than 3,200 cholera cases and more than 25 deaths between January and April 2010. Zambia had the highest numbers of recorded cases: 4,421 cases of cholera and 72 deaths [case fatality rate of 1.6 percent]. The prevalence of high levels of HIV/AIDS in countries in the Southern Africa region compounded the impact of natural disasters and political crisis. The situation of armed conflict presented an acute threat to children and women in Southern Somalia. The food security situation in the Greater Horn of Africa sub-region remained unchanged with 12 million people in need of humanitarian assistance."

In the 2010 report, UNICEF worried that many outbreaks of cholera had begun outside the typical cholera season, affecting countries where the disease was not endemic. The children's fund feared further spread in coastal areas of Central Africa where higher-than-normal rainfall was expected through the end of 2011. UNICEF identified three major cross-border cholera outbreaks: the Lake Chad Basin (Chad, Cameroon, Nigeria and Niger); the West Congo Basin (Democratic Republic of the Congo, Republic of the Congo, and the Central African Republic); and Lake Tanganyika (Democratic Republic of the Congo and Burundi). "The virulent diarrheal disease is spreading quickly along waterways between and within countries, causing an 'unacceptably high' rate of fatalities.'" Sweeping through West and Central Africa, one of the biggest epidemics in the vast region's history, cholera has infected more than 85,000 people and killed at least 2,466 at the time of the 2011 report.

Cholera is a bacterial infection of the intestines that spreads by water contaminated with human excrement (waste often carried to rivers and streams). In many parts of the world, the lack of safe drinking water and proper waste disposal are a deadly combination; and despite efforts to improve the situation, the number of cholera cases—and deaths—continues to rise.

No one can survive without water. People in these underdeveloped areas—areas neglected in essential, life-sustaining ways by many rich nations—have no choice but to use contaminated water. Men, women, and children, despite the real threat of cholera, often collect drinking water from waste-infected rivers and lakes; and they often get sick. War regresses, retards, breaks down what essential development *in cooperation* with nations and peoples could have aided, accomplished, sustained.

In her 2010 book *War Is Not Over when It's Over: Women Speak Out from the Ruins of War*, Ann Jones writes:

> Despite the conventions of modern warfare that forbid armies to target civilians, it is civilians who die in far greater numbers than soldiers do. High-tech armies' sophisticated weaponry does not shield civilians. In many conflicts, ruthless leaders use an effective strategy to destroy the civil society and culture of the enemy: a deliberate but unacknowledged war against women.

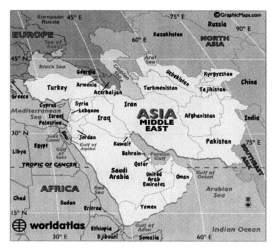

Hotspots in Crisis Excluding Libya

The UN Refugee agency's 2011 regional review for the Horn of Africa and crossing the Red Sea and Gulf of Aden showed a Somalia in displacement crisis. The breakdown by country was the following:

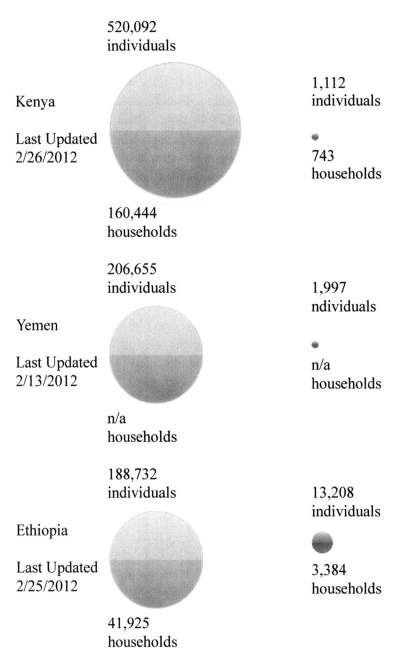

520,092
individuals

Kenya

1,112
individuals

Last Updated
2/26/2012

743
households

160,444
households

206,655
individuals

1,997
ndividuals

Yemen

Last Updated
2/13/2012

n/a
households

n/a
households

188,732
individuals

13,208
individuals

Ethiopia

Last Updated
2/25/2012

3,384
households

41,925
households

Uganda	21,629 individuals	566 individuals
Last Updated 1/30/2012	n/a households	n/a households

Djibouti	19,445 individuals	39 individuals
Last Updated 2/7/2012	n/a households	n/a households

Egypt	7,305 individuals	81 individuals
Last Updated 2/1/2012	n/a households	52 households

n/a individuals

n/a households

Eritrea	3,773 individuals
Last Updated 1/30/2012	n/a households

n/a
individuals

Tanzania   1,515
                  individuals
Last Updated   ◉
10/14/2011   n/a
                  households

n/a
households

Total Somali Refugee   Somali Refugee
Population   Arrivals in 2012

The *New Internationalist* magazine's latest report (attributing 2009 human rights organization data) of hotspots where the United States was involved included countries of the Mediterranean and Arabian Sea and Persian Gulf regions: the Horn of Africa, Iraq, China, and Indonesia.

Reported in **Egypt**: widespread torture by State Security Investigation officials and police; trials by military courts: official figures report 1,500 people detained without charge; other sources report 10,000. Egypt is the second largest recipient of U.S. aid. In

Israel: hundreds of Palestinians (including children) imprisoned in the Occupied Palestinian Territories, many held incommunicado for long periods. Most released without charge; trials held before military courts. The use of aerial drones resulted in many civilian deaths. In **Jordan**: thousands held under suspicion of being "a danger to society." In **Saudi Arabia:** barbaric punishments for vague "offenses" reported; two thousand detained in secrecy on security grounds. United States and Britain praise and promise to learn from a Saudi "reeducation" program that keeps suspects detained without charge or trial. In **Syria**: arbitrary and incommunicado detention reported widespread for people suspected of the slightest involvement in "terrorist" activity. Some seventeen thousand disappeared people, mainly Islamists, remain untraced.

Iraq: in 2008, U.S. forces held 15,500 people (despite the release of 13,000 earlier that year) without charge or trial for security purposes, and the Iraqi authorities held at least 26,000.

Afghanistan: arbitrary arrests, detentions, and torture by intelligence agents; NATO and U.S. forces have handed over detainees to them. Confessions made under torture are permissible in court. Prisoners held in U.S.-run Bagram facility have no legal representation whatsoever.

Pakistan: Interservices intelligence agency responsible for numerous

"disappearances" with the government admitting that 1,102 people had disappeared in Baluchistan Province alone. The problem exacerbated by U.S. Central Intelligence Agency bounty offers for "terror" suspects. CIA-sanctioned drones targeted to blow up "terrorists" have caused many civilian casualties in Pakistan and Afghanistan.

II

YEAR-ENDING (2011) NEWS CLIPS, COMMENTARY, CONTEXT

Official violence begets illegal violence as surely as night follows day.
—Mairead Corrigan Maguire

Harm by design: Perpetual War, Crime too Great to Conceal: Afghanistan and Pakistan, Bahrain, Yemen, Saudi Arabia, Palestine, Jordan, Syria, Iraq, Iran, Libya, Somalia, Uganda

Leading into the second weekend in December (Thursday, December 8, 2011), my blog entry was "GSRBO [short for 2012 presidential contenders Newt **G**ingrich, Rick **S**antorum, Mitt **R**omney, Michele **B**achmann, Barack **O**bama]—Presidential *Certifiables*." A former member of the U.S. Congress and himself a sometimes—presidential candidate used "insane" to characterize statements by candidates en route to the 2012 U.S. presidential election. This passes for "leadership" in America.

A former speaker of the House of Representatives, contender Newt Gingrich, had called for what amounted to "war" on the Iranian people—more strangling sanctions. Echoing the words "bomb Iran" of an earlier U.S. lawmaker in the heat of campaign, Gingrich called for government overthrow and murder. He said he would use "covert capability" to bring about "regime replacement" in Iran and "[kill] Iranian scientists to disrupt the country's atomic energy program."

Contender Mitt Romney also offered that the U.S. government should instigate regime change in Iran by using "covert and overt activities to encourage voices of dissent within the country." This high-tech armed medievalism passes for "leadership" in the United States of America.

A number of Iranian scientists reportedly have fallen by assassination over the past few years, including Professor Majid Shahriari and Professor Masoud Ali-Mohammadi. They died in 2010. "On November 4, 2011," according to press reports, "the secretary of Iran's Supreme National Security Council, Saeed Jalili, announced that Tehran had irrefutable evidence proving that the U.S. government was involved in anti-Iran conspiracies and [had] dispatched elements to carry out acts of sabotage and terrorism in Iran and other regional countries." The United States, Israel, and some of their allies accuse Tehran of pursuing military objectives in its nuclear program; and they have used this "false charge as pretext" for pushing for the imposition of ever-increasing sanctions, another form of warfare. The government of Iran consistently has argued that as a signatory to the Nuclear Non-Proliferation Treaty (NPT) and member of the International Atomic Energy Agency or IAEA (nuclear-armed Israel is neither signatory nor member), it has "the right to develop and acquire nuclear technology meant for peaceful purposes."

Responding to continued U.S. sanctions and political figures' statements urging violence, the director of the Iranian Armed Forces Center for Strategic Studies, Rear Admiral Ali Shamkhani, in December restated Tehran's view of a "dangerous Western hypocrisy . . . the West and the United States are the founders and sponsors of terrorism in the world and use terror tactics against their opponents," he said.

> *Some Western countries that promote terrorism and sponsor assassination accuse other countries and their officials of terrorism.*
>
> *Sanctions imposed on Iranian military commanders are intended to exert psychological pressure to promote propaganda.* [Emphasis added]

Whatever is Iran's intent in the use of its resources, the critical issue remains U.S. engagement in acts of aggression against a sovereign state and its people and U.S. political figures' advocacy of lawlessness.

Following a November 12, 2011, debate in which a number of Republican presidential contenders continued to make aggressive statements ranging from executing covert operations such as terrorism and assassinations to launching a military strike on Iran to subvert Tehran's nuclear program, American Iranian Eleanor Ommani suggested that the candidates were using Iran as "cover." Both major U.S. political parties and candidates, she said, are using Iran as a cover "to boost their own career and at the same time strengthen U.S. capitalism, U.S. imperialism, which has been dealt a blow by Washington failures in Iraq and Afghanistan, and changes in Egypt and Tunisia, and the fight going on in Yemen." Ommani reflected on what every student should know: that these statements by U.S. political figures represent a breach of international laws and the Constitution of the United States, documents that clearly "do not advocate assassination, killing scientists, taking down the regime."

Former U.S. senator and former presidential candidate Mike Gravel's "I" words for "insane" and "immoral" are correct characterizations. Gravel was concerned and outraged by the presidential contenders' calls for violence against Iran. "I can't tell you how dangerous this kind of rhetoric is in the United States and how the American people have been hoodwinked by these people and by U.S. mainstream media organizations that give credibility to these statements, which *have no credibility*," he said. "They are immoral, dishonest [and] wrong, internationally."

Even if weaponization were a fact in Iran, Gravel continued, "In this insanity of our global situation," to acquire such use, "is for self-defense. Morally, international law dictates that any country is entitled to pursue its self-defense." However, "to go out and advocate war . . . and for these people to be considered as presidential candidates in the United States, [this is] really a sad reflection on the state of our government . . . . The kindest thing I can say about [the candidates] is that they are morally bankrupt and somewhat insane."

Sanctions: Punishment, Acts-of-war Context

Reality was not en route to the 2012 White House. Reported in *Today's Insight News*, Saturday, May 22, 2010, Fairfield University professor Joy Gordon said sanctions described as a means of "peacekeeping" or "enforcing human rights" is counterfactual: "Sanctions are bureaucratized, internationally organized siege warfare."

Punishment is the deliberate infliction of harm to the punished party (and thus stands in clear contravention of anything like a *Hippocratic Oath*, journalist Helena Cobban wrote in a 2001 speech, "A Hippocratic Oath for international intervention? Having an effect on vulnerable others . . . ." She was writing during the George W. Bush administration in Washington. "The infliction of harm—or at the very least, a severe curtailment of rights—is not a by-product of punishment; it is intrinsic to it." Though theorists of punishment have tried to predicate the right to punish on a claimed right to undertake actions of self-defense, Cobban said,

[t]he right to self-defense is not a license to inflict any amount of harm on another person or persons. If it were, then the effect of repeated iterations of people acting in self-defense would be to fuel a rapidly escalating cycle of violence such as we have seen . . . in the Israeli-Palestinian dispute . . . . Bombings of Afghanistan and the massive military preparations preceding the bombings are seriously problematic at a number of levels. In particular, they have resulted in the infliction of widespread harm on Afghan civilians who bore no relationship to the Bin Laden networks. Harm, even if it was not directly intended, was still fairly easily foreseeable and was indeed foreseen by many international aid agencies.

Professor Joy Gordon also takes punishment in warfare to punishment in economic sanctions. "Economic sanctions violate 'just war' principles of both *jus ad bellum* and *jus in bello*," she says. "*Jus ad bellum* requires that a belligerent party have valid grounds for engaging in warfare, whereas *jus in bello* requires that the war be fought in accordance with certain standards of conduct.

To engage in warfare at all, the belligerent party must have a just cause. "*Just cause*" requires "a real and *certain* danger" such as protecting innocent life, preserving conditions necessary for decent human existence, and securing basic human rights. Under the requirement of proportionality, the damage inflicted "must not be greater than the damage prevented or the offense being avenged."

Sanctions serve hegemony and serve the punisher. They are raw acts of aggression cloaked in a "peace" mask, but aggression nevertheless—aggression for its own sake (United States against Iran or Iraq or Haiti or Somalia; Israel versus Palestinians or people of Gaza)—acts of war crafted by a self-perpetuating entrenched power.

"Sanctions of the kind imposed by the United States and Israel," Cobban writes,

have usually had the effect [a seeming irrational or uninten tional opposite effect] of . . . strengthening regimes these states do not favor. [T]he primal urge to punish, punish, punish is so strong in these countries [the United States, Israel] that simple rationality is set aside. The main aim is the sanctions themselves—often seen over the past 17 years [in the character of] Martin Indyk, the [William Jefferson] Clinton administration's Secretary of State, as an important way of weakening the regime prior to overthrowing it—rather than resolving the questions and uncertainties around Iran's avowedly civilian nuclear program.

Gordon reinforces the thought that "in certain respects, sanctions are obviously the *modern version of siege warfare*. Each [war and sanctions] involves the systematic deprivation of a whole city or nation of economic resources. Although in siege warfare this is accomplished by surrounding the city with an army, the same effect can be achieved by using international institutions and international pressure to prevent the sale or purchase of goods, and to prevent migration." She continues,

To the extent that we see sanctions as a means of peacekeeping and international governance, sanctions effectively escape ethical analysis—we do not judge them by the same standards we judge other kinds of harm done to innocents. Yet, concretely, the *hunger, sickness,* and *poverty,* which are ostensibly inflicted for benign purposes, affect individuals no differently than hunger, sickness, and poverty [emphasis added] inflicted out of malevolence. [Therefore] to describe sanctions as a means of "peacekeeping" or "enforcing human rights" is an ideological move, which, from the perspective of concrete personal experiences, is simply counterfactual.

Sanctions are, at bottom, a bureaucratized, internationally organized form of siege warfare. They should be seen and judged as such.

Endless War, Endless Abuse of Power, Endless Harm

The fourth U.S. president, James Madison, once said, "Of all the enemies of public liberty, war is perhaps the most to be dreaded because it comprises and develops the germ of every other . . . . Liberty may be endangered by the abuse of liberty, but also by the abuse of power . . . . No nation [can] preserve its freedom in the midst of continual warfare."

Worth repeating: By the end of 2011, I had counted twenty-six countries where the United States was engaged in acts of aggression against the people.

Table 1. 2011 United States at war with world's peoples and countries

Afghanistan	Bahrain
Cuba	Djibouti
Eritrea	Ethiopia
Haiti	Honduras
Iran	Iraq
Japan (Okinawa)	Kenya
Libya	Mexico
Nigeria	North Korea
Pakistan	Palestine
Russia	Saudi Arabia
Somalia	South Korea
Syria	Turkey
Uganda (dominoes the Sudan, South Sudan, Central African Republic, Republic of the Congo (Brazzaville), Democratic Republic of the Congo (Kinshasa)	Yemen

Early in 2011, as migrants (refugees, asylum seekers, and undocumented immigrants) poured across borders fleeing foreign relations conflict and war and a corresponding anti-immigrant hostility rose in the aggressor nations (Britain, France, United States, Italy, Germany, the Netherlands), I began drafting a manuscript focused on war-made migration. But U.S.-led invasions, assassination drone strikes, occupation, and destabilization spread so rapidly, accelerating daily across the Middle East and North Africa, forcing rising migrations so much so that I could not anchor the material. Constant U.S. and U.S.-led bombardments showed that violence clearly had become the first and only choice in foreign relations and global problem solving. The United Nations High Commissioner for Refugees (UNHCR) reported that the immediate region of underdeveloped and developing Africa and the Middle East—where countries such as Somalia, Kenya and Ethiopia, Syria, Lebanon, Gaza were struggling under conditions of drought, famine, disease, and conflict—took the greatest hit of internally and externally displaced people. There were repeated incidents of migrants dying at sea. Many trying to escape were turned back—often by the very foreign powers who were involved in major aggression against the migrants' countries of origin—to face continuing violence and insecurity, disease, and poverty in their homelands. The continual rise in U.S. wars and the consequential rise in refugees and homelessness, internally displaced people (IDPs, the UN calls them), asylum seekers, the stateless, mass migrants of all kinds dislodged the anchor of my manuscript; so I set it aside and kept an accounting through my blog Bennett's Study *Today's Insight News*.

In late 2011, I took the earlier notes and later blog entries throughout 2011 and resumed a manuscript centered on U.S. foreign relations violence and war-made migration.

I use the term "foreign relations" instead of "foreign policy" because I am concerned not merely with political speeches or agency records pertaining to foreign affairs but with people and the United States' act and impact (directly, indirectly, or by remote bombs) on people on the ground. Radio Netherlands World airs a weekly program whose title reflects the sense of my concern. It is called *The State We're In: How We Treat Each Other around the World*. I am concerned with U.S. government-ordered treatment of peoples (including heads of state and political leaders) of the world. I am concerned with the evidence of orders issued (orally or in writing, secretly or publicly) by political figures in U.S. executive and legislative branches of government. I am concerned with the raw evidence of relations executed by the U.S. government's official departments such as state and defense together with their contractor, mercenary, nongovernmental, nonprofit (secular, sectarian, academic) and sundry foreign (covert and overt, allied and unallied) operatives, partners, proxies, surrogates. Whatever may be the underlying or official U.S. foreign *policy* at any given time, the clearest picture of how the United States treats people and nations *around the world* is one of "violence." It is a kind of bipolar swing between arming despots against "their own people" and murdering those despots together with "their own people"; then taking to prime time telecasts, and, as sport, bragging about the kill.

The Wednesday, December 14, 2011, article at *Today's Insight News* was "High-placed Killer among Us Boasts—portrait of Peace Laureate whose Role No One Should Model." The blog entry was based on a piece by the London-based Stop the War Coalition headlined "'Peace' president Obama brags about how many people he's killed. Nobel Peace Prize winner Barack Obama is waging war in Afghanistan, Iraq, Pakistan, Somalia, Yemen and Uganda [I had counted more countries] and bragging about starting another in Iran." Recalling the U.S. president's callous outburst, the coalition wrote:

> In comments that were surprisingly bellicose even for the current political environment, President Barack Obama bragged loudly about the number of people he has killed, urging hawks who don't think he's hawkish enough to "ask Osama bin Laden and the 22 out of 30 top al-Qaeda leaders who've been taken off the field."

Stop the War Coalition suggested that the U.S. president also could have advised "[asking] thousands of Pakistanis, Afghans and Iraqis or [asking] the family of Anwar al-Awlaki, the U.S. citizen he assassinated earlier this year, but the point was already made—an Obama Administration kills lots of people and they are sure that's what voters are in the market for." Giving evidence of the United States' deepening foreign relations in violence, the president said that under his presidency, "'Iran is isolated and the world is united in applying the toughest sanctions that Iran has ever experienced' [meaning that] the Obama administration has done more to unite the world against Iran than had the preceding George W. Bush administration."

Speaking in mid-December against a measure, the National Defense Authorization Act, that would further expand U.S. global war and breach established domestic and international law, U.S. lawmaker Alcee Hastings recalled that, since September 11, 2001, the United States "has engaged in military action in numerous countries." In two wars, U.S. violence has left "hundreds of thousands" of people dead and "many more wounded." Moreover, an unconscionable U.S. "global war on terror" has become an easy pretext for elimination, a global model for lawlessness. In 2009, the *New Internationalist* magazine reported, "While many state agencies torture and kill people who stand in their way, these agencies now increasingly use counterterrorism as a justification. With the United States, the world's remaining superpower, rebranding torture [which is absolutely prohibited under international law] as a form of interrogation, and holding suspects without trial for years or hauling them before unfair military commissions, human rights have taken a beating."

Is Nobel Peace Prize Meaningless, Misnomer, or Misplaced?

Liberian President Ellen Johnson Sirleaf waves to the audience at her inauguration in Monrovia, Liberia, Monday, Jan. 16, 2006. President Sirleaf is Africa's first female elected head of state. White House 'frozen in time' photo by Shealah Craighead

The Nobel committee in 2011 awarded its "Peace Prize" to three women: Leymah Gbowee, Tawakkul Karman and, as she was standing for reelection, Liberian president Ellen Johnson Sirleaf. This committee in 2009 awarded the same prize to U.S. president Barack Obama who has waged more wars on the world than any president has in at least the past thirty years. In two of the past ten years, the U.S. president locked step with and exceeded his violent predecessors, piling up thousands of deaths and enemies. As commander in chief of United States Armed Forces and private mercenaries, the Obama government ordered the killing, maiming, and destroying of millions of lives and futures—in at least six countries. This kind of violent behavior in relations with other nations and peoples throws into question not only the legitimacy of the Nobel Peace Prize and its awarding committee but also the moral caliber and integrity of those who receive it.

Concerning Peace Prize laureate Ellen Johnson Sirleaf, Thomas C. Mountain wrote in an online *Pravda* piece that she had "received a share of one of the Western world's most prestigious awards yet residents of Liberia's capital were without running water for the six years of her presidency." As U.S. foreign relations violence spreads through North and East Africa, it also spreads westward into President Sirleaf's Liberia. Aid or the supply of skilled personnel for economic and technical development often covers the face of imperialism; developing countries not ignorant of history often fear this reality. What the imperialist calls humanitarian is likely the imperialist's strong arm of repression. "Crisis Management," Mountain wrote, "is the USA's preferred policy in Africa: Create a crisis, then manage the subsequent chaos—the better to loot and pillage West Africa's resources. [And] Liberia has long been a poster child for murder and mayhem.

"Though much hope had been placed in Africa's first 'democratically elected woman President,' after six years, beaucoup millions of dollars, and still no running water in the capital of the country, one should expect [the West's] Nobel Prize—for a job well done, at least as far as western banksters Firestone Rubber and their media minions are concerned. So it's a Nobel Prize for Liberia's President and No Water for Liberia's residents—all thanks to an unhealthy dose of western style 'democracy.'"

Early October at War

Afghanistan and Pakistan, Bahrain, Yemen, Saudi Arabia, Palestine, Jordan, Syria, Iraq, Iran, Libya, Somalia, Uganda

Neighbors (Afghanistan and Pakistan) who should be friends are not, and foreigners stir fires of violence.

Afghan lawmakers called on their government to sever diplomatic ties with Pakistan after release of a report indicating that Pakistani forces a few days in October had fired forty rockets into Afghanistan. Also headlining outside-the-U.S. news, an independent policy research organization, the Afghanistan Analysts Network, released a report saying NATO may have exaggerated the success of its operations in Afghanistan: attempting to show the ten-year (2001-2011) U.S.-led war on this country has been "successful." The network report revealed a lack of transparency in NATO—released data about raids designed to kill or capture alleged "militant" leaders between December 2009 and September 2011.

On October 14, three U.S.-led foreign troops died in different incidents of violence in eastern and southern Afghanistan. The deaths reportedly resulted from "militant" attacks and the explosion of an improvised explosive device.

In neighboring Pakistan where U.S. relations remained troubled and steeped in violence, the Obama government escalated aerial attacks, which the former George W. Bush government had initiated. Quite naturally, in the face of these unlawful attacks, relations between Islamabad, the Pakistani capital, and Washington continued to deteriorate. Pakistan officials made public statements that the airstrikes violate its sovereignty. On October 14, a drone attack by U.S. forces near the Afghanistan-Pakistan border region was the third of such attack in a forty-eight-hour period. A non-UN-sanctioned U.S. drone strike left at least four people dead in northwest Pakistan.

These killings have fueled anti-U.S. sentiment among the Pakistani people, and Pakistan's Ministry of Human Rights reportedly has asked the government to complain to the UN and other international bodies about the "extrajudicial killings."

Bahrain

In Bahrain where the United States allies with monarchy, scores of people have died. Brutal crackdowns by Saudi Arabia—backed Bahraini regime forces have arrested hundreds of peaceful protesters since anti-government demonstrations began in the Persian Gulf kingdom in mid-February 2011. Several demonstrators have been arrested in towns and villages around Bahrain's capital, Manama. In March, U.S.-allied Saudi Arabia deployed military equipment, soldiers, and police personnel to Bahrain to help the Al Khalifa regime quell mounting protests. Eyewitness reports and footage revealed the brutality of Saudi forces against Bahraini activists and Saudi involvement in the demolition of mosques and holy sites in Bahraini towns.

Reports on October 14 said a woman protester sustained serious injuries in the town of Nuwaidrat where regime forces engaged in heavy clashes with antigovernment protesters. Several peaceful demonstrators were arrested. When targeted with tear gas and sound grenades, protesters chanted antiregime slogans. Regime forces in the village of Karzakan also attacked women protesters.

Saudi Arabia

In U.S.-allied-with-monarchy Saudi Arabia, the government imposed a strict ban on antigovernment rallies in the kingdom, but protests continued. In October, antigovernment protesters took to the streets of an eastern Saudi Arabian town, demonstrating against the kingdom's ruling family and condemning violations of human rights by the Saudi regime.

Human Rights Watch accused Saudi Arabia of arbitrarily arresting civilians and called on Riyadh, the Saudi capital, to "immediately stop arbitrary arrests of relatives, rights activists, and peaceful protesters."

Yemen

Yemen/Internally Displaced Persons (IDPs) camp / Photo UNHCR/L. Chedrawl/ September 2009

From the U.S.-allied with Ali Abdullah Saleh government in Yemen, October reports came that hundreds of Yemenis had died and thousands injured since the January start of popular uprisings against the government of Ali Abdullah Saleh. After sustaining wounds in an attack on the presidential palace in June then treated in Saudi Arabia, Saleh returned to Yemen on September 23, 2011. On Thursday, October 13, the day after the UN Security Council convened to discuss the overall situation in Yemen, tens of thousands of Yemenis poured onto sixty streets of the capital, Sana'a, calling on the United Nations Security Council to take swift measures to topple the Ali Abdullah Saleh regime. Protesters chanted slogans saying Yemenis wanted a new beginning.

A woman protester reportedly called on the United Nations Security Council (permanent members: United States, United Kingdom, France, Russian Federation, and People's Republic of China) "to meet the Revolution's demands." The "Yemeni people," she said, "are being oppressed and killed. We call on the UN to take immediate measures to prosecute Ali Abdullah Saleh and his regime."

Palestine

In Palestine where the United States stands with Israel against Palestinians, the Bureau of the Committee on the Exercise of the Inalienable Rights of the Palestinian People, in an August communiqué, expressed concern over a deepening displacement or cleansing occupation: Israel's approval in August alone of 5,200 new settlement units in occupied East al-Quds (Jerusalem). On October 14, Israel's lands administration announced plans to build thousands of new settler units in East al-Quds (Jerusalem). The move represents "a continuing disregard for agreements reached with the Palestinian Authority."

The publication *Ha'aretz* reported the planned construction of 2,610 new residential units, two-thirds designated for Israeli settlers in Givat Hamatos, intended to create a settlement belt around Jerusalem. "The international community considers all settlements built in the occupied West Bank to be illegal."

Iraq

In U.S.-occupied Iraq, more than a million Iraqis have died in the U.S.-led war and occupation that began in 2003 (and these are only estimates). The week of October 9, Iraq's senior cleric Muqtada al-Sadr accused U.S. officials of plotting chaos and sectarian conflict in order to prolong the U.S. stay in this already war-scarred, devastated country.

On Wednesday, October 12, 2011, twenty-eight people died in attacks across Baghdad. On October 14, multiple bomb blasts killed at least eighteen people, including women and children, and injured scores of others in northeastern Baghdad. The day before the October 14 attacks, bombs hit the impoverished Sadr City district against the office of Muqtada al-Sadr. The senior cleric maintained his opposition to any form of U.S. military presence in Iraq beyond the 2011 agreed—upon withdrawal deadline.

Iran

In U.S.-opposed Iran, the deputy chairman of the country's Majlis (parliament) Committee on National Security and Foreign Policy, Ismail Kowsari, reportedly said that U.S. "conspiracies" against Iran "show they are struggling against the tide of the Islamic Awakening in regional nations." The lawmaker's comments came after the U.S. Justice Department on October 11 accused Iran of involvement in a plot to assassinate Saudi Arabian Ambassador to Washington Adel Al-Jubeir, with help from a suspected member of a Mexican drug cartel.

Iranian authorities dismissed Washington's accusation as a smear campaign aimed at fueling "Iranophobia" in the world. The senior Iranian lawmaker said the Islamic, European, and American awakenings raised international awareness, ultimately foiling the U.S. and Zionist conspiracies against Iran.

"President Barack Obama entered the White House with a slogan of 'change,'" Iran's permanent ambassador to UNESCO, Mohammad-Reza Majidi, told the Iranian News Agency in Paris on October 14; "but like his predecessors he is dependent on different lobbies." He described Washington's assassination plot allegations as part of the U.S. Iranophobia project and "a major insult to the intelligence of ordinary people in the U.S. and the world." The Iranian envoy went on to say that the U.S. administration had created a media hype in an attempt to cover up its failures in Afghanistan and Iraq and to divert attention from the nationwide protest rallies against poverty, unemployment, corporatism, social inequality, and other shortcomings.

Libya

In U.S.-rebel-allied Libya, serious fighting again broke out between pro—and antigovernment factions. This came two months after the alleged fall of the capital city following the U.S./NATO invasion. By mid-October, thousands of people reportedly had died in the Libyan capital of Tripoli. Many more had sustained wounds during intense fighting between government troops and revolutionary forces.

On October 14, Qaddafi loyalists held a demonstration, and the National Transitional Council (NTC) reported gun battles between forces loyal to the Libyan ruler Muammar Qaddafi and "revolutionary" fighters. By October 20, the press was reporting the Libyan dead, under suspicious circumstances.

Somalia

U.S. bombs rain down on Somalia, and cholera takes dozens of Somali lives every single day. In a twelve-hour period on October 14, at least 116 Somali children died in a southern Somalia cholera outbreak. Hundreds of children were rushed to hospitals and medical centers in Lego Town and Balad Town in southern Somalia. Germ-infested conditions linked to poor or nonexistent sewage and waste removal systems and scarcity of clean drinking water (evidence of third world regression and absence of basic vital development needs) have resulted in the spread of waterborne diseases in this country.

The United Nations' latest report in October 2011 estimated that a quarter of Somalia's 9.9 million people were either internally displaced or living outside the country as refugees.

U.S. drone attacks compounded the fears and concerns of Somalis and forced many to flee for their lives. An attack in southern Somalia by a U.S. unmanned aerial vehicle (UAV) on October 14, 2011, left at least seventy-eight people dead and sixty-four others injured. A separate U.S. drone attack the same Friday in Hoosingow District in the south of the country left eleven civilians dead and thirty-four more wounded. Somalia is the sixth country (current press estimate) where the U.S. military conducted drone strikes in 2011. In addition to Somalia, the United States has employed drones in Afghanistan, Pakistan, Libya, Iraq, and Yemen to launch aerial bombings. News stories in 2011also reported a drone plane crashed in Iran.

Uganda

The United States is in hostile engagement in Uganda where tens of thousands of people have died in a twenty-year war with security forces in the north. On October 14, in another declaration of "humanitarian warfare," U.S. president Barack Obama announced his government's intention to deploy one hundred combat-equipped troops to Uganda and, from there, into other East and Central African countries. Uganda is an east-central African country bordered on its north by the Sudan, east by Kenya, south by Tanzania and Rwanda, and on its west by the Democratic Republic of the Congo.

In a message to Congress, the president said U.S. troops "subject to the approval of national authorities could also deploy from Uganda into South Sudan, the Central African Republic and Democratic Republic of the Congo."

Casualty Sites Reporting October 14, 2011
U.S.-led War Dead
(accurate totals unknown)
Antiwar-dot-com Casualties in Iraq since March 19, 2003
(U.S. war dead since the Obama inauguration on January 20, 2009: 249) Information out of date

•

Wounded 33,151-100,000
U.S. veterans with brain injuries: 320,000
Suicides estimated: 18 a day
Iraqi deaths due to U.S. invasion: 1,455,590

Latest update on this site: October 9, 2011 http://www.antiwar.com/casualties/

•

Iraq Body Count http://www.iraqbodycount.org/
The worldwide update on civilians killed in the Iraq war and occupation
Documented civilian deaths from violence
102,953-112,504
Full analysis of the WikiLeaks's Iraq War Logs may add 15,000 civilian deaths.

•

ICasualties Figures http://icasualties.org/

Afghanistan: 1,806 United States; 2,761 coalition
Iraq: 4,478 United States; 4,796 coalition

Late October at War

Today's Insight News, Friday October 21, 2011—If a killer kills a no-longer-useful "friend," who calls the killer to account?

The U.S. reign of terror has long-term and far-reaching consequences. A country perpetually, lawlessly at war with the world can no longer claim intervention to save civilians using ridiculous rubrics such as "humanitarian" aggression, armed "peacekeeping," or war as last resort. Such statements, with all due respect to those who make them, are lies on their face. U.S. officials (executives and judges, lawmakers, and war makers), political figures of all stripes, send a clear and morally crippling message to the young and future leaders: that violence is the coin of the realm in matters of foreign relations.

Killing is the way to get what you want or to have your way. If you cannot pull it off legitimately, then orchestrate, provoke, or directly create conditions on the ground. Bribe a sufficient number of officials of member states of the UN General Assembly; squeeze the five-permanent-member UN Security Council to issue a statement corporate media transcribes and trumpets: violence "yes." Then send in the drones to take out whomever and however—labeled "bad guys": "militants," "terrorists," "rebels," and

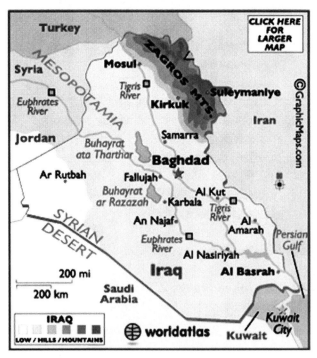

"freedom fighters;" oligarchs, dictators, authoritarian *no longer politically expedient "friends."* Destroy countries' vital structures (farms and other workplaces, schools, utilities, cultural and religious places), intertribal peaceful coexistence, and every man, woman, and child in the path of overwhelming might. Kick moneyed wealth back and forth between public governance and private profit. Hire and collude with agents, foreign and domestic, to repress peoples and nations forever. Spend billions borrowed and stolen from public treasuries of nations (including U. S. and its communities, towns, cities, states), pretending to reconstruct that which is deliberately never reconstructed and proceeding with the original intent: the perpetual destabilization, weakening, and destruction of nations.

U.S. State Department staffer Peter Van Buren gives a telling example of the U.S. foreign relations model in violence intending to do no good. In his 2011 book *We Meant Well*, Van Buren says he had been part of a reconstruction team on a one-year tour in Iraq. In an opening chapter titled "Help Wanted, No Experience Necessary" (p. 3), Van Buren writes, "The reconstruction of Iraq was the largest nation-building program in history, dwarfing in cost, size, and complexity even those undertaken after World War II to rebuild Germany and Japan. At a cost to the U.S. taxpayer of over $63 billion and counting, the plan was lavishly funded, yet, as government inspectors found, the efforts were characterized from the beginning by pervasive waste and inefficiency, mistaken judgments, flawed policies, and structural weaknesses."

In his chapter titled "What Victory Looks Like" (pp. 247-248), Van Buren asked, "How did we end up accomplishing so little when we meant well?" Part of his answer was a segregated existence. The Americans "lived imprisoned on military bases [and] had the most cursory relationships with Iraqis." U.S. reconstruction teams "were always seen as fat-walleted aliens descending from armored spaceships."

War, conflict, insecurity had forced Iraqi professionals and technocrats, doctors, and engineers "who might have been partners in reconstruction" to flee to other countries. Twenty thousand of Iraq's thirty-four thousand registered physicians had chosen exile, Van Buren said. "We were left to spend our money among thugs, thieves, tribal leaders with self-serving agendas, and corrupt government officials placed in their jobs by the United States."

Separation, violence, and deliberate incompetence to do no good, the terms "Iraqi good" or "good enough for Iraq," according to Van Buren, "stood in for any substantive quality checks."

> Soldiers would joke about "drive-by QA/QC," where a quick run past some project would replace serious quality assurance or quality check inspection. The same sloppiness applied to

staffing. If [someone] had been assistant night manager at a KFC [Kentucky Fried Chicken] back home [in the United States], he [became] a small business adviser in Iraq . . . . No Embassy leader ever received or wanted an accurate report." (pp. 248-249)

In his "Humanitarian Assistance" (HA) chapter, this veteran diplomat, who had spent a year's tour with an "embedded Provisional Reconstruction Team" (ePRT), writes, "It was almost as if a new word were needed: *disresponsible*, a step beyond irresponsible, meaning you should have been the one to take responsibility—but shucked it off." Our attention span short, our desire to examine results limited, the consequence: "Violence did not taper off and no jobs were created and the rich sheiks who controlled the territory stayed rich and in control." (p. 116)

Destruction without intent to do other than lay viciously bare, destroy utterly, absolutely forever—this is the wrenching harm of a foreign relations paradigm wherein all agencies, all departments, all programs, all effort, regardless to name, are so fixed on violence that the concept of nonviolence is alien, unthinkable, unimagined, undoable wherever the United States deploys. If you think Libya's head of state (or Bahrain's, Saudi Arabia's, Yemen's, Egypt's or Tunisia's) was corrupt, oppressive, and had ruled far too long, then you better take a look at entrenched U.S. foreign relations extending no farther back than the Nixon era, forward. You will see at least a forty-year reign of U.S. terror.

The thirty-seventh U.S. president (1969-1974), Richard Nixon, did not start the war in Southeast Asia, but he advanced it. The forty-fourth U.S. president, Barack Obama, did not start the wars of South Central Asia and North and East Africa; but he increased the wars, widened and deepened them, increased cold-blooded preemptive extrajudicial killings and a massive displacement of peoples. Through Washington's propaganda machine, its inordinate influence over non-superpowered countries, the Obama administration (as its predecessors) has lied about what the United States is doing and why the United States is involved in and actively leading global aggression. Anyone who believes the United States' reign of violence (official and unofficial) against peoples of the world is *not* akin to the barbarism of Muammar al-Qaddafi, Saddam Hussein, and Manuel Noriega (or other despots and military junta) has been living in a cave for a very long time or has been overexposed to U.S. media and other mass propaganda.

Human Rights Watch's Peter Bouckaert said on October 14, 2011, on Pacifica's *Democracy Now* news program, "The U.S. CIA and Britain's MI6 [intelligence agencies] in 2003 and 2004 were dismantling Qaddafi's weapons of mass destruction program and *at the same time* reestablishing an intelligence relationship with [Qaddafi's] Libyan government."

> In a cache of documents found in Libya by Human Rights Watch, many related to the [U.S.] rendition [unlawful abduction, kidnapping] and to the capture and rendition of Islamist "suspects" abroad. The CIA was offering to capture and render Libyan Islamists to the Qaddafi government and then they [the CIA agents] were sending to the Qaddafi government the questions they wanted [Libyan torturers] to ask.

> Many documents [show] how close their [the intelligence agencies and the Qaddafi government] relationship was . . . . They show a relationship that went way beyond the professional into the intimate, really, with a man known for his brutality and his direct role in repression, a man who probably knows a lot more about the Lockerbie bombing and other dark chapters in Libyan history than anybody else. [On December 21, 1988, a Boeing 747 (Pan-Am flight 103) en route from London to New York City exploded over Lockerbie, Scotland, leaving 270 people dead.]

> One of the documents found is a fax dated Christmas Day 2003. In it, the head of MI6 clandestine services begins the message "Dear Musa" [a title used for an African/Muslim emperor, military leader, cleric] and then expresses regret that Musa is not joining him for Christmas lunch. The fax is signed, "Your friend" and then the name of this person.

Commenting on these findings, human rights lawyer Gareth Peirce said if the Obama administration refused to investigate this collusion and torture, then worldwide organizations such as the UN Committee against Torture, the European Committee for the Prevention of Torture and others must conduct inquiries. "They must say, 'We are going to have an inquiry and we are going to investigate; and those countries that have endorsed the right for us to enter and investigate, we're going to do so.'" Peirce went on to note that people in influential Western nations had responded to recent Arab uprisings as if these were reactive to a *recent* spark.

"Without any comprehension of the history of those nations as places where the worst kind of oppression has taken place and where U.S. and British governments have constantly not just backed the wrong horse—it is not that simplistic a choice—but have backed and encouraged leaders of those countries who have been monsters, who have oppressed their people. And we have categorized the resistance and the dissent as the enemy, as Islamic extremism, radicalism, that has to be eliminated."

As questions persisted about U.S. foreign relations, its actions in Libya, what really happened in the overthrow of Libya's head of state and continued to happen in post-invasion Libya and throughout East Africa and the Middle East, I noted Chicago broadcaster Stephen Lendman's comments in the Monday, October 24, 2011, *Today's Insight News* entry "Ethos of Hegemony." In his mid-October piece, Lendman defined the U.S. Near Eastern blueprint as "regional dominance" spanning "North Africa, the Middle East, and Central Asia to the borders of the Russian Federation" and spoke of the horrific consequences of Western-led, allied violence.

"Mass graves cannot suppress a crime too great to conceal," he said "Depleted uranium, thermobaric fuel-air bombs, white phosphorous [able to burn flesh to the bone], and other terror weapons were used to commit mass slaughter. Throughout the conflict, 'rebels' committed gruesome atrocities against suspected Qaddafi loyalists, including summary executions, lynching, beheadings, and desecration of corpses. Led by United States, United Kingdom, French and other NATO Special Forces, they took full advantage if a license to loot."

The good that was, was ploughed under. Under Qaddafi's decision no. 111, Lendman wrote, "Everyone got free health care, education, training, rehabilitation, housing assistance, disability and elder benefits, interest-free loans from Libya's public bank, subsidies to study abroad, free electricity and water, generous stipends for newlyweds, and practically free gasoline. All of these are gone—replaced by impoverishment, destitution, depravation, homelessness, hunger, disease, fear, insecurity, and despair . . . . Like Iraqis, Afghans, Palestinians, and other oppressed peoples, Libyans know they are in for a long liberation struggle."

Those who survive, survive with memory of history. "Libyan loyalists [have vowed] to continue their liberating struggle and resist occupation, colonization and exploitation," Lendman wrote. Libya's state system of the masses, the Jamahiriya loyalists, will neither forgive nor forget. "Neither will the global millions raging against America's imperial monster."

What has been put forth in the world, Gareth Peirce said, is a "simplistic view that the 'enemy' [left to the West's politically expedient definition] has to be eliminated, the 'enemy' has to be gotten. If this keeps going in this way, then we will be in perpetual war—in terms of hatred and elimination—not in the quest of perpetual peace."

Refusing to see clearly acts ordered and or committed by U.S. officials, agencies, overt and covert agents, even if limited to the past forty years, is to be complicit in perpetual war: in murder and repression, the destruction of nations, families, children, societies and institutions, and their potential. I am angry and saddened by what my country is doing at home and abroad; and, yes, I want fellow Americans to engage, to act without partisan or tribal allegiance but nonviolently to right the wrongs of a U.S. global ethos of violence. "If ever there was a moment for a revolution in our thinking," Gareth Peirce said, this is it.

> We have waged war, and we are continuing to wage endless war in simplistic terms—domestically against our own Muslim citizens, against others, and against huge swaths of countries, now moving . . . to the Horn of Africa. We cannot continue in this permanence of combative aggression in our thinking, let alone our actions.

Whether they know it or not, the people of the United States are part of the people of Libya and the troubled regions of Africa and Asia where Washington continues a reign of terror. Because of the U.S. violence in relations, the American people will never enjoy true liberty free from guilt and fear (rational or paranoid)—even as narrowly envisioned in the American colonies' Declaration of Independence and in the U.S. Constitution and its amendments of the 17 and 1800s—until they uproot and move beyond an ethos of hegemony partnered in violence.

III

UNCHECKED MIGHT, HEARTBREAKING SUFFERING

To natural calamities of drought, flood, and cyclone has been added the man-made tragedy of vast proportions: I am haunted by tormented faces in our overcrowded refugee camps reflecting grim events, which have compelled exodus of these millions.
—Indira Gandhi

Conflict/war-made Displacement, Reverse Development, Civilian Death, U.S. Pageantry, Anti-American Demonstrations

Northern Afghanistan transit camp / Photo UNHCR / W. Schellenberg / August 2009

October 2011

Afghanistan

As records were showing the U.S.-led war in Afghanistan had left 5.6 million dead, the U.S. Secretary of State, Hillary Rodham Clinton, the week of October 16, 2011, flew unannounced into Afghanistan (Kabul) and neighboring Pakistan. Afghans and Pakistanis welcomed her with burnings of the former "first lady/presidential candidate" in effigy and our beloved "Old Glory" (the name given our honored Stars and Stripes in1862). American officials have an unpleasant habit not lost on people in places beyond U.S. borders: they swoop down in darkness and lecture their "hosts" from safely distanced daises. As cameras roll, they strut and swagger, then leave; and repeat this performance year after year as an ugly sideshow to the U.S. foreign relations in violence. People suffering the pain of this violence and its insulting pageantry are smoldering, enraged, ever mindful of what the United States has brought endlessly to their country and its people.

Recalling the censored memory of foreign service members assigned to Iraq, Peter Van Buren, in his "meant well" book, subtitled *How I Helped Lose the Battle for the Hearts and Minds of the Iraqi People*, recalls a child—rape and murder atrocity that U.S. soldiers had committed shortly before his assignment to the same area in which the crime occurred. "In all my preparatory briefings, no one ever mentioned" this rape and murder of a child. "Yet," Van Buren says, "I'm pretty sure the Iraqis I worked with remembered." The foreigners' memories, though, were short and without historical background. For every foreigner that swoops down on Iraq (or any other country) for a few hours or for a several-month tour, most of them "stayed no longer than twelve months and they usually believed history began when they first stepped onto Iraqi soil. Our memory barely extended back beyond a few months." "Host" country inhabitants, those who have not become refugees, never leave, and they see and suffer all the pain caused by aggressor countries and their agents. They live the horrific history of which Americans generally are oblivious. Citing an old saying, Van Buren says the Americans have "the watch," but those under invasion and occupation "have the time." Americans in Iraq "had been sent to war . . . by people [who] failed to understand that history started a long time ago."

In a November 30, 2011, *Democracy Now* interview with Amy Goodman, Van Buren seems to send a message to the sideshow political performers who swoop down in darkness and, under high security in daylight, strut and lecture people about whose culture, lives, traditions they are carelessly ignorant and contemptuous:

> I would like to propose that no VIP be allowed to go to Iraq, certainly not to announce anything using the words "victory" or "success," until he or she is willing to do that on an announced visit with the airplane landing in the daytime. As long as the visits have to be kept secret and the planes have to land at night, I would like to suggest we not use the words "victory," "success," "completion," or anything equivalent.

Images of a burning U.S. flag and a public figure burning in effigy are memorable; but far, far worse are the endless deaths, the abuse, the hunger, deprivation, and lasting adversity caused by the US-led invasion and occupation of Afghanistan. In 2011, anti-U.S. sentiment rose and intensified as the killing of civilians rose.

A United Nations report on Afghanistan issued on September 28 said that the monthly average number of security incidents recorded for 2011 until the end of August had risen by nearly 40 percent. The report also said civilian casualties, already at record levels in the first six months of 2011, rose 5 percent between June and August 2011 compared to the same period in 2010. Conflict/war forced the displacement of an estimated 130,000 people in the first seven months of the year, up nearly two-thirds from the same period one year earlier.

On October 21, in a village in the northeastern Kunar Province, a U.S.-led airstrike targeting suspected Taliban "militants" hit a house in Afghanistan's northeastern province of Kunar and left thirteen Afghan civilians dead. One day earlier, according to Press TV reports, at least one Afghan civilian died and six others were kidnapped after U.S. military forces attacked a residential area in the eastern province of Nangarhar. Sunday, October 16, U.S.-led soldiers killed an Afghan teacher and his two daughters during a night raid in eastern Afghanistan. Local officials said the troops stormed the Wardak Province house and shot and killed the teacher together with his eighteen—and twenty-year-old daughters. This was part of a pattern of endemic foreign relations violence U.S.

political figures and their agents failed to acknowledge, account for, or amend.

Asia West: U.S./NATO Destroy Afghanistan

One of the main consequences of the war on Afghanistan is the considerable increase in heroin production, Timothy Bancroft-Hinchey wrote. This war continues with seemingly no end in sight. In the October 12, 2011, news period, some reports estimated allied troop deaths at 4,600 people. More than twenty-one thousand had suffered injuries. The USA lost 1,800; Britain, 382; Canada, 157. "One of the main failures committed by the USA and its allies," Hinchey wrote, "has been the inability to win the hearts and minds of the Afghan people. Anti-American sentiments in the country have been growing steadily. Allied troops repeated nearly all of the Soviet mistakes and aggravated the situation even more."

> The local population supports the Taliban because of the occupiers' actions, for example, attacks on wedding and funeral services . . . . The Americans and their allies say they promote democracy but it appears that they cannot fully understand the meaning of "*when in Rome*, do as the Romans do." The majority of the Afghans were infuriated with attempts to have Afghan women involved in the public life of the country. Local people take such moves as intending to destroy their family values and [the occupation of their land is therefore] to destroy Islam.

In a history of plunder, invasion, occupation, and rivalry for domination, Britain and the Soviets have been in Afghanistan at least since the 1800s. Foreign affairs analyst Marvin G. Weinbaum writes in a *Britannica* article, "A rivalry between imperial Britain and tsarist Russia in the late 19th century established the modern boundaries of Afghanistan and modern Afghanistan became a pawn in struggles over political ideology and commercial influence." In the last quarter of the twentieth century and into the twenty-first century, Afghanistan suffered the ruinous impact of civil war, greatly exacerbated by foreign military invasion and occupation.

At the end of 2011, the United States was bogged down in war and its consequences in Afghanistan and Pakistan. Civilian casualties were at alarming rates. Anti-U.S. protests, the burning in effigy of leading U.S. government officials, and U.S. flag burnings were happening daily in both Pakistan and Afghanistan and in other countries where the United States sided with despots: in Bahrain, Yemen, Jordan, Israel, Saudi Arabia. The breakdown continued. On a level any sane person considers criminal, the United States continued contributing to serious oppression and regression, destruction, disruption, destabilization, and displacement. Floods of migrants, refugees, and asylum seekers fled across the Middle East Region, including Africa and South Central Asia, crossing waterways and borders farther north, east and west.

Pakistan

The U.S. secretary of state's unwelcoming in Pakistan was due in large part to the United States' continual drone (remote bomb) attacks on this country, breaching national sovereignty and leaving untold numbers of civilians dead. These relentlessly murderous attacks together with the May 2011 secret U.S. raid into Pakistan that reportedly killed al-Qaeda leader Osama bin Laden increased tensions between the nations' capitals, Islamabad and Washington, throughout 2011.

At the time of the U.S. secretary's October 21 visit, there had been new reports of "U.S. troops massing in Afghanistan along the Pakistan border, raising concerns in Pakistan about a potential U.S. plan to wage a military offensive on its North Waziristan region." From the ongoing conflict, three soldiers and more than thirty-four "militants" reportedly died in clashes between Pakistani security forces and the Taliban group in this Khyber tribal region in the northwest of Pakistan. Earlier in the week, official Pakistan issued a warning to the United States against a unilateral ground operation in the North Waziristan tribal region. Pakistani army chief general Ashfaq Parvez Kayani reportedly in an October 18 closed-door briefing told lawmakers, "Any such attack by U.S. forces from across the Afghan border would prove 10 times harder than the wars in Iraq and Afghanistan."

Hundreds of Pakistanis in their unwelcoming response to the U.S. secretary of state's visit took to the streets of the city of Multan chanting anti-U.S. slogans and slamming Washington for accusing Pakistan of harboring Afghan militants.

Bahrain (U.S. Ally)

In the home of the U.S. Fifth Fleet, the United States sides with the ruling despot as does its ally—also U.S. ally—Saudi Arabia. On October 21, the regime in Bahrain increased incarcerations of demonstrators. A military court in Bahrain's capital, Manama, sentenced twenty people to six-month jail terms for demonstrating against the ruling family. The government delayed release of a report concerning brutal crackdowns, which have been aided by Saudi Arabia.

Bahrain's court in September had sentenced twenty medical professionals to five—to fifteen-year prison terms for having treated antiregime protesters. The organization Physicians for Human Rights reported doctors and nurses' being detained, tortured, or disappeared because they had evidence of atrocities committed by the authorities, security forces, and riot police in crackdowns on antigovernment protesters.

Iraq

In the ongoing occupation and remnant of U.S. war and regional destabilization in and around Iraq, ethnic conflicts are heating up. Turkish forces backed by airstrikes on October 21 reportedly entered northern Iraq to attack the Kurdistan Workers Party (PKK) in retaliation for their killing of more than two dozen Turkish soldiers in the southeastern province of Hakkâri. The offensive apparently followed an attack two days earlier on Turkish security forces by PKK militants entering Turkey from the mountains of northern Iraq.

The United States has been accused of stirring up old rivalries and potential conflict in this country under continuous foreign occupation.

Palestine

In U.S.-allied Israel, Israeli settlers continued violence and vandalism. Israeli occupation forces continued nighttime raids and detentions, house demolitions, threatened expulsions, and other acts depriving Palestinian children of safety and a sense of security, according to UN special rapporteur Richard Falk reporting on October 20 on the situation of human rights in the occupied Palestinian territories. Reporting to the UN General Assembly's human rights committee, Falk raised concerns about the violence against Palestinian children arrested by the Israeli military and urged Tel Aviv to adopt guidelines for detained children that were in line with humanitarian law. "'Arrest procedures documented by UN agencies and reliable human rights organizations include arrests in the middle of the night, removal of children from parents for questioning, abusive treatment at detention, and conviction procedures that appear to preclude findings of not guilty."

Falk then warned of long-term human costs. "Prolonged occupation," he said, "deforms children's development through pervasive deprivations affecting health, education, and overall security."

Africa North

Africa East: NATO Destroys Libya

Libya's head of state (1969-2011) Muammar al-Qaddafi was born (1942) in a tent in the desert near Sirte (also spelled "Surt") where he reportedly died in 2011. The Sirtica Region where Qaddafi was born encompasses Sirte and is the site of one of the world's largest oil fields. The region is situated in north-central Libya fronting the Mediterranean Sea for about 300 miles (480 kilometers) along the southern part of the Gulf of Sidra and extending generally southeastward through the Sirte (Surt) Basin. Sirte (or Surt) is the main port of the Gulf of Sidra. The bulk of Libya's oil deposits are scattered throughout the Sirtica Region, particularly in the Sirte Basin. During World War II, the Gulf of Sidra had been the scene of the Battle of Sirte (March 1942), in which a British naval convoy thwarted attacks from Italian warships and German bombers.

In 1970, Qaddafi, as head of state, removed U.S. and UK military bases from his country and expelled most members of the native Italian and Jewish communities. In 1973, he nationalized all foreign-owned petroleum assets in the country. In the 1980s, Libya established a national boundary across the Gulf of Sidra and prohibited passage of foreign vessels, resulting in several brief military conflicts with the United States of America.

Commenting on the October 2011 invasion of Libya and the killing of its leader (regardless to how one feels about the Libyan leader or about colonialists and imperialists in Africa), Timothy Bancroft-Hinchey wrote, "The lesson from Sirte is an example in how low an evil invasion force [NATO] can become. It uses military hardware to strafe anything that moves. It bombs civilian structures. It mows down Libyan heroes defending their homeland against foreigners, defending their homes and families against terrorists and rapists. It shows the connivance of NATO and Islamist terrorists [visible since Afghanistan, since Kosovo, since Iraq]. It shows the callous cold-blooded disregard for human life demonstrated by a faceless and grey organization that thinks nothing of signing up desperate young men from across the Arab world and beyond and sending them to their deaths for a sign-on fee of 10,000 U.S. dollars.

"*The lesson from Sirte* is today one of resilience and resistance," Bancroft-Hinchey continued, "as it stands defiant against NATO's indiscriminate bombing and the hundreds of rockets unleashed by the terrorists it aids . . . . The lesson from Sirte will continue to be taught tomorrow: As you cannot win an election by banning the most popular party, you do not win a battle by destroying a city, by massacring thousands of people, and by killing the defenders [of their homes] to unleash on that city thousands of terrorists.

"The lesson from Sirte is that by now it is crystal clear where NATO stands . . . . It is strafing defenseless civilians and trying to impose a government of terrorists from the air."

Conflict, War, Prejudice, Forced Migration, Death Costs

Killing Qaddafi, Destroying a Land and People

Critical questions rose after the killing of another head of state. Questions were asked about high costs in ethical and legal judgments, score settling, whom to hold accountable for acts surrounding the death of Libya's head of state, which happened during the Obama government's (U.S./NATO) invasion. Was this death lawful?

The United Nations Human Rights office in October called for a probe into Muammar Qaddafi's death to determine whether he was killed during fighting or after his capture. The Office of the High Commissioner for Human Rights (OHCHR) noted that with four or five different versions of how Qaddafi died, the circumstances surrounding the ex-Libyan leader's death in his hometown of Sirte were unclear. "There are at least two cell phone videos, one showing [the former president] alive and one showing him dead. Taken together, these videos are very disturbing," said Rupert Colville of the OHCHR. "We believe there is a need for an investigation and more details are needed to ascertain whether he was killed in the fighting or after his capture."

From the start of the Libyan conflict in February 2011 until October 2011, the UN High Commissioner for Refugees and the International Organization for Migration (IOM) reported the evacuation of 37,866 third-country nationals from Egypt's Salloum border, one of the main sites for people fleeing the crisis in Libya. The geography of this area is fertile in inviting easy movement across borders but the Libyan conflict and regional warfare have made situations desperate for hundreds of thousands of people forcing them to flee for their lives. In addition to its border with the Mediterranean Sea on the north, Libya borders Egypt on the east, the Sudan on the southeast, Niger and Chad on the south, and Tunisia and Algeria on the west.

Egypt's land frontiers border Libya to the west, the Sudan to the south, and Israel to the northeast. In the north, Egypt's Mediterranean coastline is about 620 miles (1,000 kilometers). In the east, Egypt's coastline on the Red Sea (dividing Africa from Asia) and the Gulf of Aqaba is about 1,200 miles (1,900 kilometers).

All year, thousands of people sought passage and refuge outside war-torn Libya. From the start of bombing in Libya, an estimated twenty-four thousand refugees successfully made the voyage from North Africa to Italy's Lampedusa, located halfway between Sicily and the African coast. Concerning an incident in August, UNHCR reported calling for assistance from NATO after the Italian coast guard came to the aid of a refugee boat packed with three hundred people bound for Lampedusa Island. Italy reportedly asked a NATO ship in the area to come to the aid of the twenty-meter—(sixty-six-feet) long boat, but the NATO vessel failed to respond.

The United Nations Refugee Agency (UNHCR) said on October 21 that rescue efforts needed strengthening because of the growing numbers of refugees pouring out of northern Africa and losing their lives on the perilous journey across the Mediterranean Sea to Europe. At the time, an estimated 1,500 African migrants had been reported missing "since NATO launched its UN-sanctioned [*humanitarian*] bombing campaign in Libya in March 2011," according to the UNHCR.

High Costs Spanning Time and Distance

In mid-February, Libya had descended into violence, a conflict between the government and anti-government protesters. Before the middle of March, more than ninety thousand people were believed to have fled from western Libya into Tunisia and some eighty thousand into Egypt. In one twenty-four-hour period, Wednesday to Thursday the first week of March, "an estimated 9,000 people crossed into Tunisia." In that same 24-hour period, UNHCR staff reported seeing "people from more than 20 other countries [besides Egypt and Tunisia] at the border, including more than 5,300 Bangladeshi." Migrant workers in Libya, from various places in Africa (Egypt, Somalia, and sub-Sahara), were either stranded, under threat within Libya, or on the move.

March 3, 2011, UNHCR reported that conflict was forcing thousands of people out of Libya. This complicated situation was one in which people who had fled to Europe in earlier times and were later forced out of Europe to be held in Libya by an arrangement between European officials and the Libyan government, were now fleeing conflict in the country (Libya) of their supposed asylum. Thousands languished; some camped with the help of UNHCR on Libya's borders with Tunisia (west) and with Egypt (east). Registered with UNHCR were "more than 8,000 refugees and 3,000 asylum seekers" within Libya, but not all were registered with UNHCR, so the commissioner for refugees believed the real figure was much higher.

For those stranded on the border between Libya and Egypt, Salloum is the main crossing point between Libya and Egypt. The International Committee of the Red Cross had been operating at Salloum Land Port since March 2011 and reported providing breakfasts, telephone facilities, and travel documents for hordes of displaced people. A man from Ivory Coast (Côte d'Ivoire) who had spent several years working in Libya told the ICRC he was owed five months' wages, but the conflict in Libya (was) forcing him to flee—where, he did not know. His own country, as he put it, "is on fire."

The UN High Commissioner for Refugees and the International Organization for Migration (IOM) were coordinating the outflow from Libya. The IOM and the UNHCR reported, respectively, that by March 8,

> The number of people who have fled the violence in Libya has passed 212,000, including 112,169 in Tunisia, and 98,188 in Egypt.

> More than 4,000 people have arrived in Algeria by air, land
> and sea [UNHCR reports Algerian government figures],
> including evacuations from Tunisia and Egypt.

The second week in March the number of arrivals in Egypt from
Libya (since mid-February) had passed the one hundred thousand
mark, including almost seventy thousand Egyptians and more than
six thousand Libyans. More than 110,000 people had fled to Tunisia.
Third-country nationals who had been migrant workers—the majority
of them Bangladeshis and Sudanese (but also, Ghanaians, Nigerians,
and other sub-Saharan Africans)—were waiting to be flown home by
their embassies or by the International Organization for Migration.

Africa East: the Case of Somalia

In a January 2007 interview on the Pacifica program *Democracy Now*,
journalist and former spokesperson for the UN mission in Iraq Salim
Lone focused on the critical geography of the Horn of Africa, particularly
Somalia. "Somalia is one of the most strategic regions in the world, after
the Middle East," Lone said. Somalia might even be seen as touching
the Middle or Near East: "Imagine for a second that the very narrow
waterway, the Red Sea, doesn't exist then you see that Ethiopia, Somalia,
Eritrea . . . are just a few miles from Saudi Arabia and Yemen and Iraq."

Because of the wars in the Middle East, you have scores of oil tankers
and warships passing back and forth daily through the Red Sea. The
Horn of Africa is very much a part of the Middle East and for centuries
has had trade with India and countries farther east. "Somalia—also a
'newly oil-rich' country—is a crossroads, and the U.S. wants to make
sure it [the United States] dominates it fully."

In her book *Calling the Shots: How Washington Dominates Today's
UN*, Phyllis Bennis writes that in the late 1970s Somalia was "client/
proxy for the U.S," taking over from the Soviets; but after the fall of
the USSR, the U.S. government dropped this poverty-stricken country,
leaving weapons on the ground to ensure factional fighting over "scarce
resources." The declared ending of the Cold War ended all viable and
credible checks on U.S. power-grabbing militarist extremism, and nations
that needed economic assistance and protection found themselves at the
mercy of the U.S. government. Washington bribed, threatened, beat, and
browbeat these countries into submission to its will. Resisters suffered

U.S. punishment. Washington wanted a "new world order" as decreed by the George H. W. Bush government: a Middle East arranged to suit Washington's whimsical preferences and prejudices ("radical Islamists," as defined by Washington, need not apply). Power ceded to countries of the north and to their allies; perpetual poverty was the plight of countries of the south.

Somalia is south, poor, and Muslim. However, situated between sub-Saharan Africa and countries of Arabia and South Central Asia, Somalia is significant, golden; but it wanted no part of U.S. foreign relations aggression.

News reports indicated that, by 2007, Somalis had achieved peace among themselves; but even if they had not achieved a perfect peace, they had announced their stand against U.S. military interference—on the ground, by air, or by sea. Nevertheless, starting in 2001, massive foreign forces providing air support, a port of call for ships, and a base for ground personnel for the U.S.-led "war on terrorism" sat on Somalia's tiny northern-border neighbor Djibouti—formerly French Somaliland (1896-1967), strategically situated on the Bab el Mandeb Strait to the east separating the Red Sea from the Gulf of Aden.

In the spring of 2009, mass media headlines and political figures screamed "piracy" and carried on a play-by-play of Somalis-versus-the-West, leaving unuttered the critical question of what recourse is there for families driven into perpetual poverty by an endless deluge of foreign invaders, plunderers, and occupiers? Not long after the piracy headlines, the United States unmasked its *legal* aggression against the people of Somalia.

The history makes clear and Bennis and others have documented that in the post-Cold War era, the United States' unchecked domination at the United Nations has caused a breakdown in the UN charter and principles. "Arrogant, militarily powerful and lacking a viable foe to curb its contempt for international law," Hoffman wrote, "the United States government now feels 'superior' to every other country in the world, and, as a result, has become a lawless, rogue nation operating under the clandestine philosophy that 'might makes right.'"

The inordinate power of the permanent-five-member State UN Security Council (United States, United Kingdom, France, China, Russian Federation) and its overwhelming influence on the 192-member UN General Assembly has caused the UN to promote war (armed "peacekeeping") over peace and to fail States instead of helping nations build and sustain *on their own terms, in their own way*. Bennis reports that the General Assembly has decreased emphasis on "economic development, decolonization, democratization of access to technology, restraint of multinational corporations, and fighting for a more equitable international division of resources."

Horn Crossing Red Sea

Severe conditions worsened. In East Africa, the United States expediently allies with Kenya, Ethiopia, and Djibouti. Most painfully against a deeply stricken Somalia on the Horn across the Gulf of Aden neighboring Yemen neighboring Saudi Arabia, the U.S. allies with despots of the latter countries.

The United Nations 2011 reports showed that more than thirteen million people in Ethiopia, Kenya, Somalia, and Djibouti were in need of assistance. Together with being hit by the worst drought in sixty years, the region of Eastern Africa and the Horn was suffering foreign bombing campaigns. In addition to its attacks on Afghanistan, Pakistan, Libya, Iraq, and Yemen, the United States was conducting drone strikes on Somalia.

A BQM-74E remote-controlled drone takes off from the flight deck of USS Samuel B. Roberts (U.S. Department of Defense public domain image)

Somalia was under constant military attack in 2011. The press outside North America reported a U.S. drone strike on October 21 killed twenty-two people in Kudhaa Island in southern Somalia near the border with Kenya. On the same day close to Ras Kamboni town in the Badhaadhe District of the Lower Juba region near the border with Kenya, another attack by a U.S. unmanned aerial vehicle (UAV) killed at least forty-four civilians and injured sixty-three others in southern Somalia. Earlier headlines in the same period reported: "U.S. Drone Attacks Kill 26 in Somalia," "Kenyan Jets Strike

'Militants' in Somalia," "U.S. Drone Attack kills 46 in Somalia," "U.S. Drone Attack Kills 18 in Somalia," "U.S. Drone Crashes in Somalia Killing Five."

Disease

That October news day also reported Mogadishu, the capital of Somalia, whose people were suffering increased rates of waterborne diseases, had lost sixty-five more children to cholera. A physician told Press TV the children died the morning of October 20 in the capital's Hodan neighborhood and added that more than 160 other children, suffering from cholera and waterborne diseases, also were taken to Banadir and Digfeer hospitals in southern Mogadishu for medication. Earlier news headlines in the same October period reported: "80 More Somali Children Die of Cholera," "Cholera Claims 195 More Lives in Somalia," "Cholera Kills 116 Children in Somalia," "Cholera and Hunger Kill 83 More Somali Kids." In Mogadishu, a combination of poor or lacking sanitation systems, scarcity of safe and clean drinking water and overcrowding leads to the spread of waterborne diseases.

Yemen school girls in front of school. Photo UNHCR /P. Rubio Larrauri/ March 2012

Refugees: Famine, Flight, Fear, more Flight—Somalia to Yemen and Back

Though supporters and opponents of (U.S.-allied) Yemen's president Ali Abdullah Saleh were fighting during most of 2011, Somalia had had two decades of factional warfare together with foreign aggression and was hit harder still in 2011 by one of the worst food crises in memory. At the time of the UN report that year, four million people had been affected: Somalia's dead totaled in the tens of thousands of people, with 750,000 more expected to be at risk of death in the months to come. Those who were able fled for their lives.

Many Somalis left their country with the hope that they would be able reach Yemen and other gulf countries and find work, but the deteriorating security situation in Yemen curbed their movement. Work opportunities for refugees were rapidly shrinking in the fall of 2011, and refugees had little choice but to return to their troubled country. On October 21, the United Nations Press Service reported the High Commissioner for Refugees saying, "Some of the nearly 200,000 Somalis who have sought refuge in Yemen from violence and famine in their own country are now considering going back home due to worsening security in the Arabian Peninsula nation."

November 2011

Pakistan and East Africa

Pakistan

(East Africa into Asia): Somalia /
Bosasso Beach. Photo UNHCR/
A Webster / December 2006

Jacobabad, Pakistan, displaced people.
Photo UNHCR /P. Kessler
September 2010

Kenya / Refugee camps outskirts of Dagahaley. Photo IOM/
UNHCR / Brendan Bannon. 2011

Foreign governments continued to weaken South Central Asian and
African countries. Like vultures, these "democracies"—armed with
NGOs, belligerents, proxies, mercenaries, militaries, and unmanned
drones—descended and devoured. Examples aside from Afghanistan

and Iraq were preemptive wars by remote on Pakistan and Somalia.

Some of the world's biggest humanitarian emergencies were in Pakistan. The country continued to be "scarred by conflict and buffeted by earthquakes and floods." Regardless to and or because of "*humanitarian* assistance," Pakistanis continued to suffer. In 2010, floods affected a fifth of the population; that was twenty million people. After inspecting the flood damage, UN Secretary-general Ban Ki-moon said it was "one of the worst humanitarian emergencies [he had] witnessed."

Under the Obama government, the United States conducted continuous violence against the sovereignty of this neighbor of Afghanistan and against the Pakistani people, pushing them to their knees. Also throughout 2011, this government continued its war on Somalia and its suffering people, pushing them as well to their knees. Conflict, frequent drought, and rampant inflation have made Somalia one of the world's worst humanitarian crises. Huge numbers of Somalis have been displaced within the country. The United Nations said more than a million Somalis—many from the capital, Mogadishu—fled their homes in 2007.

In 2006, Islamists (Islamic Courts' Union [ICU]) ousted warlords from most of the south and took control of the capital Mogadishu; however, Ethiopian troops, siding with the transitional government, interfered and overthrew the Islamists. The Red Cross called the resulting fighting the worst in fifteen years between insurgents and Ethiopia-backed government forces. The United States under the Obama government again uses neighboring countries Ethiopia and Kenya in its violent aggression against the interests of Somalia and its people. In 2007, an African peacekeeping force arrived; Somali pirates increased attacks on international shipping, including a cargo of tanks and two oil supertankers. The North Atlantic Treaty Organization (NATO) in 2008 deployed naval vessels. Today the United States capriciously and callously sides with one faction or another, creates chaos, stirs up conflict, and continuously bombs the suffering people of Somalia. In these conditions, no one should be surprised when desperate Somalis commit acts of piracy; nor should Western leaders feign surprise and use desperate acts of an impoverished people as pretext to further a new colonialism with overwhelming military might.

If not for the violence against this country (and with the honest help of sustained impartial, nonviolent, respectful negotiation with Somalis in their public interest), the country would have a chance of rising from its knees. Though it is today one of the poorest countries in the world, researchers find that Somalia's economy could very well function and the people could survive adhering if they choose to their own cultural patterns.

Pakistan's Floods and Victims

Pakistan / Jalozal Camp Internally Displaced Persons (IDPs) /2 million had escaped conflict in Swat Valley. Photo UNHCR/H. Caux May21, 2009

These high costs, this war-caused global suffering together with suffering caused by climate and layered levels of regression across Africa, crossing the Red Sea into the Middle East, Persian Gulf, and onto the Asian subcontinent and regions farther eastward is needless suffering. It is needless because hegemony, the selfish excess of wealthy industrialized war-making nations and their regressive powers, principally the United States, my country, have callously created, exacerbated, and sustained the suffering of Africa's and Asia's nations and peoples.

Economically and industrially developed countries possess enormous wealth, knowledge, and expertise, and the wherewithal to obtain and employ these. They have the means to end suffering if not for the paradigm, this ethos of foreign relations violence and the absence of sufficient moral energy to abandon it—to mature, to progress beyond violence as the tool of relations. This cruelty, this deliberate carelessness that conducts a "global war on terror" all the while terrorizing and destroying global society, this willful failing of the United States of America and its public figures and a long line of entrenched civilian governments and their foreign and domestic agents and allies is heartbreakingly beyond criminal.

IV

Human Costs—War-Made Refugees

[W]hen killing is viewed as not only permissible but heroic behavior sanctioned by one's government or cause, the fine distinction between taking a human life and other forms of impermissible violence gets lost; and rape becomes an unfortunate but inevitable by-product of the necessary game called war.

—Susan Brownmiller

Notes from Early 2011 Shelved Manuscript

Wars' Defenseless

Refugees and those who seek asylum have left their homes not because they yearn to traverse great waterways and live in lands foreign to their culture but because violence (war and invasion, conflict, and occupation) has robbed them of their homes and land, their safety, and their future. People fleeing for their lives move across cities and towns and state and regional borders; they traverse seas and oceans, or try to, and attempt to make their way by land to what they believe or hope to be a safe harbor. They take great risks because they cannot stay in their homes on their land; and even after a time, they find they cannot return, or they find the "safe harbor" is itself in turmoil.

Somalia / Internally Displaced Persons (IDPs) / Photo UNHCR /A. Webster / December 2006

Mogadishu, Somalia / Maajo IDP Settlement Internally Displaced Persons (IDPs) in drought and famine stricken southern Somalia. Photo UNHCR / S. Modola / August 2011

At the end of 2009, approximately 43.3 million people were "forcibly displaced worldwide." This figure, according to the United Nations High Commissioner for Refugees' Global Trends report (released June 15, 2010), represents "the highest number of people uprooted by conflict and persecution since the mid-1990s." At the same time, the report said, "The number of refugees voluntarily returning to their home countries

has fallen to its lowest level in

twenty years." Leading the list of people seeking asylum in industrialized countries, according to UNHCR statistics, were Iraqis, Afghans, and Somalis. António Guterres, the head of UNHCR, said, "Conflicts in Afghanistan and Somalia fueled increases in asylum seekers and [these conflicts] showed no sign of being resolved." In places such as Iraq and southern Sudan, conflicts appeared to have been ending or were on the way to being resolved but had stagnated. This report, of course, did not foresee the 2010-2011 (continuing in 2012) uprisings and backlash in Africa and the Middle East and subsequent huge migrations from the region and across it.

"Persisting conflict," the UNHCR report said, "makes voluntary return to countries of origin—the solution preferred by host countries and refugees—more difficult because of the growing resilience of conflict. More than half of the refugees under UNHCR's care are in protracted situations"; thus, 2009 was a bad year for voluntary repatriation, the worst in twenty years. The repatriation norm had been a million people annually, Guterres said; but in 2009, "only 251,000 refugees went home." A majority of the world's refugees, before the new totals, "[had] been living as refugees for five years or more"; and increased numbers of refugees "are living in cities, primarily in the developing world," contrary to the popular view that "refugees are inundating industrialized nations."

Asylum Seekers

The number of new individual asylum claims worldwide grew to nearly one million, with South Africa receiving more than 222,000 new claims in 2010, making it the single largest asylum destination in the world.

Internally Displaced Persons

Within their own countries, the report showed, the number of people uprooted by conflict grew by 4 percent (to 27.1 million) at the end of 2009. Persistent conflict in the Democratic Republic of the Congo, Pakistan, and Somalia mainly accounted for the increase in the overall figure.

Stateless

The annual 2009 Global Trends report, which reviews statistical trends and patterns of conflict-related displacements also covers stateless people, people claimed by no country. The number of people known to be stateless at the end of 2009 was 6.6 million, though unofficial estimates range as high as 12 million.

These people do not take to roads and seas because they hate their own countries or because they love Western Europe, Canada, or the United States of America; or because they prefer cultures other than their own. This oft-repeated notion is nonsense. Refugees, stateless people, asylum seekers are people who have been forced to migrate from and across South Central Asia, the Middle East, the Horn of Africa.

Afghanistan

Northern Afghanistan returnees from 20-year exile in Iran. Photo UNHCR / W. Schellenberg, August 2009

Individual experiences of war and human rights violations, such as forced labor and kidnapping—combined with insecurity, widespread poverty, political instability, poor educational prospects, and a declining hope for a brighter future—are all fuelling migration flows—and expanding smuggling networks. Afghan youth are trying to reach Europe for several reasons, including the continuing conflict in Afghanistan and shrinking protection space in neighboring countries; and movement itself is fraught with peril.

Afghanistan's children in growing numbers, says UNHCR's 2010 report, were making a difficult and dangerous overland journey to Europe, a journey that is particularly perilous for defenseless children unaccompanied by their parents. Along the way, these children have been subjected to human rights abuses.

Looking into the reasons for migration, the routes the children took, and the reception they received on arrival at one or another destination, the report found that some children traveled "more or less directly from Afghanistan." Others had lived for years in Iran or Pakistan. Published by UNHCR's Policy Development and Evaluation Service, the study documented more than 5,900 Afghan children, mostly boys, who sought asylum in Europe in 2009. This figure contrasts with the 3,380 Afghan children in 2008. Afghan youth in 2009 made up 45 percent of asylum claims from unaccompanied children, almost three times those made by Somalis. Somalis comprised the second largest group. The refugee high commissioner believed that there were other Afghan children who did not apply for asylum but who were on the move.

Though "children face shocking hardships along the way," the director for Europe said, "they feel an obligation to their families to continue their journey. As a result," Judith Kumin concluded, "they are victimized over and over again."

Multiple, Multilayered suffering

Civilian casualties have far-reaching impact on families. When a member of the family dies in these conflicts, it is not just one death. The whole family suffers loss of wherewithal: loss of income, loss of place, loss of future, loss of food, loss of business, loss of standing, loss of peace of mind, loss of security, loss of balance, loss of traditions, loss of culture.

In 2009, more civilians died in the Afghanistan conflict than in any other year, up to that year, since the United States invaded that country in 2001. More Afghans suffered injury and property loss. These figures continued to rise in 2010 and throughout 2011. According to Afghanistan's mental health minister quoted in a news article in the fall of 2010, decades of war have severely scarred the Afghan people. Confirmed by the World Health Organization, "more than 60 percent of Afghans in an estimated total population of 28 million suffer stress disorders and mental health problems as the result of decades of war." To treat the suffering, Afghanistan, according to WHO representative Peter Graaff, has only two hundred beds for psychiatric services with only two psychiatrists to cover the entire population.

Extreme poverty, insecurity, violence, and gender disparities aid in worsening the mental health of the Afghan people.

January 16, 2011, news sources from Afghanistan reported violence was at its worst since the 2001 overthrow of the Taliban government. In previously peaceful areas like the north, violence was spreading rapidly. Civilian and military casualties were at record levels. The attacks over the weekend of the sixteenth and the previous week near the border with Pakistan followed, at that time, the end of the bloodiest year of a war that had "dragged on for more than nine years." The United Nations reported 2,412 civilians had died and 3,803 suffered wounds between January and October of 2010, a 20 percent increase over 2009. By 2011, the rise was 40 percent.

In its 2010 report, the group Campaign for Innocent Victims in Conflict wrote that *conflict harm "weaves an interconnected web of destruction* [emphasis added]. Injuries, deaths, loss of property, displacement, lost livelihoods, emotional trauma, destruction of infrastructure, and breakdown of communities compound one another to create a devastating and untenable situation." If, for example, a husband dies, the death "often means the loss of a key breadwinner." If a wife dies, this death "often leaves children and their household without the primary caretaker." In addition, "medical expenses, cost of travel, loss of property, and higher living expenses place substantial financial burdens on families, trapping them in debt and poverty. Underdevelopment, lack of infrastructure, poverty, and gender inequality as well as weakened coping mechanisms and displacement due to conflict magnify the shock and impact of war victims' losses. These factors exacerbate the challenges of recovering from harm."

Pakistan Floods: millions displaced by the worst floods and landslides northwest Pakistan has seen in decades (UNHCR).

Pakistan

Civilians in Pakistan live in a dangerous and deadly environment, and their losses "are often long lasting and complex, destabilizing families and entire communities."

In its 2009 interviews with policymakers, nongovernmental organization officials, and more than160 Pakistani civilians suffering direct losses from the conflict, the Campaign for Innocent Victims in Conflict (CIVIC) found that, since 2001, the conflict in Pakistan's northwest involving Pakistan's government, U.S. forces, and militant groups "[had] killed and injured thousands of civilians, destroyed countless homes and livelihoods, and displaced millions." In one of the poorest countries in the world, more than 1.4 million of its people "are currently displaced as a result of conflict."

Much of the Pakistani population is grieving: widows mourn husbands, parents mourn children, and children mourn their caretakers. The disabled suffer marginalization. Conflict pushes families into poverty or traps them in debt as they struggle to cope with losses. Many people CIVIC interviewed had both a combat loss in their family and had been displaced from their home. They had been forced to live with host families, in rented accommodation, or in refugee camps. Forced to find jobs and housing in a market saturated with other displaced persons severely strains families' finances and coping mechanisms. Relatives they would typically rely on were themselves often also displaced and struggling to make ends meet. "The majority of those displaced in 2009 fled the Pakistani military offensive in Swat and the surrounding districts.

By the end of 2009, most had returned; but ongoing and newly initiated military operations in different areas of Federally Administered Tribal Areas [FATA] had led to additional waves of displacement." In its report, CIVIC detailed more than 220,000 displaced in Bajaur; more than 180,000 in Mohmand, approximately 428,000 in South Waziristan; 56,000 to100,000 in Khyber; approximately 128,000 in Kurram; and approximately 200,000 in Orazai. In the summer of 2010 (July), "an estimated 2 million IDPs [internally displaced persons] remained displaced by the conflict—1.4 million of whom had been able to register with the government."

Federal Washington seated a new executive administration with an unchanged foreign relations model. Wars (invasions, occupations) intensified. Matters worsened for peoples and nations of Afghanistan and Pakistan and the entire region. On January 23, 2009, three days after the new U.S. president took the oath of office, the United States hit Pakistan with drone strikes.

"Instead of striking a Taliban hideout, the missiles struck the house of Malik Gulistan Khan, a tribal elder and member of a local pro-government peace committee. Five members of his family died." (U.S. drone attacks continued and escalated throughout 2010 and 2011 and into 2012.) Mass media headlines locked on "horrors of terrorism"; but the millions of people being hurt, forced from their homes, on the move were not "terrorists," "militants," "combatants," or "extremists." They were ordinary people caught in the crossfire of the West's wars.

In the Crossfire

CIVIC's research found that civilians suffer greatly from a much broader range of conflict-related violence. Caught in the crossfire between militants and Pakistani military forces, civilians also suffer the consequences of extrajudicial killings, sectarian violence, landmines, explosive remnants of war (ERWs), and U.S. drone strikes. Drone strikes increased dramatically.

From 2004 to 2007, there were nine drone strikes. In 2009, there were fifty-three. As CIVIC released its report in 2010, there were already more than seventy drone attacks. Nearly all the attacks were in South or North Waziristan.

Killing by Remote: the Without-cost Delusion

Pakistani media reported U.S. drone attacks killed "more than 700 civilians in 2009, approximately 90 percent of deaths overall. Between 2006 and April 2009, 687 civilians died, approximately 90 percent overall during that period. From 2006 to April 2009, 687 civilians died as the result of drone attacks." The Campaign for Innocent Victims in Conflict (CIVIC) report also found that civilian casualties in U.S. drone strikes were almost certainly higher than what the United States admitted. Though security constraints and government-imposed limits on access prevented exact calculation of civilian casualty figures—as has been routine in these intense years of U.S.-led wars in South Central

Asia—estimates indicated that civilian casualties in Pakistan were likely higher than in neighboring Afghanistan.

From faraway places, killers fire deadly missiles by remote control, attacking towns and villages. "While allowing for the legal use of drones on established fields of battle," says a professor of International Dispute Resolution at Notre Dame University in the United States, "international law cannot justify the use of unmanned aerial vehicles capable of dropping bombs and firing powerful missiles outside of the battlefield. In cities and towns and in rural areas where there is no armed conflict going on it is not appropriate to use battlefield weapons and tactics," she told Deutsche Welle news. Professor Mary Ellen O'Connell added that just because people, at some point, took part in an armed conflict, they cannot be indefinitely regarded as participants.

> There are times when the use of force under international law comes under scrutiny, such as the NATO bombing campaign in Kosovo in 1999, which prompted discussion about the use of force and humanitarian intervention.

London School of Economics International Relations lecturer Kirsten Ainley said drone use per se does not trigger the need for an update in international law, as there is no legal requirement that a human being be close to where weapons are fired. "What is challenging international law," she said, "is how we define what the battlefield of a war is."

By 2010, the United States was openly at war with the Pakistani people—even as this country was suffering a climate disaster. On its Independence Day, August 14, 2010, Pakistan abandoned the celebrations because the country had been hit by a flood disaster; but the disaster did not stop the United States' incessant "drone bombing attacks on defenseless Pakistani villages." U.S. drone attacks in September 2010 had reached a record high. Before U.S. president Barack Obama took office, he said, in the rhetorical tone of his immediate predecessor, that the United States would hunt down suspected terrorists and kill or capture them wherever they could be found. As experts debated "the limits international law places on drone use," the Obama government ramped up drone attacks in the Pakistani tribal regions.

Africa Crossing Red Sea

(Crossing Red Sea and Gulf of Aden): Cliffs of Mareero, Somalia / Asylum seekers, migrants await smuggler's boat to Yemen. Photo UNHCR/ K. McKinsey/ February 2006

Africa's War-made Homeless

Africa in 2008 was the most affected continent, with 11.6 million IDPs in 19 countries. By the fall of 2010, UNHCR reported, "more than 32,000 African refugees and migrants from Somalia and Ethiopia [had] made the perilous crossing to Yemen, escaping war and persecution." In recent years, the Red Sea, between the Horn of Africa and Yemen, has been one of the busiest and deadliest refugee routes in the world.

On the Horn of Africa, thousands of Somalis have abandoned Mogadishu, the capital city, to live in shelters skirting the city. They are some of the 1.7 million people internally displaced by the war. Ongoing violence in Somalia has forced more than two million people to flee their homes: most are displaced within Somalia; others live as refugees in neighboring countries. At the time of the UNHCR report, there were some 1.46 million IDPs within Somalia; 614,000 Somalis were living as refugees mostly in neighboring countries. All were constantly at risk. If bullets and knives did not get them, hunger, thirst, and disease probably would. In the period between 1991 and the time of the report, an estimated one million people in Somalia had died from war, disease, and famine. For some, the life support for a lifetime is a diet of no more than bread and beans. Six hundred families waited in tents for a later move into shelters, but without cash to build more than 250 new shelters, many of the people reportedly languished "without four walls to call home."

Somalia's neighbor across Gulf of Aden, Yemen

Treacherous Crossing

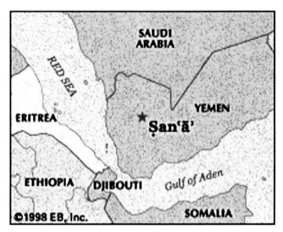

In early January 2011, Agence France Presse reported a Red Crescent official saying the Yemeni coast guard had retrieved only three bodies of dozens of African migrants (approximately forty-one passengers), believed to have drowned off south Yemen. Mostly Ethiopians were aboard the boat that capsized near the Bab al-Mandeb Strait, which links the Red Sea and the Gulf of Aden. Migrants frequently enter by boat into south Yemen, one of the world's poorest countries; then move north toward the border with oil-rich Saudi Arabia.

Tens of thousands of Ethiopians and Somalis each year make the perilous crossing to Yemen in the hope of escaping the economic deprivation, persecution, and conflicts of their home countries. Many die aboard often-small overcrowded rotten boats. Others, already weakened by long journeys from the hinterland to the coast, die at the hands of smugglers.

Somali Woman Recalls journey of horrors to UNHCR

A woman, Hawo who had crossed into Kenya with her five young children told a UNHCR staffer that after her husband was killed, she had fled the Somali capital, Mogadishu, for Beled eight months earlier.

Conflict erupted in the town of Beled where she was living in a run-down settlement for the displaced, and she was again forced to flee. "I'm scared. I don't know what to do. I have nothing with me, and I'm afraid my children will not bear this situation for much longer," she said. On a dusty, scalding-hot plateau in south Yemen, an old military base turned refugee camp for her and seventeen thousand other Somalis, $15 pays for a month's work, if you can find it. Hawo stepped inside the concrete block room, its shadows dimming the bright colors of her headscarf, into the breathless air, hot as a furnace by midday. Hawo explained how in 2007, militiamen, "the enemy of civil war," she called them, broke into her home:

> They hit [my husband] badly and they wanted to rape me in front of him. He tried to protect me, but unfortunately, they killed him with a big knife. I was seven months pregnant at that time. And I decided to go out of the country because of the unsafe [conditions].

> [With her two small daughters slumped over her lap, Hawo sat cramped in a long thin skiff, designed for two dozen people, now packed with nearly fifty.]

> I couldn't make my children be quiet, and the smugglers warned me to silence them, but I couldn't. Finally, they ripped my children away from me and threw them into the sea.

"After thirteen days and nights adrift in the ocean," she said, "help finally arrived, another boat with petrol and directions to the Yemeni coast. Forced into the water by smugglers too scared to land them on the shore, many of those who had survived the journey to Yemen drowned just meters from the shore"; Hawo's unborn had died in premature birth in Kharaz camp. Hawo had managed "through seven months of Somalia and seventeen days of escape to make it to life in Yemen."

Internal conflict that broke out in the northern part of Yemen in 2004 had directly affected "some 77,000 Yemeni IDPs," and from August 2009, fighting in and around the northern province of Sa'ada (Sa'dah, also spelled "Saada" in northwestern Yemen) resulted in significant new population displacements. Quoting UN Refugee Agency figures in January, British Broadcasting reported that in 2009 Yemen took in "more than 74,000 Africans [who were] fleeing 'desperate situations of civil war, political instability, poverty, famine and drought in the Horn of Africa.'" The UNHCR reported caring for more than 154,000 refugees in Yemen, mostly from Somalia. The Yemeni government had traditionally maintained an open-door policy toward Somalis, recognizing them as refugees on a prima facie basis, but insecure conditions in parts of the Yemen began to hinder access to "people of concern." By 2011, increasing internal conflict in Yemen forced refugees doubly to become refugees. The UNHCR reported also that continual increases in mixed-migration movements (varieties of nationalities on the move) had doubly burdened Yemen's asylum system and imposed additional burdens on government and aid agencies. (In the spring of 2012, the U.S. government was waging drone attacks on Somalia and Yemen, Pakistan and Afghanistan, possibly Iran and Bahrain.)

As the twenty-first century approached its second decade and moved further into it, nine countries (Sudan, Kenya, Democratic Republic of the Congo, Iraq, Pakistan, Somalia, Colombia, Sri Lanka, and India) were reeling from large-scale displacements of hundreds of thousands of people. Moreover, the effects of such enormous forced displacements, like all human and environmental disasters, never are contained within a country or region of origin or even a continent. We are all connected.

Iraq and Its Refugees

Foreign forces left in this occupied land continue to be combatants no matter what Washington chooses to call them. People of Fallujah suffered visible killers in the form of American soldiers with weapons. Iraqis also suffered the invisible killers, residue of weapons of war: depleted uranium, the radioactivity and toxicity of which they eat, breathe, and drink. Toxicity measured in the air seeps into the water table and affects fauna and flora. In Fallujah in 2006, close to 6,000 cases (5,928) of previously unknown or rarely seen diseases showed up in medical diagnoses.

"In the first half of 2007, 2,447 seriously ill patients were admitted to medical facilities, showing mostly little known symptoms," the United Nations Human Rights Council reported in the fall of 2010. "Fifty percent were children . . . . Five years after the 2004 attacks, cancers had multiplied by four." In five years, medical personnel noted a twelvefold incidence in fourteen-year-old children. In a six-year period, birth defects rose by 25 percent.

In its Middle East and North Africa regional report in 2010, UNHCR voiced concerns "about the deteriorating situation of the nearly 1.4 million Iraqi internally displaced persons (IDPs) and the large number of Iraqi refugees in the region." The report pointed to the critical problem of "displaced women and children, many of whom are affected by sexual and gender-based violence, including trafficking, 'survival sex' and child labor."

Worldatlas map regional: Syria, Jordan, Iran, Iraq, Eqypt, Lebanon, Turkey, Red Sea, Gulf of Aden, Yemen, and Horn of Africa

Rough or Impossible Return to Country under Occupation

Iraq is an occupied country experiencing conflict between and among internal and foreign forces. "UNHCR does not envisage wide scale returns to Iraq in the short term," the United Nations High Commissioner for Refugees representative Melissa Fleming said in the commission's 2010 update on Iraqis returning to their homeland. Why is this? The majority of Iraqis who returned to Baghdad from neighboring countries found that physical insecurity, economic hardship, and lack of basic public services led them "to regret their decision to return to Iraq." Returning Iraqis reported to UNHCR staff "numerous instances of explosions, harassment, military operations and kidnapping occurring in their areas of return." (At the turn of 2011, into the spring, and through year's end, Iraq, as were nations across the Middle East and North Africa, was experiencing protest demonstrations for basic needs and jobs, uncorrupt government, and human rights.)

Sixty-one percent of Iraqis returning to their homeland reported insecurity and personal safety concerns. Almost 80 percent of those returning to Karkh and Resafa (Baghdad's west and east-bank settlements along the Tigris River) said they did not go to their original place of residence because of general insecurity or the fear of direct persecution. Eleven percent of returning Iraqis cited poor economic conditions and unemployment as reasons for not returning to their former homes and neighborhoods. The High Commissioner for Refugees reported that together with the problem of finding regular employment was the problem of inadequate access to public services: lack of adequate health care combined with, in many parts of the country, the infrequent supply of electricity.

Iraqi government statistics reported 18,240 Iraqi refugees returned from countries of asylum in the first eight months of 2010 while 89,700 people displaced inside Iraq returned home in the same period. Presenting UNHCR's survey findings to journalists in Geneva, Switzerland, Fleming said 34 percent of people attempting to return were uncertain about staying permanently in their homeland and would consider once again seeking asylum in neighboring countries if conditions failed to improve; however, countries at war with Iraq have often balked at giving refuge.

UNHCR representative Adrian Edwards in September 2010 criticized European countries for deporting Iraqis. "Car explosions, roadside bombs, mortar attacks and kidnapping" are still "daily threats for Iraqis," he reported; and Iraqis "should not be sent home to five central provinces including Baghdad [because] those areas remain dangerous." He urged focused effort on developing "conditions in Iraq that are conducive to sustainable and voluntary return."

However, many people forced to uproot cannot return home. Reporting her observations in Iraq, Ann Jones writes in *War Is Not Over when It's Over*, "What emerged from all my fractured photographs were glimpses of a civilization, among the oldest in the world, blown apart" (Jones, 239). She says she heard a single story, over and over, not only from Iraqis of every description but also from Afghans. The example Jones gives is Fatima's story. "'I want to go back,' Fatima said, 'but to what? Our world is gone.'" Jones explains the far-reaching war-caused harm.

> Families are decimated or dispersed. Fatima has seven brothers and sisters, all highly educated, multilingual professionals—professors, judges, scientists—Iraq needs; but they live and work in Australia, Canada, Egypt, Germany, Switzerland, England, and Oman. Iraq becomes another Afghanistan: citizens capable of reconstructing their country are scattered like shrapnel by the explosion of their culture, the destruction of their cities, the devastation of their land.

Jones details the horror of raped and silenced Iraqi women (20-221). It is impossible to know how many thousands of Iraqi women and girls have been raped, Jones writes, "but rape is commonplace. Of 4,516 cases of sexual violence in Iraq reported to UNHCR in Jordan, women were the victims in 4,233 cases; and for each reported case, there are countless others . . . . For Iraqi women, rape is a terrible shame . . . . Women keep silent after the fact for fear of the social stigma that attends it . . . . The refugees form no community organization, no political action committees, no support groups. Each individual, or each family, seems to be alone and afraid. One UNHCR counselor said of the raped women, 'They have been well trained to keep silent.'"

Jones goes on to report that many Iraqi women and girls dance in nightclubs in Damascus [neighboring Syria] and leave [the clubs] in cars with men who pay them for sex. To call it 'prostitution' implies a greater degree of choice than they have," Jones comments.

> "Survival sex" more accurately describes their situation. The women are desperately poor and many sex workers are single

mothers, widowed or abandoned—some after having suffered rape (Jones, 225).

Migrants' Journey Unimaginably Harrowing

For those who might be able to escape war and conflict in their homeland, the road and seas for these refugees and asylum seekers are treacherous indeed, regardless to whether there is sanctuary or hospitality or help at another port. In mid-December 2010, a wooden boat believed to have been carrying Iranian, Iraqi, and Kurdish asylum seekers smashed against the rocky shore of Christmas Island. Australia administers the island as an external territory, located in the Indian Ocean 870 miles (1,400 kilometers) northwest of Australia. In late December, fears mounted that ninety-seven missing asylum seekers from Iraq and Iran might have died at sea en route to Australia from Indonesia. The vessel had been due to arrive more than three weeks before the December 15 boat tragedy on Christmas Island when at least forty-eight asylum seekers died. Reports said the journey by sea from Indonesia to Australia usually takes two to four days.

Conflict, displacement, struggle for asylum or resettlement not only uproots and unsettles physically and emotionally; these phenomena also rob people of a sense of self, which often fuels more violence especially against women. Again, Jones writes in *War Is Not Over when It's Over* that Iraqi men in exile have lost house, land, livelihood, status—all that once identified them as men (p. 228).

> As the family sinks deeper into poverty and waiting [for asylum or resettlement] becomes intolerable, men try to reclaim their sense of identity by reasserting control over their wives and children. Domestic violence *sweeps through Iraqi refugee communities like cholera.*

Why They Come, How to Respond

How desperate does a person have to be to leave homeland and endanger life without knowing what waits at a foreign port? Bavarian public broadcaster Stefan Troendle asked in a February 2011 opinion piece in

Deutsche Welle. The migration is "all because of the hope for a better life—or simply the hope to survive." Many societies in North Africa find themselves in upheaval, "and Europe, having no unified immigration policy, has provoked and enabled xenophobic policies of individual European countries. The refugee problem is not Italian. It is European." Though focused on Europe, Troendle could have been speaking about the United States as the responsibility applies equally and even more to the United States: for its global wars and fueling of conflict, its human rights abuses, and its comprehensive model of foreign relations in violence.

In an interview with Network Europe's Andrew David, Lincoln University professor Richard Keeble said, "most Western powers—having supported dictators—obviously bear enormous responsibility, and for the consequences including the thousands and thousands of refugees fleeing what's going on." Media organizations have played "an enormous role in fueling animosity to all things foreign," and governments must counter this by "criticizing media for discriminating against ethnic minorities" and by "welcoming immigrants." In a March 1, 2011, article, Dr. Jürgen Wiemann of the Multilateral Trading System and Development Cooperation at the German Society for International Cooperation (GIZ) concluded:

> We can build no wall in the Mediterranean nor can we send all the boat people back out to sea. Only if we offer . . . cooperation will it be possible to avoid cultural clashes and worse.

Yes, but more than a platitude or reactionary attitude is required. We must address the prior act of violence and its consequential severity in the costs paid by human beings—war-made refugees and far-reaching pain, upheaval and suffering endured needlessly by women and children, men and families, peoples and cultures and futures, countries and continents across the world.

In Ann Jones's findings and in the direct words of the Campaign for Innocent Victims in Conflict is a truth we must take to heart—conflict harm "weaves an interconnected web of destruction"—and having understood this truth, set about ending the cycle of violence and suffering modeled in relations among nations.

V

WASTE TRUMPS WANT
(PRICE OF PRESIDENCY, COSTS IN LIVES)

The only moral virtue of war is that it compels the capitalist system to look itself in the face and admit it is a fraud. It compels the present society to admit that it has no morals it will not sacrifice for gain.

—Helen Keller

Islanded in Criminal Excess as World's Majorities Languish

In the 1960s arriving in Africa as a U.S. Peace Corps teacher, my culture-shocking experience was the daily contact with beggars on the streets of Freetown, Sierra Leone's capital city. Twenty years later, while working in the capital of the United States of America, I watched beggars lying in the shadow of the capitol dome, standing with cup in hand and help-me signs along church-lined boulevards of the capital's affluent suburbs. As the years passed and growing numbers of people were dumped unhealed from mental institutions, pushed untreated from hospitals, shoved from homes whose boarded-up sores further sickened cities, begging rose and spread to more streets, under run-down bridges, in tunnels, into cardboard boxes in open spaces, and in the shadowed undergrounds of the United States of America. In late December 2011, as the floods and refuse of war and callous neglect continued rising, the "elected" elite took their leisure, laying back, licking their chops like royalty separate and apart peering through opera glasses high above the stage at Kennedy Center—and millions across the globe continued suffering the impact of Washington's endless violence.

"We cannot exist as a little island of well-being in a world where two-thirds of the people go to bed hungry every night," Eleanor Roosevelt warned America more than fifty years ago.

Dagahaley refugee camp / Kenya / Somali refugees / Dahira / 20-days' travel by foot 11-year-old girl fleeing drought holds her severely-malnourished sibling. Photo UNHCR / B. Bannon /July 28, 2011

Today the contrast between U.S. waste and other peoples' want is staggering, unconscionable. Combined with overwhelming evidence that the United States callously causes and contributes to others' want, their insecurity, their poverty, and scarcity of even the no-frills essentials of life—shelter, food, running water, electricity, work, and the right to their own resources—makes this state of affairs deeply immoral and indeed criminal.

Waste Trumps Want

How to define what is criminally cruel—so cruel as to be unspeakable yet seemingly unseen by so many? Cholera claims Somalia's children as U.S. bombs regularly attack them.

Drone image at Press TV November 6, 2011, http://www. presstv.ir/detail/208633.html "At least 99 people have been killed in a single day in the airstrikes carried out by the U.S. assassination drones in southern Somalia."

The U.S. foreign relations paradigm in violence has concomitant consequences in U.S. domestic affairs—NO LAND AN ISLAND, No PEOPLE APART. In announcing the formation of a new political party, the Justice Party USA, and his candidacy for the office of U.S. president, former Salt Lake City, Utah, mayor Rocky (Ross C) Anderson in November 2011said, "[In the past decade], outrageous, expensive wars have wasted lives and tax dollars . . . . We have been voting against our own interests . . . interests . . . undermined by these folks in Washington, both in the White House and in Congress." Instead of doing "what is in the public interest . . . they are acting as if they're on retainer with their largest campaign contributors."

Americans cannot escape the taint of a morally bankrupt, a criminal ethos that wastes critical resources and ravages peoples across the globe. In *The Conscience of a Liberal: Reclaiming the Compassionate Agenda*, former U.S. senator and educator Paul Wellstone (b. 1944-d. 2002) wrote:

> Too few people have too much wealth, power, and access, and too many people have too little . . . . Big money undercuts representative democracy at every turn. Powerful economic interests have the capital to hire lobbyists that march on Washington every day. [These coalitions] have easy access to legislators and their staffs, as well as to the executive branch.

The most highly visible, even celebrated example of the United States' criminal waste while creating and deepening the world's want is the corrupt process surrounding high public office. The U.S. presidency is a bought office, and those who buy the U.S. presidency or any high office purchase governance and purchase official decisions and policy. They buy the endless execution of a foreign relations paradigm in violence that not only takes lives but also robs futures.

Waste

U.S. presidential campaign fund-raising tallies reported in mid-October 2011 showed incumbent Barack Obama's take was at a staggering "$70 million." The Center for Responsive Politics highlighted candidates' totals in the previous quarter ending in June.

Candidate	Raised	Spent	Debts	Cash on Hand	Large Indivs	Small Indivs	End Date
Barack Obama (D)	$48,662,185	$80,235,455	$412,878	$37,110,346	$11,158,236	$21,220,058	Jun 30, 2011
Mitt Romney (R)	$18,284,223	$5,575,690	$0	$12,715,495	$17,130,766	$1,103,457	Jun 30, 2011
Ron Paul (R)	$4,514,166	$1,547,989	$0	$2,966,177	$2,258,984	$2,259,452	Jun 30, 2011
Tim Pawlenty (R)	$4,473,673	$2,472,583	$1,915	$2,001,090	$3,964,958	$460,880	Jun 30, 2011
Michele Bachmann (R)	$3,636,523	$257,456	$364,120	$3,379,067	$546,804	$1,092,919	Jun 30, 2011
Herman Cain (R)	$2,552,835	$2,070,941	$0	$0	$903,765	$1,146,571	Jun 30, 2011

Candidate	Raised	Spent	Debts	Cash on Hand	Large Indivs	Small Indivs	End Date
Newt Gingrich (R)	$2,094,866	$1,772,644	$1,030,628	$322,222	$1,154,630	$921,286	Jun 30, 2011
Rick Santorum (R)	$582,098	$352,983	$0	$229,115	$442,261	$139,587	Jun 30, 2011
Fred Karger (R)	$266,511	$264,208	$0	$2,304	$23,280	$13,222	Jun 30, 2011
Gary Johnson (R)	$180,237	$174,230	$227,360	$6,007	$135,751	$44,485	Jun 30, 2011
Buddy Roemer (R)	$95,635	$76,577	$10,000	$19,058	$60,560	$0	Jun 30, 2011
Thad McCotter (R)	$33,055	$54,636	$0	$478,780	$3,250	$6,520	Mar 31, 2011

Center for Responsive Politics, OpenSecrets.org

Latest update before *NO LAND AS ISLAND* went to press

Candidate	Total Raised	Apr 2012 Raised	Spent	Debts	Cash on Hand	% From Small Indivs	End Date
ObamaBarack Obama (D)	$217,052,304	$25,380,444	$104,198,269	$1,200	$115,157,433	44%	Apr 30, 2012
TerryRandall Terry (D)	$163,367	$0	$158,031	$9,200	$5,337	40%	Mar 31, 2012
RoemerBuddy Roemer (I)	$678,128	$-21,754	$563,632	$0	$114,495	82%	Apr 30, 2012
JohnsonGary Johnson (L)	$807,273	$59,448	$797,374	$150,181	$9,899	30%	Apr 30, 2012
RomneyMitt Romney (R)	$97,963,836	$11,332,456	$88,765,540	$0	$9,211,335	12%	Apr 30, 2012
PaulRon Paul (R)	$38,733,202	$1,981,498	$36,268,205	$0	$2,464,997	44%	Apr 30, 2012
GingrichNewt Gingrich (R)	$23,131,362	$750,581	$22,324,411	$4,777,006	$806,951	47%	Apr 30, 2012
SantorumRick Santorum (R)	$21,812,492	$1,227,060	$20,805,171	$2,275,458	$1,007,322	50%	Apr 30, 2012

Candidate	Total Raised	Apr 2012 Raised	Spent	Debts	Cash on Hand	% From Small Indivs	End Date
PerryRick Perry (R)	$19,704,786	$-61,749	$19,287,579	$14,464	$417,207	5%	Apr 30, 2012
CainHerman Cain (R)	$16,672,939	$0	$16,631,078	$450,000	$41,861	54%	Mar 31, 2012
BachmannMichele Bachmann (R)	$9,244,228	$0	$8,885,504	$1,055,924	$358,725	52%	Dec 31, 2011
HuntsmanJon Huntsman (R)	$7,835,277	$0	$7,788,171	$5,469,145	$47,107	6%	Mar 31, 2012
PawlentyTim Pawlenty (R)	$5,151,118	$0	$5,151,118	$0	$0	11%	Mar 31, 2012
McCotterThad McCotter (R)	$547,389	$0	$540,315	$105,367	$7,074	8%	Sep 30, 2011
KargerFred Karger (R)	$538,184	$28,382	$529,231	$0	$8,954	5%	Apr 30, 2012

Center for Responsive Politics, tp://www.opensecrets.org/pres12/index.php

Former United Nations Secretary-general Kofi Annan said in 2006, "The challenges of our time are many, complex and interconnected—[challenges that] cannot be tackled by any one country acting alone—no matter how wealthy or powerful that country might be . . . . We all live in the same boat; nations need not fear the success of another." Speaking before an Indonesian audience, Annan offered insight into global reality and the urgency of a new kind of leadership. The years between 2001 and 2006 "have seen severe global food shortages, soaring energy costs and the gravest economic crisis in more than 60 years. No continent, no country or community has escaped the fall-out."

The multiple crises Annan mentioned—including extreme poverty (job, income, and opportunity losses, tens of millions added to an already scandalously high number of people living below the poverty line); famine; conflict; disease; and climate-change-causing natural disasters—all worsened as did a deepening sense of urgency for a higher caliber of global leadership in the years following that 2006 speech. While acknowledging that leadership in solving the world's problems cannot come solely from politicians and governments and that "all need to accept our responsibility," Annan argues further:

> Our common values and international solidarity require that we do more to tackle the inequalities in our world, not allow them to widen further [therefore] Political leaders will need to find the courage and vision to set aside special interests and ignore the tyranny of the electoral cycle. Focus instead on the implications of failure and the appalling burden this will place on future generations.

> Old certainties of the political and economic order are disappearing [and] the scale and urgency of the challenges demand a new style of leadership—one that looks beyond narrow national interests and recognizes that durable solutions will only come through multilateral action based on shared values and agreed goals.

> We need to get out of the old mindset that the national security and economic growth of *one* country need come at the expense of another. In the modern inter-connected world, power and prosperity are not a zero-sum game. We all live in the same

boat and nations need not fear the success of another. *Not competition but cooperation* will lead to sustainable progress and durable peace. Putting our common values of fairness and humanity into action will heal divisions, spread prosperity, and bring stability.

It is time to make further progress. Our world depends upon it.

VI

AGGRESSION-CORRUPTION-OPPRESSION
PROTESTS

[U]nder conditions of terror, most people will comply; but some people will not . . . . Humanly speaking, no more is required and no more can reasonably be asked, for this planet to remain a place fit for human habitation.

—Hannah Arendt

U.S. at War

November 2011

Before leaving for a writing retreat at Niagara Falls, my *Today's Insight News* December 17, 2011, article was "Washington's WARS Far from Over." It was the eve of the Stop the War Coalition's Sunday antiwar protest focused particularly on UK Prime Minister Cameron's and U.S. President Obama's driving intensification of aggression against the Persian country of Iran. It was within some of the latest days of continuing carnage in Afghanistan aided by assassination drone killings on Pakistan's border with Afghanistan and throughout the Middle East, South Central Asia, and North and East Africa. The Nobel Peace laureate president this week had declared Washington's war on Iraq a *mission accomplished* but a flood of reports and commentaries declared otherwise.

U.S. Foreign Relations Violence Causes Retrogression

The Iraq Example: Women Suffer Most

The president of the Organization of Women's Freedom in Iraq, Yanar Mohammed, appearing on the December 16 *Democracy Now* program reported that the U.S. war had made widows of more than one million women. Some reports give higher figures.

"These widows try to survive on a salary of $150," but because of internal displacement, most widows "cannot get this salary." Yet the 1 percent of Iraqis living in the (Baghdad) Green Zone—where there had been a $40 billion loss from the annual budget—"drowns in a sea of money." After nine years, Yanar Mohammed said, "we have the most corrupt government in the world and nobody is accountable for it." The biggest losers are the women, she said. "Poverty and discrimination against women has become the norm." Under the new constitution "are articles referring to the Islamic Sharīah according to which "women are worth half a man legally and one-quarter of a man socially in a marriage." The Organization of Women's Freedom in Iraq, she says, meets women daily "who are vulnerable to being bought and sold in the flesh market."

The land and people suffer destruction without restoration. "Iraqi cities are now much more destroyed than they were" before the U.S. invasion and years of foreign occupation. "All the major buildings are still destroyed. If you drive in the streets of the capital, your car cannot survive more than one month because all the streets are still broken. There was no reconstruction for the buildings, for the cities." Because of the policies that were imposed in Iraq, Yanar Mohammed said, "we have turned into a society of 99 percent poor and 1 percent rich . . . . Destruction is everywhere. Poverty is for all the people except the 1 percent who live inside the Green Zone."

In a seemingly endless déjà vu, a reflection of destruction piled upon destruction, Erika Munk (1939-) had written in 1997 "The world turned upside down," *The women's review of* books, Vol. XIV, No. 8, May 1997] about the Bosnian conflict, another Washington war. The conflict is not over, she wrote. "Even if larger-scale violence does not recur, nothing has been solved—the refugees aren't home, the country is not being rebuilt; its political structures are a sham and war criminals lounge untouched in sidewalk cafes."

In 1995 and again in 1999 the North Atlantic Treaty Alliance [its major military Atlantic command headed by the Supreme Allied Commander Atlantic (SACLANT) headquartered in Norfolk, Virginia (USA)] attacked Serbia from the air purportedly to end the Bosnian conflict. After that came a Dayton, Ohio, agreement together with more force deployed in Bosnia, an international enforcement force of more than sixty thousand. The 1990s Bosnia conflict left tens of thousands (estimated) dead and millions displaced.

Before the 2003 U.S. invasion of Iraq, "the average number of slum dwellers in Iraq was 20 percent." A 2009 United Nations report Foreign Service Officer Peter Van Buren cites in *We Meant Well* says, at the time of the UN study, "fifty-seven [57] percent of all Iraqis lived in slums. In the worst areas, such as Maysan and Diyala, more than 80 percent lived in slums."

Yanar Mohammed said her people "are living in a huge military camp" and in a country divided in which Shiites rule and Sunnis want to secede from Iraq. "We are . . . on the verge of the division according to religions and ethnicities. It has already happened."

Irrevocable Malevolence: Countless Lives Lost and Silenced

In an article Press TV republished online, Chris Floyd (author of Empire Burlesque) observed that in the U.S. president's announced ending of the U.S. war on Iraq, he failed to mention "the thousands and thousands and thousands and thousands and thousands of Iraqis killed by this 'fulfilled mission,' this 'extraordinary achievement,' this 'success.' These human beings—these sons and daughters, fathers, mothers, kinfolk, lovers, friends—cannot be acknowledged; they cannot be perceived. It must be as if they had never existed. It must be as if they are not now dead."

Helen Fremont has written that war *silences* all of us. "I had been living my life with flawed vision, stumbling in the dark, bumping into things I hadn't realized were there," she says. "No one acknowledged anything yet each time I walked into my parents' house, I fell over something, or dropped into something, a cavernous silence, an unspoken, invisible silence . . . . Perhaps the war had not changed them so much as [it had] . . . made them rigid. Their secret their armor . . . a mask of silence imposed on all of us" (Fremont).

U.S. Foreign Relations Violence Meets BREAKDOWN in U.S. Domestic Affairs

Institute for Policy Studies vice chair Saul Landau spoke in interview about U.S. breakdown and Americans' flawed vision. "There is a level of denial in the ruling group of Americans, the political class and Congress and in the administration," Landau said. "They are denying climate change. They are denying the extent to which the economy has tanked and really is close to going under in certain places, or indeed, has gone under; and they continue to equate the Republic, which is in terrible shape.

"We see empire: look at the defense budget that passed, $700 billion not counting the money that goes for various wars, for nuclear weapons, for the CIA [Central Intelligence Agency] all of that totals almost a trillion dollars." Money goes for a new fighter plane nobody wants and absolutely nobody thinks is necessary—all the while U.S. schools are closing, people have no access to health care, and the cushion people used to be able to fall back on has diminished. For "really poor" Americans, the cushion no longer exists, and they are falling onto hard concrete. "The system is collapsing," he said, "and government officials and those running for office are not facing it . . . . They want to cut, but not the military—a military power greater than any in the world—because the military stands for the empire."

Landau correctly charges that there is an ongoing *disconnect* in the United States and an ever-rising new *enemy*. Again, enemy number one is Iran, "the bane of the new Cold War." Continuing this line of thought, Chris Floyd says, in its "divorce from reality," the United States "is beyond description. It is the all-pervasiveness of the disassociation that obscures its utter, its obvious insanity. There is something intensely primitive and infantile in the reductive, navel-gazing, self-blinding monomania of the U.S. psyche today."

> The Iraq War has not ended. Not for the dead, not for their survivors, not for the displaced, the maimed, the lost, the suffering, not for all of us who live in the degraded, destabilized, impoverished world it has spawned, and not for the future generations who will live with the ever-widening, ever-deepening consequences of this irrevocable malevolence.

In his firsthand account, Van Buren writes, "After years of seeking a military solution, followed by years of building ineffective privies through our embedded [with military] Provisional Reconstruction Teams [abbreviated ePRTs], we [the United States] simply declared victory and started to pack up." Referencing a sheik he spoke to, Van Buren says the Americans "dug a deep hole in 2003 and now are walking away leaving it empty." In hanging on to an infantile patriotism in trying to excuse the inexcusable, Van Buren speaks a kind of truth in what I view as part of the criminal pattern of U.S. government offenses against (though not only) the Iraqi people. He says, "Hubris stalked us."

> We suffered from arrogance and we embraced ignorance . . . .
> [W]e lacked the courage to be responsible. It was almost as
> if a new word were needed, *disresponsible*: a step beyond
> irresponsible, meaning you should have been the one to take
> responsibility but shucked it off.

Exacerbated Strife Drives Wedge

Iraq and Iran are neighbors as are Iran and Afghanistan and Pakistan and Afghanistan. There are long-standing conflicts, extending back, in recent history, at least to 1947, between India and Pakistan and between Kashmir and India. The West and the East (Britain, Russia, France, the United States) have played a part in these conflicts. This is South Central Asia where conflicts have long existed among political and religious, ethnic, and class varieties; the rich, desperately poor, and preyed upon; and between entrenched rulers and ordinary people. Some level of civil strife occurs in all countries, and in South Central Asia and Persia, the differences have lived together for years as they had done in Iraq. However, the United States together with its World War II and Cold War allies (and allies of expediency or vested interests) have exploited and exacerbated, ramped up, and sustained these conflicts. For their own purposes, U.S. political figures and foreign heads of state, militaries, corporations, and agents of "civil society" have created and worsened conflict among neighbors. They have used emotional or cultural issues or prejudices (including their own) to drive a wedge between people; to maintain and inflame conflict; and to justify superpowered invasion, occupation, illegal declarations, and the waging of war against the general welfare of all sides, but especially against those holding least power: struggling families, women, children.

Background

KASHMIR REGION MAP

Afghanistan/Kashmir Region
Landlocked, strategically situated along important trade routes connecting southern and eastern Asia with Europe and the Middle East, Afghanistan is a multiethnic country at the heart of South Central Asia 300 miles (480 kilometers) north of the Arabian Sea
Afghanistan borders Pakistan (including those areas of Kashmir administered by Pakistan but claimed by India) to the east and south; Iran to the west; and the Central Asian states of Turkmenistan, Uzbekistan, and Tajikistan to the north. Afghanistan also has a short border with Xinjiang, China, at the end of the long narrow Vākhān (Wakhan) Corridor, a mountainous region, in the country's extreme northeast. It is the prize long sought by empire builders. Great armies for centuries have attempted to subdue an unbowed country in which an entire generation, in relatively recently times—because of British, Russian, and U.S. twentieth—and twenty-first-century invasions—has entered adulthood knowing nothing but war.

Iran, Afghanistan, Pakistan, Kashmir Region, China

Neighbors in the Kashmir Region: Afghanistan, Pakistan, Kashmir, India, and China; Southern and southeastern portions constitute the Indian state of Jammu and Kashmir. The Indian—and Pakistani-administered portions are divided according to a 1972 agreement to a "line of control" recognized by neither country as an international boundary.

Eastern Portion

China became active in the eastern area of Kashmir in the 1950s. Since 1962, China has controlled the northeastern part of Ladakh (the easternmost portion of the region).

Neighbors Islamic Republic of Iran, Afghanistan, and Pakistan have endured more than two decades of U.S. war, occupation, assassination drone strikes, and provocation.

Since partition of the Indian subcontinent in 1947, the region (total area estimated at 85,800 square miles or 222,200 square kilometers) has been the subject of dispute between India and Pakistan.

Jammu and Kashmir

Jammu and Kashmir is a state of India located in the northern part of the Indian subcontinent close to the Karakoram and western Himalayan mountain ranges. The state is part of the larger region of Kashmir that, since the 1947 partition mentioned, has been the subject of dispute between India, Pakistan, and China. The area is critically complex: on the northeast of Jammu and Kashmir is the Uygur Autonomous Region of Xinjiang; on the east are the Tibet Autonomous Region (both parts of China) and the Chinese-administered portions of Kashmir. On the south are the Indian states of Himachal Pradesh and Punjab. On the southwest is Pakistan; and on the northwest is the Pakistani-administered portion of Kashmir. Formerly, one of the largest princely states of India, Jammu and Kashmir's administrative capitals is Srinagar in summer and Jammu in winter (area: 39,146 square miles or 101,387 square kilometers; population, 2008 estimate: 12,366,000).

Early November Wars, Resistance, Retaliation

Today's Insight News, Friday November 4, 2011, "U.S. Enters Thanksgiving month shopping while Shedding Blood: the Fatally Flawed in Power, Their Politics, Policies, and Consequences"

"Over the past half-century, the U.S. has been directly or indirectly involved in military interventions in tens of countries," Press TV quoted statements by Tehran's Friday Prayers leader Ayatollah Seyyed Ahmad Khatami. Reacting to calls for blood from members of the U.S. Congress, calls to assassinate Iranian officials, the cleric said, "Washington, who claims to be the flag bearer of the war against terrorism and has used this as a pretext to attack and occupy Iraq and Afghanistan, is now implicitly issuing assassination orders."

The world will not forget the U.S. history of committing crimes against humanity, the nuclear bombing of Japan, Ayatollah Khatami said. "Siding with the Zionist regime [of Israel] against Palestinians, giving the green light for atrocities to be committed in Bahrain are all among the U.S. crimes against humanity."

As U.S. bloodletting continued and Libya continued to break down in the wake of the U.S. North Atlantic Treaty Organization's destruction there, Phyllis Bennis spoke with *Democracy Now* about protracted U.S. and NATO violence in Africa.

Arab Spring Morphed into Western Invasion

Bringing U.S. and NATO forces into Libya, Bennis said, "Transformed what had begun in the context of the 'Arab Spring' popping up all over the region and turned that into a Western invasion—a Western assault on another North African, Middle Eastern, Arab country." NATO emerged as the air force of a self-appointed leadership of the uprising (the National Transitional Council or NTC), and within a short period, militias who had fought Libyan president Muammar al-Qaddafi made known their position that the NTC was an illegitimate creation to which they owed no accounting.

Again, U.S. NATO belligerence leaves a country more broken and more violent: "a country glutted with weapons," Bennis reported, but no clear leadership structure or accountability, and feeling a deepening dependency on their invader, the "U.S./NATO military presence and military action."

Furthermore, the carnage Libyans experienced is but a piece of the pattern of U.S. NATO malevolence across this continent.

Killer "Humanitarians": Cold War-NATO Rises as AFRICOM Invaders

"It is an example, potentially, of the look of NATO expanding its own self-defined mandate," Bennis said. From a creation of the Cold War initially designed to defend its own members (see appendix), the North Atlantic Treaty Organization now rises with the U.S. Africa Command (AFRICOM) on a continent that "provides more oil to the United States than the entire Middle East." Bennis cites the Western-fueled conflict within and between African nations suffering severely not only from internal conflict but also from natural disasters and nonexistent or sorely inadequate infrastructures. People are dying needlessly for lack of running water and proper sanitation systems, exposure to the elements, and starvation or severe undernourishment; and Western nations are bombing them and arming other nations (often, other African nations) to bomb them.

U.S.-allied "Kenyan troops claiming to be going after the [al-Shabab, an Islamist youth movement not unlike South Central Asia's 'Taliban' or 'al-Qaeda' or other variations on the 'terrorist' or 'extremist' themed] militia," she reports, "[are] moving massively into Somalia . . . bombing a refugee camp, leaving a number of people dead and dozens injured." These troops were "going after the refugees and internally displaced Somalis [are] fleeing the violence." In this manufactured chaos, governments of Kenya and Somalia (as peoples of Libya and Syria) are being forced into a deepening unhealthy dependence on the United States and Europe using NATO to engage militarily. Bennis concludes with the dire consequence in human suffering. "Escalating the war in Somalia by bringing in NATO is a very bad example," she said. More NATO engagement—"bringing in outside forces, bringing in more military forces, more combatants with guns—leads inevitably to more, not fewer civilian casualties."

War with Africa—United States Allied against Somalia

Somalia is the sixth country where the United States has used remote-controlled drone aircraft to launch deadly missile strikes.

Friday, November 4, 2011, in Somalia's capital city, Mogadishu, fighting reportedly between al-Shabab and transitional government troops left at least eleven Somali soldiers dead. One day earlier, another forty-one people had died and thirty-three suffered wounds "in a U.S. assassination drone attack near Somalia's border with Kenya." On the same day, a U.S. assassination drone struck a town in Somalia's southern Jubbada Hoose region, leaving twenty-eight people dead and dozens more wounded.

Wednesday, November 2, against Somalia's central region of Galguduud on Qeydar and Marodile villages situated between Guriceel and Balanbale districts, the U.S. remote-controlled assassination drones launched aerial attacks. The country's elders reported at least thirty-eight people died and more than seventy-four people suffered injuries in the strikes. Also on that early November Wednesday, twenty people were left dead and sixty were wounded after a U.S. assassination drone launched a strike on the outskirts of Kismayo, a strategically important port city on Somalia's Indian Ocean coast located some 500 kilometers (310 miles) south of the Somali capital. Over a two-day period, at least 127 people reportedly died in separate U.S. assassination drone strikes in Somalia and in Pakistan's northwestern tribal region bordering Afghanistan.

A BQM-74E drone launches from the USS Boxer's flight deck in the South China Sea, U.S. Navy photo by Airman Paul Polach http://www.defense.gov/ transformation/images/photos/2005-07/ Hi-Res/050713-N-3455P-003.jpg

Meanwhile, in Pakistan's northwestern region of North Waziristan on Thursday, November 3, at least three people died in the "non-UN-sanctioned U.S. assassination drone attack." The attack occurred in Darpa Khel village located about four kilometers (two miles) west of Miranshah, the main town in the district of North Waziristan. Local security officials said a drone had fired two missiles on a compound.

United States officials on October 28 had admitted flying unmanned aerial vehicles from Ethiopia. These attacks, all of them, under United Nations process are unlawful.

U.S.-occupied Nigeria

In a world of immoral and indeed criminal inequalities, amid oil wealth and corporate plunder, people increasingly employ the ancient tactic of piracy. Pirates of East and West Africa raid ships of privilege. The *privileged* deem attacks in and around Nigeria, with its important resources of oil, metals, and agricultural products for world markets, as threats to an emerging trade hub. Reported the first week in November was an incident that allegedly happened at the end of October. An official of the International Maritime Bureau told the press that presumably pirates had captured an oil tanker with a twenty-five-member crew off the coast of Nigeria. Another Nigerian oil tanker whose whereabouts on November 2 were unknown but had presumably been attacked off the Niger Delta region.

Without suggesting approval or supporting violence from any sector, it may be fair to say that under the impunity of a relentless, terrorizing imperialism, piracy may be the only recourse of a defenseless and suffering people.

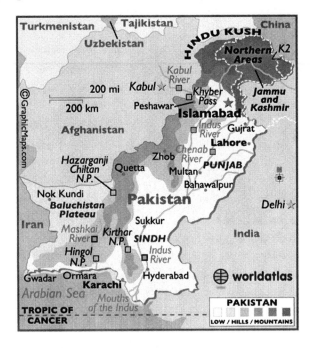

Antiwar with Asia—United States Allied against Pakistan (Protests)

The drone strikes of the imperialists in late 2011 were one of the major reasons behind growing anti-U.S. sentiments in Pakistan. Independent organizations compiled figures showing that since 2004 more than two thousand people—*most of them civilians*—had died in U.S. assassination drone attacks.

Activists held an exhibition in Islamabad, Pakistan's capital, "to bring to light the truth of U.S. assassination drone strikes." On display at the exhibition organized in collaboration with the British charity organization Reprieve were close to a dozen exploded and twisted U.S. missiles, accompanied by photographs of their victims. (News reports at year's end also revealed U.S. drone plane crashes in Somalia and Iran.)

The exhibits reportedly showed the kind of sophisticated heavy weaponry used by the United States in its drone attacks in Pakistan's Federally Administered Tribal Area (FATA), located on the Pakistan-Afghanistan border. Reprieve founder Clive Stafford Smith told the press, "The exhibition shows that when the CIA says there have been no innocent victims of drone missiles in the last 15 months, [the statement] is simply not true. What we have are parts of missiles that actually killed children . . . . That [evidence] is very solid, concrete proof that the CIA is not telling the truth."

The question shouted in protest against the U.S. presidency in the 1960s came hauntingly to my mind in 2011: "USA, USA—how many kids did you kill today?"

Pirates in Africa, Retaliatory Explosives in Pakistan (Protests)

NATO Protest image Stop The War Colalition-UK

"Militants" frequently target trucks carrying supplies for U.S.-led foreign soldiers in Afghanistan. On November 2, Taliban-linked militants in Pakistan reportedly attacked a NATO supply convoy carrying supplies for U.S.-led foreign troops in neighboring Afghanistan. Officials told Press TV that gunmen riding on motorcycles opened fire at a NATO container at a bypass area of Chaman in southwestern Balochistan Province. In the attack, the container sustained damage and the driver was injured.

Pro-Taliban "militants" claiming responsibility for attacks often say the assaults are in retaliation for non-UN-sanctioned airstrikes by U.S. assassination drones on Pakistan's tribal regions.

U.S. Allied Against/Occupied Afghanistan (Protests)

November 3 in Western Afghanistan, a bomb attack hit a NATO logistics base in the city of Herat near Herat airport. Seven people died; three others suffered injuries.

The year 2011 saw violence rising and rampant throughout Afghanistan—despite or because of an estimated 150,000 U.S.-led foreign troops invading and occupying the land. A September 28 United Nations report noted that the 2011 monthly average of recorded security incidents through the end of August had climbed nearly 40 percent. The report said civilian casualties—already at record levels in the first six months of the year—rose 5 percent between June and August 2011 compared to the identical period in 2010.

U.S.—allied India versus Kashmir, Central Asia (Protests)

Protesters took to the streets and risked arrest in Indian-administered Kashmir amid allegations accusing New Delhi's forces of torturing minors they were holding in their custody.

Hundreds of youngsters rounded up in almost daily street protests against the Indian rule over the disputed valley of Kashmir remained in detention. Police in this Muslim-majority region reportedly had launched a campaign (as in Yemen, Bahrain, Saudi Arabia, Syria, and other Near Eastern nations) to crack down on minors participating in protest rallies.

U.S.—occupied Iraq, Asia/Middle East (Protests)

As attacks targeting the army and police rose in Iraq, Prime Minister Nouri al-Maliki blamed foreign countries for fueling trouble. Maliki said in November that some nations are "spending money and effort" to destabilize Iraq. "The Iraqis do not want to build an aggressive country that will replace others," he said. "They want a country that will help in achieving local and regional stability."

This was not the first time Iraq's prime minister had apparently accused foreign countries of meddling in his country. Leaked U.S. State Department cables showed that the prime minister had long criticized foreigners, particularly U.S-ally Saudi Arabia, for conspiring against Baghdad.

U.S. Allied with Entrenched Autocratic Yemen (Protests)

Hundreds of thousands of Yemenis continued to hold antigovernment demonstrations demanding an end to the rule of Ali Abdullah Saleh whom they accused of nepotism and corruption. Hundreds of protesters died, and many more suffered injuries in government crackdowns.

Despite attacks by regime loyalists, deadly regime crackdowns, and deaths of nineteen people on November 3, Yemenis on the following day held massive antiregime demonstrations in the capital, Sana'a, and the southern city of Taizz. "The Yemenis' voice is one," they chanted. "We will bring corrupt Saleh to justice." Their Friday refrain: "Remaining peaceful is our choice."

U.S. Allied against Palestine, Pro-Israel (Protests)

In the Occupied Territories, U.S.-allied Israel again used force against a Gaza-bound aid flotilla. On November 4, according to a Press TV correspondent onboard one of the ships, "the two vessels were shadowed by Israeli warplanes and naval vessels in international waters as they approached the besieged Gaza Strip." The report said, "Eight Israeli warships made radio contact with the aid ships, calling on them to change course towards Egypt or to turn around. Israeli marines [then] boarded the vessels about 50 nautical miles from Gaza after pro-Palestinian activists refused to turn back."

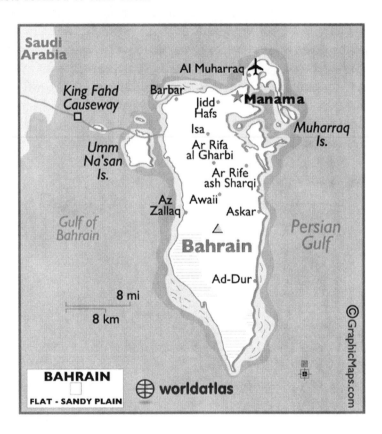

Called Freedom Waves to Gaza, the mini aid flotilla had left the Turkish port city of Fethiye on Wednesday, November 2, and intended to reach the Gaza Strip two days later. The Canadian ship *Tahrir* (*Freedom*) and the Irish ship *Saoirse* (*Freedom*) reportedly carried twenty-seven activists, including journalists and the crew, along with $30,000 worth of medicine. Activists on the Freedom Waves to Gaza were from Canada, Ireland, Egypt, United States, and Australia. Their stated international humanitarian mission was "to challenge Israel's ongoing criminal blockade of the territory."

Saoirse

In 2010 (May 31), Israeli commandos had attacked the Gaza Freedom flotilla in international waters, killed nine Turkish activists, and injured dozens of others.

Also in this early November international press news period, the Palestinian Authority's Ministry of Detainees reported nearly two hundred Palestinian inmates had died in Israeli confinement either under torture or because of medical negligence. At the time of the news reports, the estimate of Palestinian prisoners in Israeli prisons was 6,530. A November 4 statement by human rights groups charged Israeli doctors with neglect in documenting cases of torture and mistreatment of Palestinians detained in Israel. In a sixty-one-page report compiled by the Public Committee against Torture in Israel and Physicians for Human Rights were cases of one hundred detainees held by Israel since 2007. This report presented evidence that many doctors allowed "security service interrogators to use torture; approve the use of forbidden interrogation methods and the ill-treatment of helpless detainees; and conceal information, thereby instituting total impunity for the tortures."

U.S. Allied with Entrenched Autocratic Jordan (Protests)

On November 4, hundreds of Jordanians demonstrated in the capital, Amman (with similar protests in Karak, Maan, and Tafileh), urging the new government to carry out promised reforms and to fight corruption. After protests began in January 2011, King Abdullah II fired two prime ministers reportedly in an attempt to stem demonstrations. The country's third appointed premier in 2011 was Awn al-Khasawneh, a judge at the UN International Court of Justice.

Jordanians continued their street protests, driven by motivations similar to Yemenis and Bahrainis, demanding the election of a prime minister by popular vote and an end to corruption. These protesters made no calls for the king's removal. On the streets of Amman, demonstrators chanted, "No reform with the security fist."

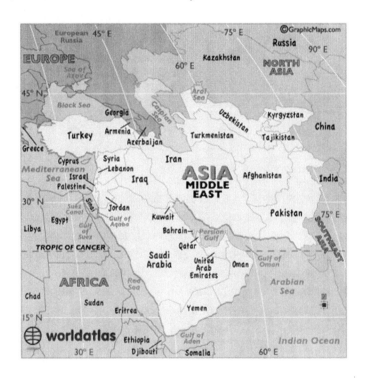

U.S. Allied with Entrenched-regime Bahrain (Protests)

Beginning in mid-February 2011, Bahrain became the scene of protests against the Saudi—and U.S.-backed Al Khalifa dynasty. In mid-March, at the request from Manama, the Bahraini capital, Saudi Arabia and the United Arab Emirates deployed military equipment and troops to quash Bahrain's antiregime protests. As the year was ending, the international press reported that forces loyal to Bahrain's ruling regime had killed scores of antigovernment protesters and jailed and tortured hundreds.

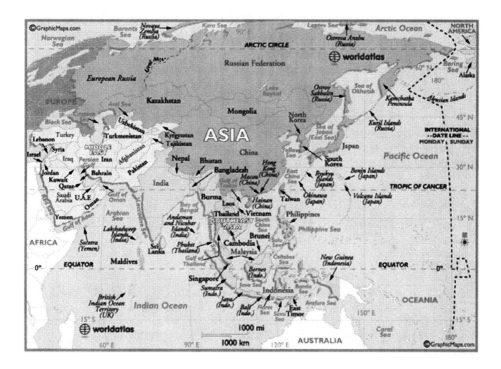

In early November, Saudi-backed Bahraini forces fired tear gas and used armored vehicles in an attempt to disperse the continuing hundreds of antiregime protesters marching in Manama. This latest use of brute force against a routine *After-Friday-Prayers event* intended to put down a huge turnout and massive funeral procession called by protest organizers after the announced death of seventy-year-old Ali al-Dayhee killed by regime forces.

The chronicle of events across Africa and Asia in 2011 and well into 2012 proves that many thousands—in the face of a calculated brutality in U.S. foreign operations, an alliance with criminal and corrupt rulers, and an almost unheard-of boorishness in the language of U.S. "diplomats"—hundreds of thousands of demonstrators steadfastly refused to be either docile or silent.

VII

Despite Protests, Sound Advice

The chief reason warfare is still with us" is neither the human species' secret death wish nor an irrepressible aggression instinct nor . . . economic and social dangers inherent in disarmament—but rather that no person or agency or judgment holding an alternative philosophy and decision-making authority "in international affairs has yet appeared on the political scene."

—Hannah Arendt

(United States at War, October/November/December 2011)

U.S. Heedlessly Terrorizing Afghans and Pakistanis

Writing in 2008, the Revolutionary Association of the Women of Afghanistan (RAWA) pointed to the duplicitous nature of U.S. dealings in Afghanistan and its culpability in the suffering of the Afghan people. The leading Afghan activist Zoya said that in 2001, "under the banners of 'liberating Afghan women,' [pro-] 'democracy' and [the] 'war on terror,' the U.S. government and its allies were successfully able to legitimize their [illegal] military invasion on Afghanistan and deceive the people of the U.S. and the world." However, she said, "The U.S. government has never supported democratic organizations."

> Contrary to the aspirations of our people and expectations of the world community, the Northern Alliance—brethren-in-creed of the Taliban and Al-Qaeda—are again in power and

generously supported by the U.S. government . . . . Combating armed and alien forces in [Afghanistan] without speaking out against Talibi and Jehadi enemies [means] welcoming the misfortunes of fascism and religious mafia; struggling against this enemy without fighting the military presence of the United States, its allies, and its puppet government means falling before foreign agents.

The duty of all "progressive and independence-seeking people," she said, is "to rise in a constant and decisive struggle for independence and democracy by taking the support of our wounded people as the independent force against the presence of the U.S. and its allies and the domination of Jehadi and Taliban criminals."

Afghanistan

A pregnant Afghan woman died and four other women suffered wounds on December 17 when U.S. forces raided a house in Afghanistan's southeastern Paktia Province. News reports said the raiding force detained two sons of Hasibullah Ahmadzai, the director of Paktia Province's counternarcotics department.

Since the United States invaded Afghanistan in 2001 under the pretext of eradicating Taliban militants, countless civilians have died or been injured. The nearly 150,000 U.S.-led foreign invading and occupying forces in Afghanistan at the end of 2011 have succeeded in sustaining and increasing a volatile security situation.

The slaughter of civilians together with retaliation for this aggression often compounds physical harm and heightens insecurity. The war on Afghanistan has caused deep anger among Afghans and prompted violent demonstrations throughout the country. On Friday, December 16, in Kabul, a police station came under attack. In the Kotai Sangi area, a bomber exploded a "suicide" bomb at a police station. The same day a group of armed "militants" reportedly broke into police headquarters and detonated an explosive.

Taliban militants' most lethal weapons against foreign troops, Afghan forces, and civilians are reportedly roadside bombs and improvised explosive devices (IEDs).

On Thursday, December 15, in Afghanistan's northwestern province of Badghis, at least two Afghan soldiers died and two others sustained injuries when their vehicle hit a roadside bomb. The same day in Afghanistan's western province of Farah at least four civilians died and eight others sustained injuries when a roadside bomb exploded. A minibus had come upon the explosive device on a road in the province's Malai area of the Pur Chaman District. On Wednesday, December 14, a roadside bomb killed an anti-Taliban district governor and two of his bodyguards in the southern Helmand Province.

As Taliban explode suicide and roadside bombs, the United States employs cluster bombs and chemical weapons that kill now and into the future.

Children run across cluster bombs' unexploded "bomblets" that have remained on the ground. This material explodes, causing severe wounds and fatalities. To end this maiming and killing, the United Nations established the Convention on Cluster Munitions. One hundred and eleven (111) countries have signed the Convention on Cluster Munitions. The United States is *not* among the signatories.

Ratified States (76) or Participants to the Convention on Cluster Munitions (CCW, Convention on Conventional Weapons)

Afghanistan	Albania	Antigua and Barbuda
Australia	Austria	Belgium
Benin	Bolivia	Bosnia and Herzegovina
Bulgaria	Burkina Faso	Cameroon
Canada	Cape Verde	Chile
Colombia	Costa Rica	Croatia
Cyprus	Czech Republic	Denmark
Djibouti	Dominican Republic	Ecuador
El Salvador	France	Germany
Guatemala	Guinea Bissau	Honduras
Hungary	Iceland	Ireland
Italy	Jamaica	Japan
Lao PDR	Lesotho	Liberia
Liechtenstein	Lithuania	Luxembourg

Macedonia FYR	Madagascar	Mali
Malta	Mexico	Moldova, Republic of
Monaco	Montenegro	Nauru
Netherlands (The)	New Zealand	Nicaragua
Niger	Nigeria	Norway
Panama	Paraguay	Peru
Philippines	Portugal	Senegal
Seychelles	Sierra Leone	Slovenia
South Africa	Spain	Sweden
Switzerland	Togo	Tunisia
Uganda	United Kingdom	Uruguay
Vatican (government of Roman Catholic Church)		

However, though the United States is not a signatory to the Convention on Cluster Munitions, the government, before last year's (November 14-25, 2011) Convention on Conventional Weapons Fourth Review Conference in Geneva, lobbied member states to quietly sign a new law allowing what more than hundred nations have banned. This action would have signed the death warrant of increased thousands of children. "Under pressure from several military powers opposed to the Convention on Cluster Munitions and its comprehensive ban," Avaaz reported,

> States Parties to the Convention on Conventional Weapons are attempting to introduce new international legislation that would allow continued use of cluster munitions banned under the Convention on Cluster Munitions and proven to cause unacceptable harm to civilians.

The particular problem with cluster bombs—beyond their callous use as part of the United States' immoral and criminal foreign relations violence—is that these particular bombs never stop killing long after a political figure announces an end to war. In addition, those who drop these bombs never take full responsibility in clearing them from the lands of people they have bombed. The killers simply pack up and move on to the next war (Kuwait to Iraq to Kuwait to Iran, Afghanistan to Pakistan to Bahrain to Yemen to Somalia)—a perpetual state of carnage.

The May 30, 2008 (Dublin), conveners of the Diplomatic Conference for the Adoption of a Convention on Cluster Munitions had serious concerns that only the criminally callous persist in ignoring. Conference conveners were concerned with civilian populations and individual civilians continuing to bear the worst of armed conflict. In particular, that cluster munition remnants

- kill and maim civilians including women and children,
- obstruct economic and social development including through the loss of livelihood,
- impede postconflict rehabilitation and reconstruction,
- delay and prevent return of refugees and internally displaced persons,
- negatively affect national and international peace-building and humanitarian assistance, and
- have other severe consequences that can persist for many years after use.

In not only the use of cluster bombs, drones, and other criminally lethal and inhumane arms and materiel, U.S. decision makers have claimed the exclusive "right" to kill with chemical weapons. The chemical weapons used by Saddam Hussein against Iran in the 1980s had been supplied by the Western "democracies" who later orchestrated the killing of Hussein, Iraq's head of state.

F-22A Raptor from the 27th Fighter Squadron, Langley Air Force Base, Va., fires an AIM-120 Advanced Medium Range Air-to-Air Missile at an aerial target drone over the Gulf of Mexico. U.S. Air Force photo by Master Sgt. Michael Ammons http://www. defense.gov/transformation/images/ photos/2006-02/Hi-Res/IMG0052.jpg

Despite its opposition to *certain* other governments' development of deadly material (Iran, no; India and Israel, yes), the United States of America has continued to oppose implementation of a Chemical Weapons Convention; but as one of the main victims of chemical weapons, Iran has called on the United States to abide by international law. In advance of the December 2, 2011, Conference on the Prohibition of Chemical Weapons convened at The Hague, the United States voiced its intent "to keep its arsenal of chemical weapons for many years to come." Joined by five countries (Russia, China, India, Israel, and Belarus), the United States attempted to push through changes to extend by a decade the April 2012 deadline obliging states signatories to the international Chemical Weapons Convention to dismantle their chemical weapons. This time the mission failed.

U.S. Drones Kill Pakistani Civilians 50:1

In late November, reports of casualty figures indicated that aerial bombings had left hundreds of Pakistani civilians dead. According to Pakistani sources, "U.S. drone strikes leave some 50 civilians dead for every militant killed." During the same week, Pakistani officials announced their intention "to complain to the UN Human Rights Council about non-UN-sanctioned U.S. drone strikes in its [Pakistan's] northwestern tribal belt near the border with Afghanistan." The parliament intended "to collect data about civilian deaths caused by U.S. assassination drone strikes against Pakistan's territory" and then (Press TV attributes antiwar.com) use the data in lodging a complaint about the terror attacks.

Aerial (drone) attacks that began during the George W. Bush administration increased under the successor government. The United States regularly carried out attacks by unmanned aircraft on Pakistan's tribal regions—strikes local people reported to have taken *mostly civilian* lives.

The onslaught continued into December, as did Pakistani protests and "official" statements demanding that the United States stop its assassination drone strikes on this neighbor to Afghanistan. On Thursday, December 15, at the Pakistan embassy in Washington, Pakistani officials reportedly made a presentation about the November 26, 2011, U.S.-led NATO cross-border attacks that left dozens of Pakistani officers dead. Senior Pakistani officials presented evidence they said could prove that what happened in NATO's deadly assault on a pair of Pakistan's army border outposts at the Afghan border was no mistake. Acting Pakistani envoy Iffat Imran Gardezi said, "We want to offer our view of the incident as we see it." The evidence presented to international journalists also showed that the shooting by helicopter gunships continued for an hour after NATO forces told Pakistani officials at the posts that it would stop. The same Thursday, the fifteenth, in the eastern city of Lahore, hundreds of Pakistanis took to the streets to voice their anger over the NATO cross-border airstrikes that had killed the two dozen Pakistani soldiers in that late November attack. NATO helicopters and fighter jets on November 26 had attacked two military border posts in northwest Pakistan; twenty-four Pakistani troops died. Protesters lit candles to mourn the dead Pakistani soldiers, and as in previous demonstrations, protesters burned NATO in effigy and chanted anti-U.S. slogans.

On Friday, December 16, Pakistani Prime Minister Yusuf Raza Gilani met with the U.S. ambassador to Pakistan, Cameron Munter, and warned that Islamabad would continue blocking NATO convoys. He said the United States had to guarantee its commitment to cease breaches of Pakistan's borders. Gilani said the United States "must respect Pakistan's red lines as well as the Central Asian nation's national sovereignty and territorial integrity." Pakistan had closed the border crossings used by the Western military alliance to send fuel and other supplies to the U.S.-led forces in landlocked Afghanistan.

A year earlier (October 2010), a report by the UN special envoy on extrajudicial killings had said the U.S. drone attacks "were undermining the rules designed to protect the right of life." Philip Alston said he "feared that the drone killings by the U.S. Central Intelligence Agency could develop a 'PlayStation' mentality."

U.S. Drones Kill Afghan children

Also around November 24, 2011, in the week of American Thanksgiving, the U.S.-led International Security Assistance Force reportedly had launched an air strike in Zhari district of Kandahar Province on a residential area in southern Afghanistan that left at least seven civilians—*mostly children*—dead.

Expressing the cruelty of the war on Afghanistan, Press TV commented that Afghan civilians have paid a heavy price since the U.S.-led invasion of the country in 2001. "Insecurity increases and deepens." The report repeated the estimated count of 130,000 people displaced by the conflict in the first seven months of 2011—an increase of nearly two-thirds over the same period in 2010. As mentioned earlier, the monthly average of security incidents recorded for 2011 through the end of August rose nearly 40 percent. Civilian casualties between June and August 2011—already at record levels in the first six months of 2011—rose by 5 percent.

In early December, the head of the human rights subcommittee of the Iran Majlis (parliament) said there were documents "to prove that American authorities have official meetings with 'terrorist' groups in Afghanistan." Referring to explosions targeting Afghan Muslims on Ashura (a holy day), Zohreh Elahian charged: "Western occupiers are responsible for terrorist attacks in the country." [Ashura is a Muslim holy day that is voluntary among Sunnis and a major festival among Shiites, a period of expressions of grief commemorating the death of Ḥusayn, grandson of Muhammad, and of pilgrimage to Karbala (present-day Iraq).]

Reported by Fars News Agency on December 7, Zohreh Elahian said, "The UN Security Council and human rights bodies should question the U.S. about terrorist attacks [in Afghanistan] on Ashura and the occupying forces should be held accountable in this regard." She charged the UN Security Council with responsibility "for investigating terrorist attacks in Afghanistan." The day before her statement, press reports said at least fifty-four Afghans had died in two separate explosions in Kabul and Mazar-i-Sharif when Muslims were participating in mourning rituals commemorating the martyrdom anniversary of the grandson of Islam's prophet Mohammad (PBUH) and third Shia imam, Imam Husayn (PBUH).

"The massacre of Afghans," Elahian said, "has increased Afghans' hatred toward the United States."

The December 6 attacks came a day after one thousand leaders from more than one hundred countries and international organizations had met in Bonn, Germany, on Afghanistan. Their purported concern was with "drawing up a roadmap for the transfer of security responsibility from foreign forces to Afghan authorities over the next three years" (2011-2014). This group also voiced "continued support for the security and development of Afghanistan." However, whatever the publicly stated concerns and promises of the Bonn conferees, the Afghan lawmaker was skeptical.

She said the United States was sowing discord between Shia and Sunni in Afghanistan. The Iraqis have also charged the United States with using this tactic in the Middle East/Persia. Regrettably, Elahian said, the

Bonn conference "[fell] short of discussing terrorism in Afghanistan"; but since both "Shias and Sunnis consider the U.S. and its allies their common enemy, [they] will show self-restraint by not playing in the ground prepared by the enemies of Islam."

U.S. Drones Kill Suffering Somalis

A people in turmoil, displaced, in the Horn of Africa's worst drought in six decades are also under attack by U.S. assassination drones and NGOs. Whether in the Americas, in Africa, or in South Central Asia, countless NGOs will do no good for the countries they occupy, countries of whose inhabitants they are contemptuous and feel superior, countries on which they descend then leave, descend and leave. So-called nongovernmental organizations receive funding not unlike mercenaries for hire to occupying oppressive foreign governments or private interests (or both). Also, like religions groups, they are selfishly self-perpetuating and thus prone to doing more harm than good (predator priests/preachers preying on the defenseless). Unless and until the United States ends its foreign relations in violence, developing nations such as Somalia will never develop, never come into their own, and never gain their liberty and justice for all.

December news from Somalia reported that in a twelve-hour period during that month, fifty children died in refugee camps between Mogadishu and Afgoye. Cholera and malaria had broken out in the camps of this famine-stricken country where there are insufficient medicines to help those stricken with diseases. Close to 580 children went to hospitals. Drought and famine have affected millions of people across Somalia, Kenya, and Ethiopia. United Nations reports said a quarter of Somalia's 9.9 million people are either internally displaced or living outside the country as refugees. Reports have also revealed over several months that the Somali people have come under repeated attack by U.S. killer drones.

Today's Insight News, Tuesday, November 8, 2011, "West Worsens Conditions in Africa"

A BQM-74E drone launches from the USS Boxer's flight deck in the South China Sea,

U.S. Navy photo by Airman Paul Polach http://www.defense.gov/
transformation/images/photos/2005-07/Hi-Res/050713-N-3455P-003.jpg

A U.S. unmanned "spy plane" crashed on Monday, November 7, in southeastern Somalia near the Somali port city of Kismayo as it was reportedly helping Kenyan troops monitor the port city, according to a Press TV correspondent attributing Somali military officials.

In October 2011, U.S.-allied Kenya (Somalia's southwestern neighbor) had dispatched soldiers to Somalia and begun air and ground offensives against "al-Shabab fighters." A civil conflict over control of towns in south Somalia allegedly has fueled growing tensions between a Kenyan military-backed Somali government and al-Shabab fighters. U.S. drone attacks further fueled the conflict and added to the misery of Somalia's people. U.S. action by proxy or directly with Somalia—not unlike the U.S. pattern in Iraq, Afghanistan, and Pakistan—is a blatant example of the U.S. seeding and executing regional, as well as intra—and internation conflict, chaos, division, and violence whose further consequences are regression.

> November 18, 2011
> "U.S. Terror Drones kill 42 More in Somalia"—at least 42 people died when U.S. assassination drones launched two separate aerial attacks in southern and central Somalia.

> November 17, 2011
> "U.S. Drone Crashes in Central Somalia"—a terror drone operated by the U.S. military crashed in central Somalia near the border with [Somalia's northwestern neighbor] Ethiopia.

> November 16, 2011
> "U.S. Terror Drones kill 35 more in Somalia"—at least 35 people died after U.S. assassination drones launched aerial attacks in southern Somalia near the border with [Somalia's southwestern neighbor] Kenya.

> November 15, 2011
> "U.S. Drone Strike Kills 17 in Somalia"—17 people died and nearly 67 others suffered wounds when a U.S. assassination drone strike hit southern Somalia.

October 8, 2011
A U.S. drone strike killed at least 16 civilians and injured 50 others in southern Somalia near the border with Kenya.

October 5, 2011
"U.S. Drone Strike Kills Six in Somalia"

U.S.-UK Drone Collusion Questioned

British officials in December were questioned about their collusion with the United States in drone strikes. In the face of mounting reports implicating UK intelligence in setting up people (alleged "militants") for CIA drone assassination, attorneys with the law firm Leigh Day and Co, acting on behalf of Noor Khan, called on the British foreign secretary, William Hague, "to clarify the role of the British intelligence in CIA drone attacks . . . . Reveal how British intelligence has assisted America's 'targeted killing' campaign in Pakistan." Among hundreds of Pakistani civilians killed by drone strikes was Noor Kahn's father, a victim of U.S. drone strikes in northwest Pakistan.

The head of Leigh Day and Co's human rights department raised the issue of legal grounds for a UK-U.S. CIA collusion that targets people for assassination and conducts assassination drone attacks. "Unless it is categorically denied that the UK continues to pass such information to the U.S. government forces," he said, "we require a clear policy statement of the arrangements which are in place and circumstances in which the UK considers it to be lawful to do so."

Balancing Dangerously in North Africa

Liberation at Al-Tahrir Square and the taking down of Egypt's head of state turned to business as usual under U.S.-backed military rule; so protesters—as in Jordan, Yemen, Bahrain—returned to the streets demanding substantive change. The second week of December was ending in Cairo, and two people lost their lives when the Egyptian army attacked protesters demanding an end to military rule in the country. Close to a hundred people were injured. The Egyptian protesters accused the military junta of carrying on with practices used by the former ruler, Hosni Mubarak. They called for his successor, the Supreme Council of Armed Forces, to hand over power to a civilian government. Where there is violence, United States' presence leads, looms, or lurks.

The week of the U.S. Thanksgiving, Deutsche Welle news had reported on the U.S.-led West's "dangerous balance" dealing with Egypt's military. The United States—as well as a number of European states—has continued to supply the oppressive Supreme Council of Armed Forces (SCAF) with "the military hardware, tear gas and rubber bullets being used against the crowds in Tahrir Square," the report said. "Much the same way as it supplied more than $60 billion in unconditional aid to the Egyptian military during [former Egyptian president Hosni] Mubarak's 30-year reign of corruption and oppression." The West's continuing support for Egypt's Supreme Council of Armed Forces (a pattern demonstrable in U.S. alliances with Libya's Transitional National Council and with despots across Red Sea) "is sending irreparably damaging signals to the prodemocracy movements in Egypt and across the region," North Africa/Middle East expert Kristian Ulrichsen told Deutsche Welle. "It reinforces perceptions that the West would rather see a narrow change of elites than a thorough revolution based on ideas of equality, dignity, social justice and democracy."

In addition to late-year protests in Egypt (and in some African countries farther west), protests and military-style crackdowns also continued in Bahrain and Yemen, to some extent in Saudi Arabia, and in Syria where the United States here too swings as politically expedient. Those beaten into submission have risen in retaliation. Casualties have risen as superpowers have recast their expedient enemies into allies and their expedient allies into enemies. An interesting concept, expediency, embraced by all political figures, it describes an act or entity that is useful for one's purposes, for a time, for achieving a particular end. That which is immediately advantageous—*without regard for ethics or consistent principles.*

Today's Insight News, Friday, October 28, 2011: "Misguided Policies Eventually Unravel, Blow Back, Boomerang"

Middle East/Syria/Persian Gulf

In late October, Alastair Crooke at Conflicts Forum commented on meddling and mistakes, who uses, and who is used in the Middle East's U.S. or the U.S.'s Middle East theaters of war. "Europeans and Americans and certain Gulf states may see the Syria game as the logical successor to the supposedly-successful Libya 'game' in remaking the Middle East," Crooke wrote. "It will not be for the first time Western interests sought to use others for their ends—only to find they have instead been used . . . the very tools that are being used on their behalf are highly combustible and may yet return to haunt them—as was experienced in the wake of the 1980s 'victory' in Afghanistan."

From the outset of the Syrian upheaval in March, "the Saudi king has believed regime change in Syria would be highly beneficial to Saudi interests," Crooke writes; (and) the real danger is that the Saudis, with their back to the wall, might once again fire up the old jihadist network and point it in the general direction of Shiite Iran.

> (Saudi Arabia and Iran are neighbors on either side of the Persian Gulf—Iran north and east [eastern neighbors Afghanistan/Pakistan] of the gulf, Saudi Arabia west [northern neighbor Iraq] of the gulf. Syria is west of Iraq, north of Jordan, northeast of Palestine/Occupied Territories.)

"[T]hat is exactly what is happening," Crooke continues, "but the West does not seem to have noticed . . . . Saudi [Arabia] and its Gulf allies are 'firing up' the Salafists [Sunni Islamists], not only to weaken Iran; but mainly in order to do what they see is necessary to survive—disrupt and emasculate the awakenings which threaten absolute monarchism. Salafists are being used for this end in Syria, in Libya, in Egypt . . . in Lebanon, Yemen, and Iraq."

Crooke may be right; but people should not have to beg or make threats for their liberty and justice, as seems inherent in Crooke's words, "Implanting Western paradigms, by force if necessary, into the void of fallen regimes"—the Hillary Clinton-devised response to the Arab awakening—will be seen as "a 'cultural war on Islam' and will seed further radicalization." There is more involved than if-then grounds. There is a ground of morality and law on which to base action, as *Pravda*'s David Hoffman suggests. The U.S. government has created a lawless nation (illegal judge, jury, jailor, abductor, torturer, and murderer in the name of a manufactured "war on terror"), a rogue nation operating under the clandestine philosophy that "might makes right" while openly (and hypocritically) cloaking itself in the garments of "freedom," "justice," and "human rights." The character and actions of entrenched ruthless governance have leave death: a country barely distinguishable "from the third-world dictatorships it claims to abhor—a country controlled by a plethora of sadistic, amoral, venal and ruthless reprobates who relentlessly manipulate the fear of terrorism to promote their own agendas and propagate their own brand of terror throughout the world."

There was indeed an enormous amount of wisdom, sound advice, and common sense abroad in the world in 2011; but the arrogance of federal Washington refused to listen or take heed. Officials continued the global carnage, but I believe, not alone in spring uprisings, there is light for the long term. Where countries and peoples connect—lands and waters meet—as neighbors. Where great majorities including these neighbors come together in mutual cognizance and concern that all our lives and futures are under attack by inordinate, unchecked power, is too an illegal and immoral use of power—there is healing, tremendous potential to be acted upon constructively, nonviolently for progress.

> Freedom requires people to think for themselves [Hoffman], to gather facts and information necessary to formulate reasoned judgments or opinions. Freedom . . . means making difficult, sometimes life-altering decisions with no guarantee those decisions will reap any positive results.

The chronicles presented in these chapters may at times seem repetitious. Some of that is deliberate to illustrate and emphasize the deeply harmful nature of the U.S. foreign relations model. Repetition in the span chronicled is also indicative of a constant in character, *in the grain*: violence as first choice, never last resort in U.S. foreign relations. This model in foreign relations is prejudiced and preemptive in the sectors (Somalia, Yemen, Bahrain, Iran, Afghanistan, Pakistan and others) which claim the focus of this work: Africa crossing the Red Sea and Gulf of Aden into South Central Asia. This character, this first choice as violence is not only a constant but, in the past two to three years, it has grown more and more and more reckless, heartless and severe.

The most sadistic and illegal example (together with targeted assassination of high-level foreign figures, mutilation and trophy making of human body parts) is likely the U.S. use of drone strikes, remote controlled missiles, on defenseless people; and lying about it. As U.S. violence increased in these years, so did angry reaction from government leaders and retaliation from ordinary people on the ground.

As U.S. violence rose in the countries invaded and occupied by the United States, so did civilian deaths, although actual categories and numbers of dead and wounded were always questionable.

In-country officials and foreign officials, including U.S. officials, routinely banned impartial coverage and censored information or members of the press self-censored. Information could not be trusted because it usually came from people within or allied with governments; or from people in the general population who, in an era of social networking, had their own agendas *as terrorist-labeling to settle old scores*. So foreign relations violence was constant, repetitious and reckless; and published numbers and categories of dead and wounded and the manner and causation of casualties were always suspect, unclear and very likely inaccurate. Reporting by the press or governments on far-reaching consequences of U.S. foreign relations in violence was virtually nonexistent.

VIII

CREDIBILITY LOSS
UNITED STATES-INTERNATIONAL

The first step in the direction of a world rule of law is the recognition that peace no longer is an unobtainable ideal but a necessary condition of continued human existence.
—Margaret Mead

Reckless Impunity, Global Lawlessness

Law is what we do for ourselves as society writ as large as the world and as small as local communities. Law enables society, allows us to live interdependently *with* one another—*neither islanded nor apart.*

Law is not a convenience or expediency (rather, it should not be) or caprice enacted by holders of enormous wealth or inordinate power. Law is not selective, holding some but not others to account. Law is not so much a kibosh on liberty as it is the guarantor of rights.

Law is a discipline, not mere punisher or avenger. In imposing a check on power, law secures liberty for all. Law knits society—whether society consists of one family or many, one sect or many, local municipalities, states of nations, countries of the world and the peoples who dwell within the global construct—allowing people together with their enterprises to live together within, to *share* a space. To be just, law must be incorruptible, applied without prejudice or partiality, without fear or favor.

When inordinate power or any power is permitted to create its own laws unchecked by an impartial superordinate orbiter, assembly or standard, such power enshrines its own impunity the consequence of which is universal lawlessness: endless cycles of offense, suffering and retaliation. Power unchecked is a world at war with itself, a society in breakdown.

Reckless Impunity

F-22A Raptor from the 27th Fighter Squadron, Langley Air Force Base, Va., fires an AIM-120 Advanced Medium Range Air-to-Air Missile at an aerial target drone over the Gulf of Mexico. U.S. Air Force photo by Master Sgt. Michael Ammons http://www.defense.gov/transformation/images/photos/2006-02/Hi-Res/IMG0052.j

A head of state or any person or entity holding enormous power and under cover of office commits crimes, covers up crimes, or shields from prosecution those who have committed crimes is undermining global and domestic rule of law—contributing to the breakdown of society.

In that October 2011 piece, *Pravda* legal editor David R. Hoffman observed "Nobel Peace Prize Winning Barack Obama and his cronies [doing] everything in their power to promote illegal detentions, torture and the extrajudicial executions of American citizens." The Obama government's "attorney general, Eric Holder, a self-professed paragon of 'integrity'—who demonstrates far too little of it—refused to prosecute corrupt CIA officials who [had], in defiance of a court order, destroyed videotapes that depicted the torture of detainees," Hoffman continued,

> [In] a revelation exposed by [the whistle blowing website] WikiLeaks, it was discovered that [President] Obama strong-armed foreign governments to prevent them from filing torture and/or war crimes charges against [former U.S. president George W] Bush and/or his minions. An Associated Press article and other sources suggested that in at least one respect, the current U.S. president might have exceeded

the extremes of his predecessor in that he "is the first U.S. president intentionally to target an American citizen for extrajudicial execution."

The December 2011 North American protests that continued a push for the forty-third U.S. president to face a court of justice for grave violations of law may be an example of the rule of law trying, in the hands of the public, to assert itself in an era of unchecked high crimes.

Hundreds of Canadians declaring "George W. Bush responsible for 'mass murders' and 'torture' and 'commander of the utterly illegal war on Iraq that caused the deaths of over 1.2 million Iraqi people'" took to the streets opposing the former president's visit to Canada and calling for his arrest. Amnesty International had argued that George W. Bush is a war criminal and urged the Canadian government to arrest him the moment he entered the country.

Global Lawlessness

World society descends into chaos—a deliberately engineered chaos—when and where relations, interactions, dealings among agents and states conduct themselves continually in violence. Breakdown occurs when principles of societal *care* are violated, when law impartially drawn is thrown to the winds. Timothy Bancroft-Hinchey's October opinion piece in *Pravda* correctly observes that, though international law exists, those holding power and inordinate influence apply it with "tribal" bias and unequally. The law is twisted, manipulated, and insulted. "Under international law, the Libya Question," he said, "was an internal affair of the Jamahiriya government of Libya."

> [I]t was a rebellion sponsored from abroad [illegal], financed, aided and armed from abroad [illegal], planned and programmed well in advance by the French, British and Americans [illegal] whose selfish interests were being blocked by Colonel [Muammar al-] Qaddafi and his African projects. The North Atlantic Treaty Organization [NATO] received the go-ahead by the United Nations after a false-flag event. The international organization took sides in an internal conflict [war crime], strafed civilian structures with military hardware [war crime], targeted the water supply [war crime], interrupted electricity and food supplies [war crime],

murdered civilians [war crime], placed troops on the ground [breach of international law], armed the rebels [breach of international law] and used mercenaries [breach of international law].

A wide view of the Security Council as Members unanimously adopt resolution 1969 (2011), extending the UN Integrated Mission in Timor-Leste (UNMIT) for one year, until 26 February 2012, UN Photo/JC McIlwaine|

"It matters not whether the majority of the members of the international community shrug and look the other way, accept bribes and trade influences and interests, allow themselves to be bullied and pushed into accepting the new status quo," Bancroft-Hinchey said. *"The law is the law. What is right is right. What is wrong is wrong"* [Emphasis added].

International Criminal Court (ICC) facade 2005
©ICC-CPI / Wim Cappelen. Reprinted and republished by Permission of ICC Public Affairs Unit (Amielle del Rosario)

Libya's (U.S.-backed) "rebel" terrorists who committed "ethnic cleansing, murdering the Negro population, raping women, torching buildings, killing children, destroying public and private property; who [took] up arms against their government and sided with foreigners—these are the scum the international community recognizes as the new Government of Libya." However, "under international law, this community has no right to recognize them as the government of anything, therefore the United Nations together with this community has lost all its legitimacy."

Hoffman lays out fact and consequence (quoted earlier in this book) of this breakdown—this reckless impunity of inordinate, unchecked power—in his "America Is Still Dead" article:

> Arrogant, militarily powerful and lacking a viable foe to curb its contempt for international law—the United States government feels "superior" to every other country in the world. As a result, it has become a lawless, rogue nation operating under the clandestine philosophy that "might makes right" while openly (and hypocritically) cloaking itself in the garments of "freedom," "justice" and "human rights."

By the spring of 2012, before my work went to press, former U.S. President George W Bush, his Vice President Richard Bruce (Dick) Cheney, his Defense Secretary Donald Rumsfeld and five of their legal advisers had been ruled guilty of war crimes by a war tribunal in Kuala Lumpur, Malaysia (May 15, 2012, http://www.presstv.ir/usdetail/241362.html).

Tribunal president, Judge Tan Sri Lamin Mohd Yunus said the eight accused (tried in absentia) were also individually and jointly liable for crimes of torture in accordance with Article 6 of the Nuremberg Charter. The War Tribunal sent transcripts of the five-day trial to the chief prosecutor at the International Criminal Court and to the United Nations Secretary-general, General Assembly and Security Council.

The Nürnberg (also spelled Nuremberg) Trials were a series of trials held in Nürnberg, Germany (1945-46) in which former Nazi leaders were indicted and tried as war criminals by the International Military Tribunal. The former Nazi leaders were indicted on four counts: crimes against peace; crimes against humanity; war crimes; and "a common plan or conspiracy to commit" the criminal acts listed in the first three counts (*Britannica*). Nuremberg Principle VI holds that the following "are punishable as crimes under international law":

- Crimes against peace (planning, preparation, initiation or waging of a war of aggression or a war in violation of international treaties, agreements or assurances; participation in a common plan or conspiracy for the accomplishment of any of the acts mentioned);
- War crimes (violations of the laws or customs of war which include but are not limited to murder, ill-treatment or deportation of slave labor or for any other purpose of the civilian population of or in occupied territory; murder or ill-treatment of prisoners of war or persons on the Seas, killing of hostages, plunder of public or private property, wanton destruction of cities, towns, or villages, or devastation not justified by military necessity);
- Crimes against humanity (murder, extermination, enslavement, deportation and other inhumane acts done against any civilian population, or persecutions on political, racial, or religious grounds, when such acts are done or such persecutions are carried on in execution of or in connection with any crime against peace or any war crime) (*Wikipedia*).

IX

WHAT'S IT TO BE?

*Don't you see, there has been no real progress; only a big
circle in which individuals march around and around—each
one with a picture, one's own little mirage, of the future.*
— Lorraine Hansberry

Stand with the Dead or Move Constructively Forward?
Regress or Progress?

People living in Western industrialized sanitized nuclearized
spaces—people in high places striped left, right, elephant, donkey or
Zebra—enjoy the luxury of ignorance or feigned ignorance of history
("I hadn't been born back then"), arms folded, eyes closed, ears covered,
comfortably wrapping themselves around the status quo.

In the United States, the political Right has its Newt Gingrich, Jesse
Helms (dead), Rush Limbaugh, Ronald Reagan (dead), Pat Robertson,
Strom Thurmond (dead). The political Left has its Noam Chomsky, Tom
Hartmann, Tom Hayden, any (dead) Kennedy, Martin Luther King (dead),
Howard Zinn (dead)—all men, mostly dead, passé or programmed in
talking-point banalities capable of being recited while sleeping. These
men and those who summon their names and sayings are as pawns on
boards of chess or checkers: each side constantly cognizant of the other's
move, each moving according to script—staying the status quo.

Nothing changes. The Left "select" and the Right "select" want it
this way: their select perpetually selected in print and broadcast media,
on stage and screen, the expected, the experts delivering the same lines
and holding the line. These instruments in regress (named and unnamed)

paraded repeatedly on to the public space are the obstructionists standing in the way, for example, of Grace Lee Boggs's exciting notion of "Reimagining the World." What I term a continuously forward constructive progress (all progress is not constructive or forward moving). What some contemporary Progressivist women thinkers have termed a human "evolutionary process."

Vast majorities in the world have not the luxury of the male messiahs, their followers, fans and promoters. Vast majorities are *living* horrendous histories, enduring consequences strewn against them by old empires (the same men or their mirrored kind) and latter-day despotic imperialists (the United States, Portugal, Spain, Britain, France, Italy, Roman Catholic Central, Israel, influential figures among Muslims, Jews, Christians) and their "allies."

The world's majorities cannot forget human costs, the hurt they suffer at the hand of U.S. foreign relations in violence, a model endorsed by every political stripe in the game of an infantile luxury of real or feigned, insensible ignorance. The world's majorities have not the luxury of ignorance or forgetfulness. They cannot forget nor will they forever endure the status quo. Implied in the worldview NO LAND AN ISLAND NO PEOPLE APART is a commitment to stand against any of world's people being subjected to regression, the tyranny of the status quo.

Perpetual War, Perpetual Disease

The issue of health and disease is perhaps the most tangible illustration of the sensibility I offer in this book: NO LAND AN ISLAND NO PEOPLE APART. Here is clear evidence of the lethal consequences of regression. Epidemics believed long banished have returned more powerful than before. Diseases and health threats once eliminated or prevented are now spreading because global governments bent on violence in relations among nations (waging war, creating chaos, stoking conflict and arming the world) have ignored or deliberately neglected prevention, cure, continuous comprehensive education, unbiased research, monitoring and maintenance of health. People languish, as I have reported earlier in this text, without clean water (Western country leaders in the pockets of irresponsible corporations pollute water and air with impunity) or sanitation or proper shelter, known contributors to ill health and disease. Polio, tuberculosis, Ebola and cholera are but a few of the deadly diseases of the past that have returned (or persisted because of for-profit health, for-profit education, limited scientific research) with added force.

Polio—American physician Jonas Salk developed the polio vaccine in the early 1950s and heath professionals administered the vaccine to schoolchildren with the result that later years saw the incidence of polio in the United States drop from eighteen cases per 100,000 people to fewer than two per 100,000. However, in 2009, polio was spreading across the Horn of Africa, affecting the peoples of northern Sudan, Kenya, and Uganda, Ethiopia, and southern Sudan.

Tuberculosis—Because of drugs developed and administered in the 1950s, England and Wales saw the rate of tuberculosis deaths drop from 190 per 100,000 in 1900, to seven per 100,000 in the early 1960s. The same period in the United States saw a drop from 194 per 100,000 to approximately six per 100,000. However, tuberculosis of the drug-resistant type (XDR-TB) reached twenty-seven countries in 2009. These are countries in which at least four thousand new cases of drug-resistant TB occur annually; or, according to the World Health Organization, countries in which a tenth of the total number of new cases are drug resistant.

Ebola—The Ebola virus, of which there are several strains, causes internal bleeding, crosses continents, breeds in animals and human beings, and crosses species. Virus strains discovered in the 1960s and 1970s have a fatality rate of 50 to 90 percent; and to date, there is blood and plasma treatment to control bleeding but no treatment for Ebola fever. In the 2000s, Ebola hit the United States and Europe. The government of the Philippines, in January 2009, reported the first known case of Ebola virus transmission from pig (animal) to human being.

Cholera—The twentieth century brought a medical breakthrough in the discovery that human beings' small intestine's absorption of sodium, the principal ion lost during an acute cholera attack, is linked to the absorption of glucose; and that administering a solution of sodium, glucose, and water in the intestine would overcome the loss caused by the cholera enterotoxin, and maintain hydration. Thus, oral rehydration salts (ORS) became the principle treatment for all diarrheal illnesses, including cholera. However, for-profit health, war and conflict, poor infrastructural support systems, and the manufacture and maintenance of poverty meant that majorities of people continue, needlessly, to die of this disease.

Cholera reaches back at least to the early nineteenth century. It was a disease of global importance in 1817; it spread in the United States and Canada in the 1930s, through Asia in the 1960s, to the Middle East in the 1970s and reached Africa where it had not appeared for seventy years.

In 2005, studies reported cholera in nearly 120 countries. It added to the already-heavy burdens borne by impoverished nations—deepening disparities between industrialized and less-developed countries. Experts predicted cholera would become endemic to many parts of the world, much as it has been for centuries to the Ganges Delta (the region in West Bengal State, India, and Bangladesh).

In the past two centuries, seven pandemics (global epidemics) of cholera have carried the disease to countries around the world.

This is regression. Health and disease is a global issue worsened by powerful nations' failure to cooperate with and care for all nations as a global society.

We are in a state of arrested development. I should say *arrested progress* so as not to confuse my meaning with property development or consumerist culture: flipping houses, building and abandoning property resulting in the rise of homelessness; making chips for one after another version of cellular device or other throwaway gadget resulting in overflowing, toxic landfills. The arrested development I see involves political figures and allies bearing a variety of colors, all in lockstep with regressive precedent. War, occupation, assassination, massacre, bullying, threat, torture, plunder, displacement are their chosen means of relating to the world. They destroy wellbeing, arrest human development, and annihilate all that is life and potential and promise.

Government Propaganda, Media Programming

I receive many e-mails from the political Left and often what I read is bickering, name-calling, an air of superiority over the "religious Right" or the "right wing." When I listen to local radio broadcasts featuring the Right, I hear bickering, name-calling, expressions of superiority. The attitude and language in both positions are not only extreme but are also vacuous and false.

No one is superior to any other one. Superiority is an illusion often passed from one generation to another. In arguments (or talking points), except for the truly ridiculous or advocacy of violence, there is usually something to look into, some measure of merit sufficient to engage further in civil discussion. Extreme positions and personal attacks are wasted energy all round, serving the status quo, regress.

Those who hold the stage hold the line. All the while, huge majorities across the world suffer and die for lack. Not lack of "charity" (the West's NGO, nonprofit, sectarian self-serving drive-bys); but for lack of cooperation, human sensibility, mutual respect and responsibility, a broadly informed and independent media, moral and competent leadership.

Missed Opportunity

The Left, Right, Center model in U.S. public affairs programming has serious drawbacks not least being its (islanded) insularity and exclusivity, its cloned feel, its nostalgic, anachronistic nature. What is missing in public affairs (domestic and international-focused) programming is the public: a wide array of imaginative, intelligent, thoughtful people, perspectives, ideas and developing ideas, questions, issues and developing solutions.

What is missing in U.S. public affairs programming is, of course, *quality*; but also a model that lends itself to color and variety of thought: the intelligently-produced "conversation" or "discussion" model concerned with the broad public interest, instead of "my" shows and personality, celebrity-driven, self-aggrandizement affairs.

What is missing is a constantly changing intelligently produced "panel" of discussants or conversationalists. A panel format of participants drawn from independent journalism and private/corporate journalism, from freelance, grassroots, arts and entertainment, and scholarly communities, from random studio audiences and activist communities, and from at least as many countries as are represented in the UN General Assembly (193).

The problem is, as Erika Munk puts it, "We are back at the gates of Troy or the sack of Rome, but with better technology"—in a "world turned upside down."

It does not have to be this way. We can at least increase the quality of content: direction and production, message and messengers. Accept the challenge to end a long era of regurgitated war propaganda and mass distraction. Enable a progressive era that aids in the transformation from a foreign relations model in violence to a journey in nonviolence. One of the greatest contemporary women standing steadfastly for peace says nonviolence involves more than the silence of guns. "Such a silence is merely the dim early enlightenment of anti-violence," Mairead Corrigan Maguire says. The commitment "to live without arms *no matter what happens*, requires a much deeper pilgrimage."

Choice of Progress

It seems to me that progressivism presumes a commitment to nonviolence. Nonviolence presumes true progressivism, an embrace of constructive, forward movement. Progressivism, in my view, does not throw away the past or the Left, Right, or Center. It critically judges, selects, and incorporates the best ideas and ethics to inform current action. It also improves upon what is, what was, and asserts what ideals dream. Progressivism is both rational and human centered. Conceived within it is a preference for the creative self *within* the collective over centered-on-self individualism; the preference for a cooperative style over a combative character; a "we," instead of "us/them" sensibility; a sense of a global society of equals, interdependent in respectful social contract, mutually responsible with and for one another as human beings sharing the universe.

The current U.S. foreign relations model in destruction violates domestic and international laws and human rights conventions, and lacks moral standing among the world's peoples. It is antithetical to progressivism. Destruction and progress cannot coexist. Either we go forward or we go backward.

For at least two decades, we have intensified a backward trend, a breakdown—a breakdown that is harmful to the world's peoples. And not only that. We are part of *not apart from* the world and the impact of violence ordered and executed from Washington hits us on our soil. Every dollar for war subtracts from science, health, education, the arts, community infrastructures; in other words, justice, domestic tranquility, the common defense and general welfare promised in the Constitution of the United States. Every hostility, every occupation, every assassination drone, every abduction and detention without charge, legal counsel or trial, every sale of arms in the Middle East, South Central Asia, East Africa and beyond further ingrains cycles upon cycles of violence and retaliation. Global BREAKDOWN. Whatever rationales or pretexts politicians and mass media give for this carnage, we must stand for ending it now or we fail the future.

What's it going to be?

What I said in *Same Ole or Something New*, I still believe: We can do better. If we refuse to be divided or wedged on issues (for example, personal choices concerning marriage and reproduction and religion) or set against one another on partisan or ideological grounds, we can together change the status quo and move continuously, constructively forward for the greater good. I believe lifelong internationalist Progressivists who do not tire or ease up in the struggle can accomplish this. A final thought brings a bit of the best of the past forward. I have updated the language only slightly. The educator Helen Keller nearly a hundred years ago expresses what I have tried to convey in my worldview *NO LAND AN ISLAND NO PEOPLE APART*.

> I look upon the whole world as my homeland and every war to
> me has the horror of family combat. I look upon true patriotism
> as the society of human beings and the service of all to all.

We cannot exist islanded in well-being as the world's majorities hunger, Eleanor Roosevelt said; nor even more: when the character of our relations is the cause of far-reaching costs, endless human suffering. No land is an island. No people are apart.

Sources and Notes

INTRODUCTION: Paradigm of U.S. Foreign Relations in Violence Causes Regress in Global Society

Carolyn LaDelle Bennett, *BREAKDOWN: Violence in Search of U (you)-Turn: Nature and Consequences of U.S. International and Domestic Affairs Geopolitics Occupation Human Rights Historical Contexts (Notes and Commentary)*, 2009.

Chapter 2, Part 1: Violence at the Heart of Relations Foreign and Domestic

Encyclopædia Britannica Standard Edition, s.v. "United Nations."

Phyllis Bennis, *United Nations Peacekeeping, Calling the Shots: How Washington Dominates Today's UN* (Olive Branch Press).

Director of the New Internationalism Project at the Institute for Policy Studies Phyllis Bennis is a fellow of Transnational Institute (TNI) and the Institute for Policy Studies in Washington D.C. She directs IPS's New Internationalism Project and specializes in U.S. foreign policy issues, particularly involving the Middle East and United Nations. Bennis worked as a journalist at the UN for ten years and currently serves as a special adviser to several top-level UN officials on Middle East and UN democratization issues. She is a frequent contributor to U.S. and global media. She has authored many articles and books—particularly on Palestine, Iraq, the UN, and U.S. foreign policy.

Democracy Now (Phyllis Bennis interviewed) "State of the Union 2005: Bush Pushes Aggressive Foreign Policy of Spreading Democracy," New York, accessed February 3, 2005, at http://www.democracynow. org/2005/2/3/state_of_the_union_2005_bush; Phyllis Bennis, *Before & After: U.S. Foreign Policy and the September 11th Crisis* (New York: Olive Branch Press, 2002); Bennis, *Calling the Shots: How Washington Dominates Today's UN* (New York: Olive Branch Press/Interlink Publishing).

GlobalSecuritydotorg, "The Horn of Africa"; "Operation Enduring Freedom, Horn of Africa, Djibouti," Alexandria, Va., GlobalSecurity. org in the News: 27-04-2005 15:32:25 Zulu; http://www.globalsecurity. org/military/library/report/1984/GA.htm; http://www.globalsecurity. org/military/ops/oef-djibouti.htm

Democracy Now (Salim Lone interviewed) "U.S. Launches Targeted Assassination Air Strikes in Somalia, Many Reported Killed," New York, accessed January 9, 2007 at http://www.democracynow.org/ article.pl?sid=07/01/09/1454252

Salim Lone is a columnist for Daily Nation in Kenya and former spokesperson for the UN mission in Iraq.

Carolyn LaDelle Bennett, *Same Ole or Something New: Uprooting power ENTRENCHMENT* (p. 124). Bloomington, 2010.

_____ "War for 'liberation' was a lie—Afghan women spoke truth from the ground" (ZOYA), Wednesday, October 28, 2009, p. 123-124.

> "Our freedom is only achievable at the hands of our people," says Zoya and the Revolutionary Association of the Women of Afghanistan. Zoya is a pseudonym because this Afghan woman cannot reveal her identity. She was speaking on several radio programs in the United States and Canada. RAWA takes the position that there should be no expectation of either the U.S. or any other country to present Afghans with democracy, peace, and prosperity.

_____ "Women injected clarity into U.S. 'war on terror'" (Leading Afghan women's activist, Zoya), Saturday, November 21, 2009, p. 221

> "The U.S. government has never supported democratic organizations . . ." (Elsa Rassbach's interview with Zoya of the Foreign Committee of RAWA) May 24, 2009. In June 2008, the Afghan activist Zoya (pseudonym) of the Revolutionary Association of the Women of Afghanistan (RAWA) testified before the Human Rights Commission of the German Parliament (Bundestag) in an effort to persuade the German government to withdraw its troops from Afghanistan. At that time, Elsa Rassbach, a U.S. citizen living in Germany, interviewed Zoya in Berlin. In light of the U.S. House of Representatives' approval at that time of tens of billions in further financing for the continued war and occupation in Afghanistan, Zoya and Rassbach believed the interview might be of interest to U.S. citizens.

The Revolutionary Association of the Women of Afghanistan (RAWA) established under the leadership of Meena in Kabul, Afghanistan, in 1977. The group was originally made up of a number of Afghan women intellectuals. Meena was assassinated in 1987 in Quetta, Pakistan, by Afghan agents of the then KGB in connivance with fundamentalist band of Gulbuddin Hekmatyar. RAWA's objective was to involve an increasing number of Afghan women in social and political activities aimed at acquiring women's human rights and contributing to the struggle for the establishment in Afghanistan of a government based on democratic and secular values, http://www.rawa.org/rawa.html.

> "Let's rise against the war crimes of U.S. and its fundamentalist lackeys!" was RAWA's Statement on the massacre of over 150 civilians in Bala Baluk of Farah Province by the U.S. "The only way our people can escape the occupant forces and their obedient servants is to rise against them under the slogans of: 'Neither the occupiers! Nor the bestial Taliban and the criminal Northern Alliance—long live a free and democratic Afghanistan!'" http://www.rawa.org/rawa/2009/05/07/lets-rise-against-the-war-crimes-of-us-andits-fundamentalist-lackeys.html

"America is still dead" (column by David R Hoffman, legal editor of Pravda.ru), October 3, 2011—English pravda.ru)

Libya

"Qaddafi Killing Could Be War Crime: ICC [International Criminal Court]." December 16, 2011, http://www.presstv.ir/detail/215990.html.

Related:

"'Justice dies when the law is co-opted for political purposes.' Gareth Peirce, one of our key human rights lawyers, talks to Stuart Jeffries" "Why I Still Fight for Human Rights," interview with Stuart Jeffries and Gareth Peirce, October 11, 2010, http://www.guardian.co.uk/law/2010/oct/12/gareth-peirce-fight-human-rights.

"Human Rights Watch has uncovered hundreds of letters in the Libyan foreign ministry proving the Qaddafi government directly aided the extraordinary rendition program carried out by the CIA and the MI6 in Britain after the 9/11 attacks. The documents expose how the CIA rendered suspects to Libyan authorities knowing they would be tortured." "Discovered Files Show U.S., Britain Had Extensive Ties with Qaddafi Regime on Rendition, Torture," September 7, 2011, http://www.democracynow.org/2011/9/7/discovered_files_show_us_britain_had.

Gareth Peirce is one of Britain's key human rights lawyers.

Democracy Now (Peter Bouckaert interviewed) "Discovered Files Show U.S., Britain Had Extensive Ties with Qaddafi Regime on Rendition, Torture—Human Rights Watch has uncovered hundreds of letters in the Libyan foreign ministry proving the Qaddafi government directly aided the extraordinary rendition program carried out by the CIA and the MI6 in Britain after the 9/11 attacks. The documents expose how the CIA rendered suspects to Libyan authorities knowing they would be tortured," accessed September 7, 2011, at http://www.democracynow.org/2011/9/7/discovered_files_show_us_britain_had

Peter Bouckaert is emergencies director at Human Rights Watch and helped find the documents in Tripoli.

"Alleged Inhumane Conditions for Post-9/11 Suspects Sparks Global Scrutiny of U.S. Detention Policies," *Democracy Now*, New York: In this program discussion of U.S. detention policies since 9/11 were Tarek Mehanna's brother, Tamer, and Gareth Peirce, one of Britain's best-known human rights lawyers. Peirce She had represented WikiLeaks founder Julian Assange and many prisoners held at the U.S. military base at Guantánamo Bay, http://www.democracynow.org/2011/10/14/alleged_inhumane_conditions_for_post_9 accessed October 14, 2011

NOTED:

"Ten years after the 9/11 attacks, detention policies in the United States are facing increasing scrutiny both here and abroad. American citizen Tarek Mehanna is set to stand trial this month on charges of 'conspiring to support terrorism' and 'providing material support to terrorists.'

"Mehanna is accused of trying to serve in al-Qaeda's 'media wing.' When arrested in October 2009, he was 27 years old. Since his arrest, he has been held in solitary confinement.

"Mehanna was originally courted by the FBI to become an informant.

"Meanwhile, the European Court of Human Rights is hearing a case on the legality of extradition of terror suspects to the United States on the grounds that inmates are subjected to inhumane conditions of confinement and routine violations of due process. This could become a landmark case in human rights law, potentially damaging the international reputation of the U.S. legal system."

I. Heartache and Hotspots

U.S. War Regions
Arabian, Iranian Basin, Somali Basin, Persian Gulf (Gulf of Aden, Red Sea, Arabian Sea): Iraq, Kuwait, Iran, Bahrain, Yemen, Horn of Africa, Somalia

Arabian Sea: Pakistan, Afghanistan, Iran
Mediterranean Sea gateway to Europe: Libya/Egypt (south), Palestine
(east)

People images Press TV
World Atlas maps
IOM [International Organizations on Migration]

IOM works in the four broad areas of migration management:
migration and development, facilitating migration, regulating
migration, and addressing forced migration. Crosscutting activities
include the promotion of international migration law, policy debate
and guidance, protection of migrants' rights, migration health and the
gender dimension of migration. IOM works closely with governmental,
intergovernmental and non-governmental partners. IOM Headquarters:
17 route des Morillons • C.P. 71 • CH-1211 Geneva 19, Switzerland,
www.iom.int

External Situation Report, IOM International Organizations on
Migration in Response to Libyan Crisis, October 10, 2011 http://www.
iom.int/jahia/webdav/shared/shared/mainsite/media/docs/reports/
IOM-sitrep-MENA.pdf

AFRICA AND MIDDLE EAST

"IOM Tackles the Spread of Scabies among Migrants and Refugees
at Salloum Border Crossing," http://www.iom.int/jahia/Jahia/media/
press-briefing-notes/pbnAF/cache/offonce/lang/en?entryId=30769

ICRC [International Committee of the Red Cross]—Salloum

For those stranded on the border between Libya and Egypt, Salloum is
the main crossing point between Libya and Egypt. Operating at Salloum
Land Port since March 2011, the ICRC (International Committee of the
Red Roses) has helped these displaced people by providing breakfasts,
telephone facilities and travel documents, http://www.icrc.org/eng/
resources/documents/field-newsletter/egypt-libya-newsletter-2011-09-
20.htm

Egypt

Egypt (officially Arab Republic of Egypt) is located in the northeastern corner of Africa. Its land frontiers border Libya in the west, the Sudan in the south, and Palestine in the northeast. (Israeli forces occupied the Sinai Peninsula and the Gaza Strip in eastern Egypt after the Arab-Israeli War of 1967. In 1982, the Sinai returned to Egypt.) In the north, Egypt's Mediterranean coastline is about 620 miles (1,000 kilometers); in the east, its coastline on the Red Sea and the Gulf of Aqaba is about 1,200 miles. Egypt's capital is Cairo.

Egypt was the home of one of the principal civilizations of the ancient Middle East. Like Mesopotamia, it was one of the very earliest urban and literate societies.

Libya

Libya (officially Socialist People's Libyan Arab Jamahiriya, formerly Libyan Arab Republic or People's Socialist Libyan Arab Republic) is in North Africa; bounded by the Mediterranean Sea on the north; Egypt on the east; the Sudan on the southeast; Niger and Chad on the south; and Tunisia and Algeria on the west. Libya is largely composed of the Sahara, and the population is concentrated along the coast, where the de facto capital, Tripoli (Ṭarābulus), and Banghāzī (Benghazi), the de jure capital, are located.

UNICEF [United Nations International Children's Emergency Fund] reports

"Cholera epidemic spreads in west, central Africa: UN—The virulent diarrheal disease is spreading quickly along waterways between and within countries, causing an 'unacceptably high' rate of fatalities, the U.N. Children's Fund UNICEF said," October 11, 2011, http://www.worldbulletin.net/?aType=haber&ArticleID=80093
UNICEF, http://www.unicef.org/health/uganda_53862.html
UNICEF Humanitarian Action Mid Year 2010 Review, http://www.unicef.org/files/HAR_Mid-Year_Review_2010.pdf

Images IOM http://www.iom.int/jahia/Jahia/media/photo-stories/lang/en

Ann Jones, *War Is Not Over when It's Over: Women Speak Out from the Ruins of War* (New York: Metropolitan Books, 2010) p. 7.

New Internationalist magazine http://www.newint.org/features/2009/11/01/427-08-war-on-terror.jpg http://www.newint.org/features/2009/11/01/world-of-counterterrorism/

II. Year-ending (2011) News Clips, Commentary, Context

Harm by design: Perpetual War, Crime Too Great To Conceal: Afghanistan and Pakistan, Bahrain, Yemen, Saudi Arabia, Palestine, Jordan, Syria, Iraq, Iran, Libya, Somalia, Uganda

James Madison (1751-1836) was the fourth President of the United States (1809-1813).

"Newt Gingrich Advocates Assassinating Iranian Scientists as Drum Beat for War Continues at GOP Debate," November 12, 2011, at http://videocafe.crooksandliars.com/heather/newt-gingrich-advocates-assassinating-iran.

Daniel Larison, "Newt Gingrich's Dangerous, Self-aggrandizing Foreign Policy, *The Week*, http://news.yahoo.com/newt-gingrichs-dangerous-self-aggrandizing-foreign-policy-104800717.html.

"Santorum: Dead Foreign Scientists a 'Wonderful Thing,'" October 27, 2011, http://videocafe.crooksandliars.com/david/santorum-dead-foreign-scientists-wonderful-t.

"U.S. presidential hopeful Newt Gingrich has openly called for sabotaging Iran's nuclear program through terrorism and assassinating Iranian scientists as part of Washington's policy." "U.S. Gingrich Says Kill Iranian Scientists," November 14, 2011, http://www.presstv.ir/detail/210013.html.

Press TV has conducted an interview with cofounder of American-Iranian Friendship Committee Eleanor Ommani.

Eleanor Ommani is co-founder of American-Iranian Friendship Committee

"Republican presidential hopefuls Newt Gingrich and Rick Santorum U.S. Republican presidential candidates have renewed calls for covert operations including acts of sabotage, assassination and aid to terrorist groups against Iran." "'Insane' U.S. Politicians to Wage More Wars," Press TV, December 8, 2011, http://www.presstv.ir/detail/214513.html.

Background: Sanctions

Today's Insight News, Saturday, May 22, 2010, "'Just War,' Sanctions, Punishment Masked as 'Peace'" *In siege warfare, armies surround cities. With sanctions, international powers prohibit migration and sale or purchase of goods.* Both are types of war that destabilize and fail states, inflict and exacerbate injustice: human rights abuse, hunger and homelessness, sickness, disease and perpetual poverty. Warfare and sanctions do what they purport to undo. The current administration in Washington carries on its predecessors' legacy of punishment and hegemony. "Economic sanctions, just war doctrine, and the 'fearful spectacle of the civilian dead" (Joy Gordon): "Sanctions like siege intend harm to civilians and therefore cannot be justified as a tool of warfare," (Cross Currents), http://www.crosscurrents.org/gordon.htm

Dr. Joy Gordon is professor in philosophy and director of legal studies at Fairfield University in Connecticut, http://www.fairfield.edu/about/about_contact.html

Helena Cobban, "A Hippocratic Oath for international intervention? Having an Effect on Vulnerable Others: Two Aspects of the Present U.S. Actions toward Afghanistan," *Christian Science Monitor*, teach-in panel discussion on ethical dimensions of crisis held at the University of Virginia, October 9, 2001, http://helenacobban.org/.

Helena Cobban is a veteran writer, researcher, and program organizer on global affairs. She is author of *Re-engage! America and the World after Bush* (2008) and publishes the blog Just World News centered on international issues.

Martin Sean Indyk is Vice President for Foreign Policy at the Brookings Institution in Washington, D.C. and was U.S. ambassador to Israel and Assistant Secretary of State for Near East Affairs

(William Jefferson Clinton administration). Indyk was a lead U.S. negotiator at the Camp David talks and framer of the U.S. policy of dual containment [U.S. policy of 'dual containment' (isolating both Iran and Iraq) sought to depict Iran as a 'rogue' State that supported terrorism.]. Iraq and Iran were viewed as Israel's two most important strategic adversaries (*Wikipedia*, s.v, "Martin Indyk"; *Encyclopaedia Britannica*, s.v. "Martin Indyk").

Camp David (Maryland) Accords

Agreements between Israel and Egypt signed on September 17, 1978. These agreements led in the following year to a peace treaty between Israel and Egypt, the first such treaty between Israel and any of its Arab neighbors. The 39th U.S. president, James (Jimmy) Earl Carter Jr., brokered the accord between Israeli Prime Minister Menachem Begin and Egyptian President Anwar el-Sādāt. The official title of the accord was "Framework for Peace in the Middle East." The agreements are widely known as the "Camp David Accords" because the negotiations took place at the U.S. presidential retreat at Camp David, Maryland (*Britannica*)

"Just War" Concept from the Middle Ages

Just war (*jus ad bellum*) is a notion rising from Classical Roman and biblical Hebraic culture containing religious and secular elements that first coalesced as a coherent body of thought and practice during the Middle Ages [medieval times running variously between the 5th and 15th centuries]. The idea is that the resort to armed force (*jus ad bellum*) is justified under certain conditions; and the notion that the use of such force (jus in bello) should be limited in certain ways. "*Just war*" in the Western context is a byproduct of canon law and theology. *A "just war" most scholars agree must meet several jus ad bellum requirements.* Four most important ones are:

- The war must be openly declared by a proper sovereign authority—the governing authority of the political community in question
- The war must have a just cause—e.g., defense of the common good or a response to grave injustice

- The warring state must have just intentions—i.e., it must wage the war for justice rather than for self-interest
- The aim of the war must be the establishment of a just peace

"Just war" conditions added at the end of World War II:

- There must be a reasonable chance of success
- Force must be used as a last resort
- The expected benefits of war must outweigh its anticipated costs

Western thought distinguishes the "just war" concept from the Islamic concept "jihad" (Arabic: 'striving' or holy war) which is, in Muslim legal theory, the only type of "just war."

Background: U.S. and Iran

Nuclear notes

"Want, nuclear rise; peace ops fall—SIPRI [Stockholm International Peace Research Institute] Report." *Today's Insight News*, Thursday, June 30, 2011

The Stockholm International Peace Research Institute (SIPRI) on June 7, 2011, released findings assessing current state of international security, armaments and disarmament. The summary of its findings were, "resource competition raises tensions; Nuclear forces 'leaner but meaner'; Peace operation numbers fall."

Key findings:

- New levels of global resource demand could destabilize international relations.
- Continuing cuts in U.S. and Russian nuclear forces are offset by long-term force modernization programs.
- Number of peace missions fell to the lowest level since 2002.

Excerpt from report highlights [Nuclear weapons]

- Falling numbers
- Little progress toward disarmament
- The United States, Russia, the United Kingdom, France, China, India, Pakistan and Israel possess more than 20,500 nuclear weapons, a drop of more than 2,000 since 2009.
- More than 5000 of these nuclear weapons are deployed and ready for use, including nearly 2,000 that are kept in a state of high operational alert.
- The United States and Russian Federation agreed to modest cuts in their strategic nuclear forces in April 2010 under the New Strategic Arms Reduction Talks (START) treaty, but both countries [at the time of this report] either are deploying new nuclear weapon delivery systems or have announced programs to do so and appear determined to retain their nuclear arsenals for the indefinite future.

SIPRI Senior Researcher Shannon Kile says that it is "a stretch to say that the New START cuts agreed by the USA and Russia are a genuine step towards nuclear disarmament when their planning for nuclear forces is done on a time scale that encompasses decades and when nuclear modernization is a major priority of their defense policies."

Meanwhile, India and Pakistan continue to develop new ballistic and cruise missile systems capable of delivering nuclear weapons. They are also expanding their capacities to produce fissile material [material capable of releasing of large amounts of energy caused by splitting of atomic nucleus] for military purposes.

World Nuclear Forces 2011

Country	Deployed warheads*	Other warheads	Total 2011	Total 2010
USA	2150	6350	8500	9600
Russia	2427	8570	11000	12000
UK	160	65	225	225
France	290	10	300	300
China		200	240	240

India		80-100	80-110	60-80
Pakistan		90-110	90-110	70-90
Israel		80	80	80
Total	5027	15500	20530	22600

Source: SIPRI Yearbook 2011
*"Deployed" means warheads placed on missiles or located on bases with operational forces

Peace operations fewer

The North Atlantic Treaty Organization (NATO) International Security Assistance Force has the world's largest number of 'peacekeepers' is a misleading image.

"The vast size of the ISAF [NATO-led International Security Assistance Force] creates a misleading picture of peace," says senior researcher Sharon Wiharta, head of SIPRI's Project on Multilateral Peace Operations. "ISAF troops are mostly engaged in counter-insurgency rather than mainstream peacekeeping. Take them out of the equation and the peacekeeping surge of the 2000s appears to be largely over."

The number of active peace operations fell in 2010 to its lowest level since 2002.

Fifty-two (52) peace operations deployed 262, 842 international troops, observers, civilian police and civilian staff, an increase of 20 percent over the 2009 level (219, 278 in 54 operations). However, at 131, 730 troops, the NATO International Security Assistance Force (ISAF) in Afghanistan deployed more personnel than all the other 51 operations combined.

Non-ISAF personnel numbers actually fell by 3 percent (from 135 132 in 2009 to 131,112 in 2010).

"Resource competition raises tensions. Nuclear forces 'leaner but meaner.' Peace operation numbers fall," says SIPRI Yearbook released in early June. The Stockholm International Peace Research Institute

(SIPRI), on June 7, 2011 (http://www.sipri.org/media/pressreleases/yblaunch11), released findings assessing the current state of international security, armaments and disarmament.

Established in 1966, the Stockholm International Peace Research Institute (SIPRI) is an independent international institute dedicated to research into conflict, armaments, arms control and disarmament. SIPRI provides data, analysis and recommendations, based on open sources, to policymakers, researchers, media, and the interested public.

A decision by the Swedish Parliament established SIPRI and an annual grant from the Swedish Government is the source of a substantial part of SIPRI's funding. To carry out its broad research program, the Institute also seeks financial support from other organizations. http://www.sipri.org/about

Background: Iran, United States, and Nuclear
"Entrenched Manfactured Iran—Giraldi's Progressive Course," *Today's Insight News* February 27, 2010

Former CIA officer Philip Giraldi, asks, "*Why is Iran the target of so much rage* even though [Iran] has not threatened the United States or any vital American interest?" Israel's and its friends' influence over [the U.S.] Congress and the media is surely a large part of the answer. How else can one explain the different treatment afforded Iran and North Korea given Pyongyang's open development of nuclear weapons and ballistic missiles? Giraldi continues.

> *Unlike North Korea, Iran continues to be a signatory of the Nuclear Non-Proliferation Treaty and its nuclear sites are inspected by the UN's International Atomic Energy Agency.*
>
> *Iran is a developing country with a small economy and tiny defense budget and it has not invaded a neighbor since the eighteenth century.*
>
> *Iran does not even have the resources to refine its own oil for home consumption and must import the gasoline it uses.*

Wider consequences

If proposed Congressional sanctions are fully implemented, Iran's economy will grind to a halt but the damage does not stop there. Iran deals with many European and Asian companies in its energy industry and, if they do not break off relations with Iran, all would feel the impact of U.S. sanctions. They might not like that and might well take commensurate steps against the United States. Ultimately, the United States Navy might have to enforce the sanctions. What happens when U.S. forces stop a Chinese or Russian ship on the high seas? Did members of the U.S. Congress really think about what they were doing and what the consequences of sanctions might be? The irony is that the United States has an Iran problem largely manufactured in Washington and in Tel Aviv.

> *Tehran does not actually threaten the United States yet Washington has been supporting terrorists and separatists who have killed hundreds of people inside Iran.*
>
> *Israel, which has its own secret nuclear arsenal, claims to be threatened if Iran develops even the ability to concentrate its uranium referred to as 'mastering the enrichment cycle,' a point of view that has also been adopted by Washington.*
>
> *The White House has made repeated threats that the military option for dealing with Tehran is 'on the table' while Israel has been even more explicit in its threats to attack.*
>
> *The U.S. mainstream media are united in their desire to come to grips with the Mullahs.*

No wonder Iran feels threatened—because it is under threat. To be sure, Iran is no role model for good governance but a desire to deal with the country fairly and realistically is not an endorsement of the regime in power. Iran engages diplomatically and through surrogates in the entire Persian Gulf region and Central Asia, supporting its friends and seeking to undermine its enemies. That makes it no different from any of its neighbors and the United States—all of which play the same game.

The bottom line is that the United States has been interfering in Iran since 1978 and even before if one goes back to the overthrow of Mohammed Mossadeq by the CIA in 1953. The interference has accomplished nothing and has only created a poisonous relationship that [U.S. President] Barack Obama has done little to improve. Indeed, President Obama and Secretary of State Hillary Rodham Clinton's harsh rhetoric suggests that when it comes to Iran the Democrats are more hard line than was [former U.S. President] George W. Bush.

The drive to punish Iran supported in Congress and the media is perhaps no coincidence suggesting that those who want war are coordinating the effort. In an overwhelming voice vote at the end of January, the U.S. Senate joined the House of Representatives in passing a resolution demanding sanctions on Iran's energy imports. A joint resolution being crafted could well give the Obama government political cover to advocate even more draconian measures against Iran and its rulers. From the Iranian viewpoint, this is pretty much a declaration of war.

Far better course of action: real change

Imagine for a moment what might happen if Washington were to adopt a serious foreign policy based on the U.S. national interest. That would mean *strict non-interventionism* in troubled regions like the Middle East where the United States has everything to lose and little to gain.

- It would be the real change promised by candidate Obama if Washington were to admit that it is not threatened by Tehran and were to declare that it will not interfere in Iran's politics.
- It could further announce that it no longer has a military option on the table, and that it will *not* permit Israeli overflight of Iraq to attack Iran.
- Iran's leaders just might decide that they don't really need their own 'option on the table' which has been the threat that they might seek to develop a nuclear weapon.
- An Iran that feels more secure might well be willing to take some risks itself to defuse tension with its neighbors and with Washington. In 2003, Iran offered to negotiate all outstanding

differences with the United States—an offer the [George W.] Bush White House turned down.

The big question about Iran is not whether or not it has the knowledge and resources to build an atom bomb. It does or soon will. The real issue is whether the United States is actually threatened by that knowledge and what should be done in terms of positive policies to discourage an expanded nuclear program.

Punishing Iran is no solution.

It will not work. It closes the door to diplomacy and will only make the worst-case scenario that much more likely. Opening the door to a rapprochement by eliminating the threatening language coming out of Washington and creating incentives for cooperation is a far better course of action.

"Some Straight Thinking About Iran" (Philip Giraldi), February 18, 2010, http://original.antiwar.com/giraldi/2010/02/17/some-straight-thinking-about-iran

Philip Giraldi is a former officer of the United States Central Intelligence Agency who became famous for claiming in 2005 that the United States was preparing plans to attack Iran with nuclear weapons in response to a terrorist action against the United States, independently of whether or not Iran was involved in the action. Giraldi is a partner in an international security consultancy, Cannistraro Associates and a graduate of the University of Chicago and the University of London with masters and doctoral credentials in European History [*Wikipedia*].

Jack A. Smith, "The U.S. and Iran: A Manufactured Crisis Part 1: The Facts of the Matter," *Activist Newsletter*, September 28, 2009, http://activistnewsletter.blogspot.com/

> "If push does come to shove with Iran, it is important to remember how effortless it was to hoodwink the majority of American politicians and the masses of people into backing a completely unnecessary war against Iraq. As in the buildup to

the unjust invasion of Iraq, today's U.S. corporate mass media are playing a principal part to perfection: uncritically echoing government distortions about the danger of Iran's nonexistent nuclear weapons. The Iran situation is different but similar in terms of mass public manipulation and the possibility of a future confrontation getting out of hand."

Jack A. Smith is editor of the *Activist Newsletter,* a former editor of the *Guardian* (U.S.) radical newsweekly.

Nagasaki Peace Declaration 2010

[Excerpt]

The mayor of Nagasaki spoke boldly today (August 9, 2010) in support of nuclear nonproliferation and elimination and in condolence for the dead and suffering.

> On August 9, 1945, at 11:02 a.m., a single atomic bomb dropped by a United States military aircraft devastated Nagasaki instantly. Intense heat rays, blast winds, radiation, and ceaseless fires . . . claimed the precious lives of 74,000 people, while inflicting deep physical and mental wounds on those who narrowly escaped death . . . .

> We call upon the leaders of the nuclear weapons states never to trample on humanity's efforts for 'a world without nuclear weapons.'

> This May [2010], at the Nuclear Non-Proliferation Treaty (NPT) Review Conference, concrete steps toward nuclear disarmament with specified timelines were proposed by the Chairperson. This proposal was widely supported by non-nuclear weapons states.

> Expectations were raised among non-governmental organizations assembling in New York from around the world and among the people of Nagasaki, a city that has suffered the horror of atomic bombing.

The Chairperson's proposal was later rejected by the government representatives of the nuclear weapons states of the United States, Russian Federation, United Kingdom, France and the People's Republic of China.

The lack of sincere commitment from the nuclear weapons states toward nuclear disarmament could provoke antipathy and lead to the emergence of more new nuclear weapons states, increasing the threat of nuclear proliferation around the world . . . .

We believe that a new treaty is necessary in order to take the steps to eliminate nuclear weapons . . . .

I would like to remind everyone around the world that it is we ourselves who have the power to decide which path we should take, 'a world with nuclear weapons' filled with distrust and threat, or 'a world without nuclear weapons' based on trust and cooperation. For our children, we have responsibility for creating a future without the fear of nuclear weapons. . . .

Many people in the world are continuing their peace efforts toward the abolishment of nuclear weapons. In cooperation with them, the city of Nagasaki will establish an extensive global network of peace citizens to unite with a city that has suffered nuclear attack . . . .

We offer our sincere condolences on the deaths of the atomic bomb victims, and pledge to continue our utmost efforts together with the city of Hiroshima, until the day when nuclear weapons no longer exist on the earth . . . .

[O]n our own, each of us might be small and weak [but] by joining together we can become a force to make governments act, to create a new history. Let us convey our intention fully and clearly to our governments . . . ." (Tomihisa Taue, Mayor of Nagasaki, August 9, 2010)

"Nagasaki Peace Declaration," Nagasaki City, Peace Appeals, August 9, 2010, http://www.city.nagasaki.nagasaki.jp/peace/english/appeal/
"Nagasaki marks A-bomb anniversary," August 9, 2010, http://english.aljazeera.net/news/asia-pacific/2010/08/20108945819655132.html
"Nagasaki remembers atomic victims," August 9, 2010, http://english.aljazeera.net/news/asia-pacific/2010/08/20108913451439239.html

"Atomic Wounds"

As part of its "Witness" program, Al Jazeera-English on Sunday August 8 through Tuesday August 10 aired "Atomic Wounds"

Noting that a survivor of the 1945 atomic bomb at Hiroshima, Dr Hida, continued to care for some of the other quarter of a million survivors, the program retraced the physician's dedicated journey and revealed how successive U.S. administrations in the 1950s through the 1970s without concerned for public health concealed the terrible danger of radiation so that nuclear power could be freely developed. [Atomic Wounds," http://english.aljazeera.net/programmes/witness/2009/05/2009537181173851.html]

The Riz Khan show presented "Eliminating Nuclear weapons" from Wednesday August 4, 2010, http://english.aljazeera.net/programmes/rizkhan/2010/08/20108463955110993.html

The Obama administration Budget [in news reports February 17, 2011] Boosts Loan Guarantees for Nuclear Power Industry: the New budget plan included "$36 billion in spending to provide loan guarantees for the nuclear power industry to establish new reactors." David Wallechinsky at AllGov.com.

Related text, update—reporting on U.S. presidential candidates Bachmann, Obama, Gingrich and the backlash

U.S. Presidential candidate Michele Bachmann reveals plans to close the U.S. embassy in Iran though the U.S. has had no embassy there since 1980. The candidate reportedly told a crowd in Waverly, Iowa, "'That's exactly what I would do [if I were president]. . . . We wouldn't have an embassy in Iran. I wouldn't allow that to be there.'"

The sitting president also apparently "slipped up" when "denouncing the storming of an 'English' embassy in Tehran, which is actually 'British'"

In another verbally violent outburst, House Speaker Newt Gingrich told a Wednesday gathering of the Republican Jewish Coalition in Washington, D.C. (and the press) that he would resort to 'covert capability' to bring about 'regime replacement' in Iran. 'They only have one very, very large refinery,' he said. 'I would be focused on how to covertly sabotage it every day' (AFP quoted the former speaker).

The preceding month, Gingrich proposed that Washington kill Iranian scientists to disrupt the country's atomic energy program.

Another candidate, former senator Rick Santorum, restated the call for assassination of Iranian scientists. 'We need to say very clearly that we will be conducting covert activity to do everything we can to stop their nuclear program.' [By the spring of 2012, candidates Bachmann, Gingrich and Santorum had withdrawn from the Republican race for the U.S. presidency.]

Republican presidential contender Mitt Romney called on Washington to openly help seditionists in Iran. 'We should also have covert and overt activities to encourage voices of dissent within the country. Ultimately regime change is what's going to be necessary in that setting.' During a debate featuring a number of Republican presidential candidates, there were calls ranging from executing covert operations—such as terrorism and assassinations—to launching a military strike on Iran. Press TV and other news outlets have reported that a number of Iranian scientists have been assassinated over the past few years, including Professor Majid Shahriari and Professor Masoud Ali-Mohammadi, who were both killed in 2010. Iran has also launched investigation of these deaths.

"Oops! Presidential hopeful plans to close U.S. embassy in Iran," December 1, 2011, http://www.presstv.ir/usdetail/213227.html

GOPers call for covert ops on Iran," December 8, 2011, http://www.presstv.ir/detail/214448.html

Backlash

The secretary of Iran's Supreme National Security Council, Saeed Jalili, announced on November 4, 2011, that Tehran had irrefutable evidence proving that the U.S. government was involved in anti-Iran conspiracies and had dispatched elements to carry out acts of sabotage and terrorism in Iran and other regional countries. That statement said, "The United States, Israel, and some of their allies accuse Tehran of pursuing military objectives in its nuclear program and have used the false charge as a pretext to push for the imposition of sanctions on the country."

Affirming its "right to develop and acquire nuclear technology for peaceful purposes," Iran's officials warned of "a crushing response to any military strike against the country" and that a a strike against Iran "could spark a war that would spread beyond the Middle East."

Imperialism and neocolonialism

Source note: Imperialism is state policy, practice, or advocacy of extending power and dominion, especially by direct territorial acquisition or by gaining political and economic control of other areas. Because it always involves the use of power, whether military force or some subtler form, imperialism has often been considered morally reprehensible and the term is frequently employed in international propaganda to denounce and discredit an opponent's foreign policy.

Imperialism results from a complex of causes in which, in varying degrees, economic pressures, human aggressiveness and greed, search for security, drive for power and prestige, nationalist emotions, '*humanitarianism*,' and many other factors are [in effect].

This mixture of motivations makes it difficult to eliminate imperialism and easy for states to suspect imperialism in foreign policies and to consider themselves potential victims of imperialism.

Some states of the Third World have accused the former colonial powers [Britain, France, Italy, Portugal, Spain, Roman Catholicism (The Vatican)] and other nations [United States of America] of neocolonialism: the execution of economic and political policies by which a great power indirectly maintains or extends its influence over other areas or people (*Merriam Webster*). Third World populations fear that the granting of aid or the supply of skilled personnel for economic and technical development might be an imperialist guise. *Encyclopedia Britannica*, s.v. "imperialism."

Mike Gravel

A former U.S. presidential candidate (2008) and a former U.S. Senator (1969-1981), Maurice Robert (Mike) Gravel (b. May 13, 1930) is prominently known for his release of the Pentagon Papers, the secret official study that revealed the lies and manipulations of successive U.S. administrations that misled the country into the Vietnam War. After the *New York Times* published portions of the leaked study, the Nixon administration moved to block any further publication of information and to punish any newspaper publisher who revealed the contents. Speaking on the floor of the Senate, Gravel (a junior senator at the time) argued that his constituents had a right to know the truth behind the war and proceeded to read into the senate record 4,100 pages of the 7,000-page document. The Supreme Court ultimately ruled that Senator Gravel did not have the right and responsibility to share official documents with his constituents. Gravel then published *The Senator Gravel Edition,* The Pentagon Papers, Beacon Press (1971). What followed was the court case Gravel v. U.S. and the handing down of a landmark Supreme Court decision (No. 71-1017-1026) pertaining to the Speech and Debate Clause (Article 1, Section 6) of the United States Constitution.

Mike Gravel has been characterized as "a passionate advocate of direct democracy and the National Initiative." During the 2007-2008 presidential campaign, Gravel ran on these ideas.

The former lawmaker served in the Alaska House of Representatives (1963-66), and as Speaker (1965-66). He then represented Alaska in the U.S. Senate (1969-81) where he served on the Finance, Interior, and Environmental and Public Works committees, chairing the Energy, Water Resources, Buildings and Grounds, and Environmental Pollution subcommittees. In 1971, Gravel waged a successful solo filibuster for five months that forced the Nixon administration to cut a deal, effectively ending the draft in the United States. He was founder and president of The Democracy Foundation, Philadelphia II, and Direct Democracy, nonprofit corporations dedicated to the establishment of direct democracy in the United States, through the enactment of the National Initiative for Democracy by American voters. Senator Gravel is author of Jobs and More Jobs, and Citizen Power. He lectures and writes about governance, foreign affairs, economics, Social Security, tax reform, energy, environmental issues and democracy.

Senator Gravel served in the U.S. Army (1951-54) and as special adjutant in the Communication Intelligence Services and as a Special Agent in the Counterintelligence Corps. His academic credentials are in economics (B.S., Columbia University) and in law and public affairs (four honorary degrees). Mike Gravel was born in Springfield, Massachusetts, of French Canadian immigrants. http://www.mikegravel.us/bio

Stop the War Coalition (UK) and Press TV reporting

USA and the War on Terror . . . Nobel Peace Prize winner Barack Obama is waging war in Afghanistan, Iraq, Pakistan, Somalia, Yemen and Uganda and bragging about starting another in Iran, Jason Ditz: "'Peace' president Obama brags about how many people he's killed," December 9, 2011 (http://stopwar.org.uk/index.php/peace-president-obama-brags-about-how-many-people-hes-killed).

Britain's peace activists announce plans to hold a peace march on Sunday December 18 in protest of "the British Government's aggressive, illegal, and dangerous, policy toward Iran" and against "the unjust war in Afghanistan, which after ten years [had] reached its bloodiest level."

In stating their intent to join the "Occupy London" protesters, the Stop the War Coalition demonstrators declared that the British government's involvement in wars around the world "is only in the interest of the 1 percent—a government cabinet of millionaires and their friends in the oil and arms companies . . . The '99 percent' desire peace," they said, and "peace is essential for human well being. We believe Peace is

Possible" ("UK protesters urge policy shift on Iran," December 17, 2011, http://www.presstv.ir/detail/216215.html; "U.S. lawmaker challenges deepening BREAKDOWN," *Today's Insight News*, December 15, 2011.

ALCEE HASTINGS

Congressman Alcee L. Hastings serves as Senior Member of the House Rules Committee, Ranking Democratic Member of the U.S. Helsinki Commission, and Democratic Chairman of the Florida Delegation.

U.S. House of Representatives posted at House Press Gallery
http://housepressgallery.house.gov/

The National Defense Authorization Act for Fiscal Year 2012 passed in the U.S. House of Representatives by a vote of 283-136 but was strongly opposed by Democratic Congressman Alcee L. Hastings. ("Hastings Blasts Passage of National Defense Authorization Act," December 14, 2011, http://www.alceehastings.house.gov/index. php?option=com_content&view=article&id=1039:de

Also on this issue

Statement by Human Rights High Commissioner Louise Arbour on Human Rights Day December 10, 2007; and the Brennan Center, http:// www.brennancenter.org/page/-/pull%20quotes/investigating.pull.2.png

Congressman Alcee Hastings

U.S. Representative Alcee Lamar Hastings has been a member of the U.S. Congress since 1993. Before entering the Congress, he was a United States District Judge for the Southern District of Florida (1979-1989), a judge of the circuit court of Broward County, Florida (1977-1979), and a lawyer in private practice. Representative Hastings took his academic credentials at Howard University School of Law (Washington, D.C., Juris Doctor) and Florida Agricultural and Mechanical University (Tallahassee, Florida, 1963) and Fisk University (Nashville, Tennessee, Baccalaureate). Hastings was born in Altamonte Springs, Seminole County, Florida.

Remote-Controlled Drone

A BQM-74E remote-controlled drone takes off from the flight deck of USS Samuel B. Roberts prior to starting a live-fire exercise in the Caribbean Sea, July 19, 2005. U.S. Navy photo by Petty Officer 1st Class Michael Sandberg http://www.defense.gov/ transformation/images/photos/2005-07/ Hi-Res/050719-N-4374S-003.jpg

Wednesday, December 14, 2011, "High-placed killer among us boasts—Portrait of Peace Laureate whose role no one should model"

Stop the War Coalition said, "In comments that were surprisingly bellicose even for the current political environment, U. S. President Barack Obama bragged loudly about the number of people he's killed, urging hawks who don't think he's hawkish enough to 'ask Osama bin Laden and the 22 out of 30 top al-Qaeda leaders who've been taken off the field.'" The Coalition continued its reaction.

> He [the U.S. president] could've also advised them to ask thousands of Pakistanis, Afghans and Iraqis as well, or the family of Anwar al-Awlaki, the U.S. citizen he [presidential

orders] assassinated earlier this year, but the point was already made: an Obama Administration kills lots of people, and they're pretty sure that's what voters are in the market for.

Moving beyond that, Obama went on to more familiar hawkish territory, trotting out his usual 'all options are on the table' threat against Iran, comments which appear timed to resonate through the Republican Jewish Coalition Conference, which itself centered on potential Obama foes bragging about how quickly and on how little pretext they'd attack Iran.

'Today Iran is isolated and the world is united in applying the toughest sanctions that Iran has ever experienced,' added Obama, saying his administration had done more to unite the world against Iran than the [George W.] Bush Administration had.

Unconscionable role to model

Image *War Crimes Times* http://www.waarcrimestimes.org/2010/05/ crimes-are-crimes-no-matter-who-does.html

[Caption Echoes of former war presidents Richard M. Nixon and Lyndon Baines Johnson]

"'Peace' president Obama brags about how many people he's killed." "USA and the War on Terror," Jason Ditz, December 9, 2011; "Nobel Peace Prize winner Barack Obama is waging war in Afghanistan, Iraq, Pakistan, Somalia, Yemen and Uganda and bragging about starting another in Iran" (http://stopwar.org.uk/index.php/peace-president-obama-brags-about-how-many-people-hes-killed).

My count of countries in this entrenched U.S. global war is even higher, and I don't think my count comes close to the real total.

The United States is at *war* with the world's peoples and their countries:

- arming and bankrolling to create domestic and regional pressure
- assassination with impunity
- direct aggression
- direct/indirect threat/intimidation
- displacement/destabilization
- economic/financial sanctions
- failing nations failing to negotiate with words or nonviolent diplomacy
- provocation/incitement to protracted violence
- occupation
- unlawful search and detention
- torture

Afghanistan	Bahrain
Cuba	Djibouti
Eritrea	Ethiopia
Haiti	Honduras
Iran	Iraq
Japan (Okinawa)	Kenya
Libya	Mexico
Nigeria	North Korea
Pakistan	Palestine
Russia	Saudi Arabia
Somalia	South Korea
Syria	Turkey
Uganda (dominoes the Sudan, South Sudan, Central African Republic, Republic of the Congo [Brazzaville], Democratic Republic of the Congo [Kinshasa])	Yemen

"Washington's Wars Far from Over: Continuing Carnage in Middle East—this Week's Protests, Commentary on Lies," *Today's Insight News* (blog), Saturday, December 17, 2011.

Iran
"UK Protesters Urge Policy Shift on Iran," December 17, 2011, http://www.presstv.ir/detail/216215.html.
"U.S. Uses Sanctions as Psywar Tactic," December 17, 2011, http://www.presstv.ir/detail/216244.html.

Afghanistan
"U.S. Forces Kill Pregnant Afghan Woman," December 17, 2011, http://www.presstv.ir/detail/216210.html.http://www.presstv.ir/detail/216170.html.
"Police Station Bombed in Afghan Capital," December 16, 2011, http://www.presstv.ir/detail/216066.html.
"Bomb Blast Kills 2 Afghan Soldiers," December 15, 2011, http://www.presstv.ir/detail/215858.html.
"Roadside Bomb Kills 4 Afghan Civilians," December 15, 2011, http://www.presstv.ir/detail/215850.html.

Pakistan
"Pakistan: NATO Raids Were Deliberate," *Christian Science Monitor*, December 16, 2011, http://www.presstv.ir/detail/215958.html.
"Pakistan: U.S. Must Heed Our Red Lines," December 16, 2011, http://www.presstv.ir/detail/216099.html.
"Pakistanis Protest Deadly NATO Attacks," December 16, 2011, http://www.presstv.ir/detail/215973.html, http://www.presstv.ir/section/351020401.html.

Drones

"CIA drone strikes are killing hundreds—if not thousands—of civilians and destabilizing Pakistan." "Britain Questioned over CIA Drone Strike," December 17, 2011, http://www.presstv.ir/detail/216274.html.

Africa

Libya
"Qaddafi Killing Could Be War Crime: ICC," December 16, 2011, http://www.presstv.ir/detail/215990.html.

Somalia
"Diseases Kill 50 More Somali Children," December 15, 2011, http://www.presstv.ir/detail/215815.html.

Egypt
"Two Protesters Killed in Cairo Violence," December 16, 2011, http://www.presstv.ir/detail/216089.html.

Ann Jones, *War Is Not Over when It's Over: Women Speak Out from the Ruins of War* (New York: Metropolitan Books, 2010), p. 7.

New Internationalist magazine http://www.newint.org/features/2009/11/01/427-08-war-on-terror.jpg http://www.newint.org/features/2009/11/01/world-of-counterterrorism/

EARLY OCTOBER

"Ten Years after U.S. Invasion, Afghan War Rages on with No End in Sight," *Democracy Now* October 7, 2011, http://www.democracynow.org/2011/10/7/ten_years_after_us_invasion_afghan

Peace laureates—Is the Nobel Peace Prize meaningless, misnomer or misplaced prize?

"Liberia: Nobel for President, No-water for residents," October 13, 2011, http://english.pravda.ru/world/africa/13-10-2011/119314-Liberia_President_No_water_for_residents-0/

Thomas C. Mountain is the only independent western journalist in the Horn of Africa, living and reporting from Eritrea since 2006.

Friday, October 7, 2011

Nobel Peace Prize Committee recognizes three women

The Norwegian Nobel Committee this year awards a three-way Peace Prize whose recipients are Leymah Gbowee, Tawakkul Karman, and Ellen Johnson Sirleaf for "their non-violent struggle for the safety of women and for the rights of women to full participation in peace-building work." Nobel Peace Prize 2011 announcement at Oslo, October 7 2011, http://nobelpeaceprize.org/en_GB/announce-2011/.

Leymah Gbowee—Residence at time of award: Liberia
Tawakkul Karman—Residence at time of award: Yemen
Ellen Johnson Sirleaf—Time of award: Resident and President of Liberia

Biographical briefs of the women (October 7, 2011) at http://www. nobelprize.org/nobel_prizes/peace/laureates/2011/gbowee.html; http:// www.nobelprize.org/nobel_prizes/peace/laureates/2011/karman.html; http://www.nobelprize.org/nobel_prizes/peace/laureates/2011/johnson_ sirleaf.htm
Nobelprize.org   http://www.nobelprize.org/nobel_prizes/lists/women. html

Britannica Caption
Liberian President Ellen Johnson-Sirleaf, AP
2011 Nobel Peace Prize Captions

EARLY OCTOBER AT WAR

Afghanistan and Pakistan, Bahrain, Yemen, Saudi Arabia, Palestine, Jordan, Syria, Iraq, Iran, Libya, Somalia, Uganda

Afghanistan and Pakistan

Afghanistan
"Afghan MPs Want Pakistan Ties Severed," October 14, 2011, http:// www.presstv.ir/detail/204589.html.

"Three U.S.-led Troops Killed in Afghan War," October 14, 2011, http://www.presstv.ir/detail/204511.html.

Pakistan
"U.S. Drone Strike Kills Four in Pakistan," October 14, 2011, http://www.presstv.ir/detail/204567.html.

Bahrain
"Bahrain Forces Attack, Arrest Protesters," October 14, 2011, http://www.presstv.ir/detail/204568.html.

Saudi Arabia
"Saudis Stage New Anti-regime Protest," October 14, 2011, http://www.presstv.ir/detail/204548.html.

Yemen
"Yemenis Urge End to Saleh Rule," October 13, 2011, http://www.presstv.ir/detail/204357.html.

Palestine
"Israel to Build 1,000s More Settler Units," October 14, 2011, http://www.presstv.ir/detail/204536.html.

Iraq
"Multiple Blasts Kill 18 in Baghdad," October 14, 2011, http://www.presstv.ir/detail/204446.html; "Baghdad Bombings Claim 15 Lives," October 13, 2011, http://www.presstv.ir/detail/204429.html.

Iran
"Awakenings Foil anti-Iran U.S. Plots," October 14, 2011, http://www.presstv.ir/detail/204598.html.
"U.S. after Fueling Iranophobia in World," October 14, 2011, http://www.presstv.ir/detail/204572.html.

Libya
"Fighters, Qaddafi Forces Battle in Tripoli," October 14, 2011, http://www.presstv.ir/detail/204600.html.

Somalia
"Cholera Kills 116 Children in Somalia," October 14, 2011, http://www.presstv.ir/detail/204579.html.
"U.S. Drone Strike Kills 78 in Somalia," October 14, 2011, http://www.presstv.ir/detail/204501.html.

Uganda
"U.S. president says he is deploying 100 combat troops to Uganda to help efforts against Lord's Resistance Army rebels." "Obama Sends U.S. Combat Troops to Uganda," October 14, 2011, http://english.aljazeera.net/news/africa/2011/10/20111014174712102972.html.

LATE OCTOBER AT WAR

Peter Van Buren, *We Meant Well: How I Helped Lose the Battle for the Hearts and Minds of the Iraqi People* (New York: Metropolitan Books Henry Holt and Company, 2011).

"'Justice dies when the law is co-opted for political purposes.' Gareth Peirce, one of our key human rights lawyers, talks to Stuart Jeffries." "Gareth Peirce: Why I Still Fight for Human Rights," interview with Stuart Jeffries and Gareth Peirce, October 11, 2010, http://www.guardian.co.uk/law/2010/oct/12/gareth-peirce-fight-human-rights.

"Human Rights Watch has uncovered hundreds of letters in the Libyan foreign ministry proving the Qaddafi government directly aided the extraordinary rendition program carried out by the CIA and the MI6 in Britain after the 9/11 attacks. The documents expose how the CIA rendered suspects to Libyan authorities knowing they would be tortured." "Discovered Files Show U.S., Britain Had Extensive Ties with Qaddafi Regime on Rendition, Torture," September 7, 2011, http://www.democracynow.org/2011/9/7/discovered_files_show_us_britain_had.

Peter Bouckaert is emergencies director at Human Rights Watch and helped find the documents in Tripoli.

"Alleged Inhumane Conditions for Post-9/11 Suspects Sparks Global Scrutiny of U.S. Detention Policies," October 14, 2011.

Ten years after the 9/11 attacks, detention policies in the United States are facing increasing scrutiny, both in the United States and abroad. American citizen Tarek Mehanna is set to stand trial this month on charges of 'conspiring to support terrorism' and 'providing material support to terrorists.'

Mehanna is accused of trying to serve in al-Qaeda's 'media wing.' When arrested in October 2009, he was 27 years old. Since his arrest, he has been held in solitary confinement. Mehanna was originally courted by the FBI to become an informant . . . ."
[Also noted above in Introduction of No Land an Island]

In this program discussion of detention policies since 9/11 in the United States were Tarek Mehanna's brother, Tamer, and one of Britain's best-known human rights lawyers, Gareth Peirce. She has represented WikiLeaks founder Julian Assange and many prisoners held at the U.S. military base at Guantánamo Bay. (October 14, 2011, http://www.democracynow. org/2011/10/14/alleged_inhumane_conditions_for_post_9).

Stephen Lendman, "Mixed Messages on Qaddafi," *SteveLendmanBlog*, October 24, 2011, http://sjlendman.blogspot.com/.
"Nothing from NATO, political capitals, puppet TNC [current de facto government of Libya, the Transitional National Council] officials, and major media scoundrels is credible." "Mixed Messages on Qaddafi."

Stephen Lendman also appeared on Press TV. Lendman's blog is sjlendman.blogspot.com. He also appears with guests on the *Progressive Radio News Hour* on the Progressive Radio Network Thursdays at 10:00 a.m. Central Time and Saturdays and Sundays at noon. All programs are archived for later listening

Jamahiriya
Reference MATHABA

"Great Jamahiriya: Power, Wealth and Arms in the Hands of the People"

"The administrative system in Libya is summed up in the word Jamahiriya, which literally means the state of the masses. The Great Socialist People's Libyan Arab Jamahiriya is situated in

North Africa, stretching along the Mediterranean shoreline for nearly 2,000 kilometers. Its area is 1,775,500 square kilometers making it the fourth largest country in Africa. Egypt is on its eastern border; Sudan, Chad and Niger are to the south and Tunisia and Algeria lie to the west.

"The population of just over four million is concentrated in the cities, villages and farming areas along the coastal strip. Almost one million Libyans died during the Italian occupation from 1911 to 1944."

MATHABA (Media Active To Help All Become Aware); "MATHABA means a meeting place, platform, sanctuary."

Founded in 1999 as the first stateless news organization in history, MATHABA describes itself as "the world's leading independent news agency and a major online news network [with] the most advanced and effective news distribution."

MATHABA's mission: "Changing the world by broadcasting news and information that serves the public interest while also having over fifty different news categories, news feeds and distribution across multiple platforms for almost any type of news and information," www.mathaba.net/info/

Thermobaric

NTC

A thermobaric weapon (including the type known as a fuel-air bomb) is an explosive weapon that produces a blast wave of a significantly longer duration than those produced by condensed explosives. The longer duration increases human casualties and causes more damage to structures. Thermobaric explosives (easily used inside confined environments such as tunnels, caves, and bunkers, unsuitable for use underwater, at high altitude, or in adverse weather) rely on oxygen from the surrounding air, whereas most conventional explosives consist of a fuel-oxidizer premix (e.g., gunpowder contains 25 percent fuel and 75 percent oxidizer).

The National Transitional Council of Libya (sometimes known as the Transitional National Council, the Interim National Council, or the

Libyan National Council) is the current de facto government of Libya, established by anti-Qaddafi forces during the 2011 Libyan civil war, a war that pitted these forces against the regime of Colonel Muammar al-Qaddafi. The NTC issued a 'Constitutional Declaration' in August 2011 in which it set up a road map for the transition of the country to a constitutional democracy with an elected government. *Wikipedia*, s.vv. "thermobaric," "NTC."

Related

Middle East

"Anti-Saleh Rallies Continue in Yemen," October 28, 2011, http://www.presstv.ir/detail/207164.html.

"Jordanians Rally for Promised Reforms," October 28, 2011, http://www.presstv.ir/detail/207140.html.

"Death Toll in Iraq Twin Blasts Hits 36," October 28, 2011, http://www.presstv.ir/detail/207097.html.

"Pro-regime Thugs Attack Bahrainis," October 28, 2011, http://www.presstv.ir/detail/207043.html.

Southwest Asia

"Pakistanis Protest US Drone Attacks," October 28, 2011, http://www.presstv.ir/detail/207110.html.

Caption Press TV

Pakistanis hold a massive demonstration in Islamabad to protest U.S. assassination drone attacks in Pakistan's northwest tribal region (October 28, 2011).

"Militants Blow Up Schools in Pakistan," October 28, 2011, http://www.presstv.ir/detail/207101.html.

"Roadside Bomb Kills 4 Afghan Civilians," October 28, 2011, http://www.presstv.ir/detail/207074.html.

Africa

"33 Civilians Die in a Mogadishu Battle," October 28, 2011, http://www.presstv.ir/detail/207059.html.

"U.S. Flying Drones from Ethiopia,'" October 28, 2011, http://www.presstv.ir/detail/207015.html.

"Kenyan Airstrikes Kill 41 in Somalia," October 28, 2011, http://www.presstv.ir/detail/207044.html.

"French warships have shelled parts of coastline of the Horn of African state of Somalia with more than 20 heavy missiles." "French Warships Hit Somalia Coastline," October 27, 2011.

Kenya Caption Press TV
A Kenyan Air Force F-5 fighter jet (file photo)

"The great powers have no principles, only interests." "The Destruction of Libya and the Murder of Muammar Qaddafi," P. Ngigi Njoroge, *Empire Strikes Black*, http://empirestrikesblack.com/2011/10/the-destruction-of-libya-and-the-murder-of-muammar-gaddafi/.

Background—Middle Eastern/Asian states, a tight club, old and complex

Britannica notes

Saudi Arabia

Saudi Arabia is a monarchy ruled by the Āl Saūd, a family whose status was established by its close ties with and support for the Wahhābī religious establishment. The king combines legislative, executive, and judicial functions. As prime minister, he presides over the Council of Ministers (Majlis al-Wuzarā).

The kingdom has never had a written constitution although in 1992 the king issued a document, the Basic Law of Government (Al-Niẓām al-Asāsī lī al-Ḥukm), which provides guidelines for how the government is to be run and sets forth the rights and responsibilities of citizens.

Islamic law, the Sharīah, is the primary source of legislation but political expediency, ruling family politics, and the influence of intertribal politics, which remain strong in the modern kingdom, often temper the promulgation of legislation and implementation of policy.

The Sharīah is the basis of justice. Judgment usually is according to the Ḥanbalī tradition of Islam; the law tends to be conservative and punishment severe, including amputation for crimes such as theft and execution for crimes that are deemed more severe (e.g., drug trafficking and practicing witchcraft).

Education in Saudi Arabia

Education is free at all levels and is given high priority by the government. The school system consists of elementary (grades 1-6), intermediate (7-9), and secondary (10-12) schools. A significant portion of the curriculum at all levels is devoted to religious subjects, and, at the secondary level, students are able to follow either a religious or a technical track. Though fewer girls than boys attend school and all courses are segregated by gender, girls are able to attend school. Literacy rate among males exceeds 85 percent, among females around 70 percent.

Economy in Saudi Arabia

Petroleum and related industries dominate the economy of Saudi Arabia. With about a fifth of the world's known reserves, Saudi Arabia ranks first internationally in oil reserves. Oil deposits are located in the east, southward from Iraq and Kuwait into the Rub al-Khali and under the waters of the Persian Gulf.

Saudi King Abd Allah

Saudi King Abd Allah (also spelled Abdullah; in full: Abd Allāh ibn Abd al-Azīz, b. 1923): One of King Abd al-Azīz ibn Saūd's thirty-seven sons. For his support of Crown Prince Fayṣal (Fayṣal is also spelled Faisal) (1964-75) during Fayṣal's power struggle with King Saūd (1953-64), Abd Allāh was rewarded in 1962 with command of the Saudi National Guard. In 1975 King Khālid (1975-82), Fayṣal's successor appointed him deputy prime minister, and in 1982 King Fahd appointed him crown prince and first deputy prime minister. In 1995, Fahd suffered a debilitating stroke, and Abd Allāh briefly served as regent the following year. Although Fahd subsequently returned to power, Abd Allāh ran the daily affairs of the country and became king after Fahd died in 2005.

Abd Allāh was committed to preserving Arab interests but he also sought to maintain strong ties with the West, especially with the United States. In 2001, relations between the two countries grew strained over Saudi claims that the U.S. government was not evenhanded in its approach to the Palestinian-Israeli conflict. The situation worsened later in the year, following the September 11 attacks against the United States and the subsequent revelation that most of the attackers were Saudi nationals. Abd Allāh condemned the attacks and, in a move to improve relations, proposed a peace initiative that was adopted at the 2002 Arab summit meeting. The plan called upon Israel to withdraw from the occupied territories (the Gaza Strip, West Bank, and Golan Heights) and promised in return a full Arab normalization of relations with the Jewish country. Tensions between the United States and Saudi Arabia resurfaced, however, after Abd Allāh refused to support a U.S.-led attack on Iraq or to allow the use of Saudi military facilities for such an act.

Syria and President Bashar al-Assad

President Bashar al-Assad (b. Sept. 11, 1965, Damascus, Syria) has been in office since 2000. Bashar al-Assad succeeded his father, Ḥafiz al-Assad, who had ruled Syria since 1971. In 1994 Bashar al-Assad's older brother, Basil, who had been designated his father's heir apparent, died in an automobile accident. Bashar returned to Syria and took his brother's place. [Assad had studied medicine at the University of Damascus and graduated as a general practitioner in 1988. He then trained to become an ophthalmologist at a Damascus military hospital and in 1992 moved to London to continue his studies. Before taking office, he trained at a military academy and gained the rank of colonel in the elite Presidential Guard.]

On June 18, 2000, after the death of his father on June 10, Assad was appointed secretary-general of the ruling Bath Party, and two days later the party congress nominated him as its candidate for the presidency. The national legislature approved the nomination. On July 10, Assad ran unopposed and the election outcome resulted in his taking a seven-year term. In 2007, in what critics and opponents termed a sham, a nearly unanimous election result awarded Assad a second term. Changes Assad made in his first term were described as mainly cosmetic and economic reforms had made minor progress and the second term brought no significantly meaningful political change.

Syria the country

After Syria gained its independence in 1946, political life in the country was unstable because of intense friction between the country's social, religious, and political groups. In 1970, Syria came under the authoritarian rule of President Ḥafiz al-Assad, whose goals included achieving national security and domestic stability and recovering the Syrian territory lost to Israel in 1967. Assad committed his country to an enormous arms buildup, which put severe strains on the national budget and left little for development. After Assad's death in 2000, his son Bashar al-Assad became president.

The country is located on the east coast of the Mediterranean Sea in southwestern Asia. Its area includes territory in the Golan Heights, an area occupied by Israel since 1967. The present area does not coincide with ancient Syria, which was the strip of fertile land lying between the eastern Mediterranean coast and the desert of northern Arabia. The capital is Damascus (Dimashq), on the Baradā River, situated in an oasis at the foot of Mount Qāsiyūn.

Islamic Sects: *Sunni and Shiite, Salafists: Sunni Islamists*

Sunnite; plural: Sunni—A member of one of the two major branches of Islām, the branch that consists of the majority of that religion's adherents. Sunnite Muslims regard their sect as the mainstream and traditionalist branch of Islām, as distinguished from the minority sect, the Shīites.

Shiite; collective Shiah; plural Shiites—Early in the history of Islam, the Shīites were a political faction (Arabic shiat Alī, 'party of Alī') that supported the power of Alī ibn Abī Ṭalib (the fourth caliph [khalīfah, successor of Muhammad]) and, later, of his descendants.

Starting as a political faction, this group gradually developed into a religious movement, Shīism, which not only influenced Sunni Islam but also produced a number of important sects to which the term Shīah is applied.

Caption
Syria, Palestine: Sites important in Syrian and Palestinian religion

Qatar and Doha

Qatar

An independent emirate on the west coast of the Persian Gulf occupying a small desert peninsula that extends northward from the larger Arabian Peninsula, continuously but sparsely inhabited since prehistoric times.

The capital is the eastern coastal city of Doha (Al-Dawḥah), which was once a center for pearling and is home to most of the country's inhabitants [Diving for pearls or pearling was once a mainstay of Qatar's economy now greatly decreased to almost non-existence largely because of the Japan-dominant cultured-pearl industry].

Doha

Probably founded by Sudanese refugees from the sheikhdom of Abu Dhabi, Doha is the capital of Qatar, located on the east coast of the Qatar Peninsula in the Persian Gulf. The original quarter of the city, Al-Bida, is at the northwest. More than two-fifths of Qatar's population lives within the city's limits. Situated on a shallow bay indented about three miles (five kilometers), Doha has long been a locally important port.

UAE (United Arab Emirates)

The global economic downturn of 2009 affected all the emirates composing the United Arab Emirates (UAE). The formerly booming emirate of Dubai—whose stock exchange, real-estate values, and construction industry declined markedly causing thousands of residents and workers to leave the emirate—suffered the most and received help from oil-rich Abu Dhabi.

Though world markets in November were shaken when Dubai asked to delay interest payments for six months and Abu Dhabi was forced to extend bailout funds, Dubai in September inaugurated an ultramodern subway line, the first of its kind in any Arab Gulf country.

Tensions between the UAE and its neighbor, Saudi Arabia, rose over border issues and Gulf Cooperation Council (GCC) members' selection of Riyadh (Saudi Arabia's capital) as the headquarters of the GCC's proposed central bank. The UAE considered the decision politically motivated and dismissive of the competitive advantages of locating the bank in the emirates. Subsequently, in May the UAE decided to join Oman [the country occupying the southeastern coast of the Arabian Peninsula at the confluence of the Persian Gulf and Arabian Sea] in withdrawing from the planned GCC monetary union. This left only four countries (Saudi Arabia, Bahrain, Qatar, and Kuwait) committed to the project aimed at creating a single GCC currency.

Jordan

A young state occupying an ancient land, separated from ancient Palestine by the Jordan River, bearing traces of many civilizations, Jordan (an Arab country of Southwest Asia, capital city, Amman) sits in the rocky desert of the northern Arabian Peninsula. Slightly smaller in area than the country of Portugal, Jordan is bordered at the north by Syria, the east by Iraq, the southeast and south by Saudi Arabia, the west by Israel and the West Bank. The West Bank area (named because it lies just west of the Jordan River) was under Jordanian rule from 1948 to 1967.

Jordan's constitution declares the country to be a constitutional, hereditary monarchy with a parliamentary form of government. Islam is the official religion, and Jordan is declared part of the Arab *ummah* ('nation'). The king remains the country's ultimate authority and wields power over the executive, legislative, and judicial branches. The king appoints a prime minister to head Jordan's central government and chooses the cabinet.

Jordan's capital city, Amman, is one of the region's principal commercial and transportation centers and one of the Arab world's major cultural capitals.

Jordan's king: Abdullah II (in full: Abd Allāh ibn Ḥusayn, b. January 30, 1962, Amman, Jordan)

A member of the Hashimite dynasty, considered by pious Muslims to be direct descendants of the Prophet Muhammad, Abdullah II, the eldest son of King Hussein, has been Jordan's king since 1999. Until the age of three, he had served as the crown prince. Unrest in the Middle East caused Hussein to name Abdullah's adult uncle, Prince Hassan, heir to the throne but in January 1999, King Hussein, in deteriorating health, named Abdullah II the new heir to the Hashimite crown. Hours after his father's death on February 7, 1999, Abdullah became king of Jordan and was officially crowned on June 9. In his new role, Abdullah II continued to follow many of his father's policies. Following the September 11, 2001 attacks in the United States, Abdullah supported the United States' efforts to combat terrorism. After the U.S.-led invasion of Iraq in 2003, the king permitted U.S. forces to maintain bases in Jordan.

Abdullah was educated in Britain and the United States. He graduated in 1980 from the Royal Military Academy in Sandhurst, England, and later served in the British Armed Forces as well as in Jordan's Armed Forces in the forty-first and ninetieth armored brigades. In 1993 and until he assumed the throne, Abdullah II was (by appointment) deputy commander of Jordan's elite Special Forces.

III. Unchecked might, heartbreaking suffering

Conflict/war-made Displacement, Reverse Development, Civilian Death, U.S. Pageantry, anti-American Demonstrations

October

Afghanistan

"U.S. Blast Kills 10 [later updated to 13] Afghan Civilians," October 21, 2011, http://www.presstv.ir/detail/205834.html

"State Dept. Veteran Peter Van Buren Defies U.S. Censors to Recount Failed Reconstruction in Iraq," November 30, 2011, http://www.democracynow.org/2011/11/30/state_dept_veteran_peter_van_buren

Peter Van Buren, *We Meant well: How I Helped Lose the Battle for the Hearts and Minds of the Iraqi People* (New York: Metropolitan Books Henry Holt and Company, 2011), pp. 248-249; pp. 253-254.

Timothy Bancroft-Hinchey, "The Lesson from Sirte: NATO Protects Civilians from Terrorists by Murdering Them," October 12, 2011, http://english.pravda.ru/opinion/columnists/12-10-2011/119311-sirte_nato-0/.

Marvin G. Weinbaum is a professor emeritus at the University of Illinois and U.S. Department of State Foreign Affairs analyst. He is author of *Pakistan and Afghanistan: Resistance and Reconstruction.*

Encyclopædia Britannica Deluxe Edition, s.v. "Afghanistan.

Background: Afghanistan

In contemporary times, the Republic of Afghanistan between 1973 and 1978 (and the Afghan mujahideen in the 1980s) tried to move away from dependency on the Soviet Union and the United States and to remove foreign troops from Afghanistan but on the night of December 24, 1979, the Soviets invaded Afghanistan. This invasion and the subsequent civil war severely disrupted Afghanistan's economic development.

United Nations Security Council Powers in Afghanistan (and Pakistan) 1980s

Western sponsors viewed resistance operations in Afghanistan as an opportunity to keep the Soviet army bogged down and to bleed Moscow economically. By early 1980, several regional groups—collectively known as mujahideen (from the Arabic: *'those who engage in jihad'*)—united inside Afghanistan or across the border in Peshawar, Pakistan, to resist the Soviet invaders and the Soviet-backed Afghan army.

Toward the end of 1986, the United States, the United Kingdom, and China via Pakistan were sending more and better weapons (shoulder-fired ground-to-air missiles) from the outside world to the mujahideen. The Soviet and Afghan air forces began suffering considerable casualties.

Also during the 1980s, the United Nations sponsored talks in Geneva between the foreign ministers of Afghanistan and Pakistan but obstructing progress were (a) the Soviet troop withdrawal timetable and (b) the end of arms supply to the mujahideen. In April 1988, the parties signed peace accords. In May, Soviet General Secretary Mikhail Gorbachev began withdrawing Soviet troops; in February 1989, the last Soviet soldier left Afghanistan.

1996-2001: U.S.—allied Mujahideen becomes U.S.-opposed Taliban

The UN imposed sanctions against the Taliban in November 1999 and January 2001. Pakistan, the United States, China, and several European and Arab states (most notably Saudi Arabia, home of Osama bin Laden) provided small amounts of financial and military aid to the mujahideen. This assistance grew and the Pakistan military's Inter-Service Intelligence Directorate (ISI) assumed primary responsibility for funneling the money and weapons to Afghan resistance groups.

After a brief rule by mujahideen groups, the Taliban (an austere movement of religious students) rose up against the country's governing parties and warlords and established a theocratic regime (1996-2001) that soon fell under the influence of a group of well-funded Islamists led by an exiled Saudi Arabian, Osama bin Laden.

Mujahideen (U.S.-allied Northern Alliance versus Taliban): 2001—present

The United States then allied with the Northern Alliance, a coalition of mujahideen factions. In mid-November 2001, the Northern Alliance troops and United States Special Forces launched a ground offensive against Afghanistan. In 2005, attacks and violent exchanges between the U.S.-led coalition and the Taliban forces became more frequent, particularly in the eastern and southern provinces, and casualties increased. In July 2006, the North Atlantic Treaty Organization (NATO) troops officially replaced the U.S.-led coalition as the head of military operations in the south; in October, NATO took command of the eastern provinces, thus assuming control of international military operations throughout Afghanistan.

At the end of 2011, the United States was bogged down in war and its consequences in Afghanistan and Pakistan.

Civilian casualties were at alarming rates and anti-U.S. protesters burned U.S. flags and leading U.S. government officials in effigy. The demonstrations occurred daily in both Pakistan and Afghanistan and in other countries where the U.S. sided with despots: in Bahrain, Yemen, Jordan, Israel, Saudi Arabia. The Breakdown continued. On a level any sane person considers criminal, the United States continued contributing to serious oppression and regression, destruction, disruption, destabilization and displacement (thousands of migrants, refugees and asylum seekers) across the Middle East Region including Africa and South Central Asia.

Pakistan

"Pakistanis Protest Clinton's Visit," October 21, 2011, http://www.presstv.ir/detail/205857.html
"U.S. Warned against Pakistan Incursion," October 19, 2011, http://www.presstv.ir/detail/205451.html

Background: Middle East (Near East) Countries

The Middle or Near East consists of the lands around the southern and eastern shores of the Mediterranean Sea. These lands extend from Morocco to the Arabian Peninsula and Iran, and by some interpretations beyond. Some of the first modern Western geographers and historians who tended to divide the Orient into three regions gave the region the name "Near East."

In their three-region designations: Near East applied to the region nearest Europe, extending from the Mediterranean Sea to the Persian Gulf; the Middle East, extending from the Persian Gulf to Southeast Asia; and the Far East, encompassing the regions facing the Pacific Ocean.

The change in usage from "Near" to "Middle" East began evolving before World War II and extended through that war. The British military command in Egypt coined the term "Middle East" and, so defined, its states or territories included:

Turkey, Cyprus, Syria, Lebanon;
Iraq, Iran, Palestine, Jordan;
Egypt, The Sudan, Libya; and
Various states of Arabia proper (Saudi Arabia, Kuwait, Yemen, Oman, Bahrain, Qatar, and the Trucial States, or Trucial Oman [now United Arab Emirates]

Subsequent events have tended, in loose usage, to enlarge the number of lands included in the definition. Among these are:

Tunisia, Algeria and Morocco, three North African countries "closely connected in sentiment and foreign policy with the Arab states";

Afghanistan and Pakistan, because geography and geopolitics connect these with affairs of the Middle East;

Greece occasionally is included in the compass of the Middle East because the Middle Eastern (then Near Eastern) question in its modern form first became apparent when the Greeks in 1821 rebelled to assert their independence from the Ottoman Empire. Turkey and Greece, together with the predominantly Arabic-speaking lands around the eastern end of the Mediterranean, were also formerly known as the Levant.

Historically the countries along the eastern Mediterranean shores were called the Levant. Common use of the term is associated with Venetian and other trading ventures and the establishment of commerce with cities such as Tyre and Sidon as a result of the Crusades. It was applied to the coastlands of Asia Minor and Syria, sometimes extending from Greece to Egypt. It was also used for Anatolia and as a synonym for the Middle or Near East. In the sixteenth and seventeenth centuries, the term "High Levant" referred to the Far East. The name "Levant States" was given to the French mandate of Syria and Lebanon after World War I, and the term is sometimes still used for those two countries, which became independent in 1946. ("Levant" is from the French "lever," "to rise," as in sunrise, meaning the east.)

Use of the term "Middle East" remains unsettled, and some agencies (notably the United States State Department and certain bodies of the United Nations) still employ the term "Near East."
Encyclopædia Britannica Deluxe Edition, s.v. "Middle East."

Bahrain

"Bahrain Delays Report on Crackdown," October 21, 2011, http://www.presstv.ir/detail/205739.html.

"'Torture of Bahraini detainees persist'—Concerns grow over the health condition of detained Bahraini opposition leaders amid continuing reports of ongoing torture in the country's prisons," Press TV reports, October 20, 2011

Caption Bahrain protest
Tens of thousands of pro-democracy protesters converge from two directions to demonstrate outside the walls of King Hamad bin Isa Al Khalif's Safriya Palace in the Bahraini capital of Manama (file photo).

Iraq

"Turkish Forces Enter Iraq to fight PKK," October 21, 2011, http://www.presstv.ir/detail/205738.html.

Jordan

"In Jordan thousands have rallied in the capital, Amman, to urge prime minister-designate Awn Khasawneh to implement political reform," October 21, 2011, http://www.presstv.ir/detail/205738.html

Palestine

"UN Calls on Israel to Stop Harassing Kids—The UN has criticized Israeli violence against Palestinian children, urging the international community to scale up its protective measures for minors living under Israeli occupation," October 21, 2011, http://www.presstv.ir/detail/205736.html

Africa
Africa North
Africa east—NATO destroys Libya

Qaddafi—Libya's head of state (1969-2011), Muammar al-Qaddafi, was born (1942) in a tent in the desert near Sirte (also spelled Surt) where he reportedly died in 2011. As Libya's head of state, Qaddafi in 1970 removed United States and British military bases and expelled most members of the native Italian and Jewish communities from Libya. In 1973, he nationalized all foreign-owned petroleum assets in the country.

The Sirtica Region where Qaddafi was born encompasses Sirte and is the site of one of the world's largest oil fields. The region is situated in north-central Libya fronting the Mediterranean Sea for about 300 miles (480 kilometers) along the southern part of the Gulf of Sidra, extending generally southeastward through the Sirte (Surt) Basin. The bulk of Libya's oil deposits are scattered throughout the Sirtica region, particularly in the Sirte Basin. The Sarīr oil field is located southeast of the region. The petroleum reservoirs in the Sirtica Region are estimated to lie at depths of between 500 and 13,000 feet (150 and 4,000 meters) below the surface.

Sirte (or Surt) is the main port of the Gulf of Sidra, arm of the Mediterranean Sea. During World War II, the Gulf of Sidra was the scene of the Battle of Sirte (March 1942), in which a British naval convoy thwarted attacks from Italian warships and German bombers. In the 1980s, Libya established a national boundary across the gulf and prohibited passage of foreign vessels, resulting in several brief military conflicts with the United States of America.

Commenting on the October 2011 invasion of Libya and the killing of its leader (regardless to how one feels about the Libyan leader or about colonialists and imperialists in Africa), Timothy Bancroft-Hinchey wrote:

> The lesson from Sirte is an example in how low an evil
> invasion force (NATO) can become. It uses military hardware
> to strafe anything that moves. It bombs civilian structures. It
> mows down Libyan heroes defending their homeland against

foreigners, defending their homes and families against terrorists and rapists.

It shows the connivance of NATO and Islamist terrorists (yet again visible since Afghanistan, since Kosovo, since Iraq). It shows the callous cold-blooded disregard for human life demonstrated by a faceless and grey organization that thinks nothing of signing up desperate young men from across the Arab world and beyond and sending them to their deaths for a sign-on fee of 10,000 U. S dollars.

. . . . *The lesson from Sirte is today one of resilience and resistance, as it stands defiant against NATO's indiscriminate bombing and the hundreds of rockets unleashed by the terrorists it aids. . . .*

The lesson from Sirte will continue to be taught tomorrow: as you cannot win an election by banning the most popular party, you do not win a battle by destroying a city, by massacring thousands of people and by killing the defenders [of their homes] to unleash on that city thousands of terrorists.

. . . . *The lesson from Sirte is that by now it is crystal clear where NATO stands . . . It is strafing defenseless civilians and trying to impose a government of terrorists from the air. . . .*" (Timothy Bancroft-Hinchey, "The lesson from Sirte: NATO protects civilians from terrorists by murdering them," Pravda. Ru Opinion, October 12, 2011, http://english.pravda.ru/opinion/columnists/12-10-2011/119311-sirte_nato-0/

Libya

Egypt

Far-reaching Social, Human and Economic Ramifications of Western Relations with Middle East/North African countries

Migrant workers in Libya from various places in Africa (Egypt, Somalia, various Sub-Saharan countries) were stranded, under threat, and or on the move.

Related: conflict, war, disease, regression, flight
More needless suffering

Haiti

The United Nations World Health Organization reported that on record today in Haiti are "470,000 cases of cholera." In this figure are "6,595 deaths, which have been reported since an epidemic of the disease erupted in the Caribbean country a year ago."

Over the past year, an estimated 250,000 cholera patients had been hospitalized. If the current trend continues, a WHO representative told reporters in Geneva, the disease could infect another seventy-five thousand Haitians by the end of the year. If this happens, the cumulative total number of cases would rise to half a million.

What wars and conflict cause and create: mass migration, displacement, destabilization, suffering, and anger

This year has been a year of displacement crises like no other, said António Guterres of the office of the High Commissioner for Refugees (UNHCR). People fled not so much to far-off industrialized countries as to their neighboring countries.

Through its latest survey, UNHCR found that between January 1 and June 30, 2011, there were 198,300 asylum applications. Last year the survey reported 169,300.

Of the 44 countries surveyed, the main countries of origin for asylum seekers this year remained largely unchanged from previous surveys: Afghanistan (15,300 claims); China (11,700); Serbia (and Kosovo) (10,300); Iraq (10,100); and Iran (7,600).

By Continent or Region

Europe registered the highest number of claims, with 73 percent of all asylum applications in industrialized countries. By country, the United States received more applications (36,400) than any other industrialized country followed by France (26,100); Germany (20,100); Sweden (12,600); and the United Kingdom (12,200). The Nordic region was the only European region to see a decline in asylum applications. In Northeast Asia, applications more than doubled: 1,300 claims were lodged in Japan and South Korea compared to 600 in the first half of 2010.

Applications for asylum in developed countries rose by 17 percent in the first six months of this year, with most of those seeking admission coming from countries with a history of population displacement.

Egypt

Egypt (officially Arab Republic of Egypt) is located in the northeastern corner of Africa. Its land frontiers border Libya in the west, the Sudan in the south, and Palestine in the northeast. (Israeli forces occupied the Sinai Peninsula and the Gaza Strip in eastern Egypt after the Arab-Israeli War of 1967. In 1982, the Sinai was returned to Egypt.) In the north its Mediterranean coastline is about 620 miles (1,000 kilometers), and in the east its coastline on the Red Sea and the Gulf of Aqaba is about 1,200 miles. The capital is Cairo.

Egypt was the home of one of the principal civilizations of the ancient Middle East, and like Mesopotamia, it was one of the very earliest urban and literate societies.

Libya

Libya (officially Socialist People's Libyan Arab Jamahiriya, formerly Libyan Arab Republic or People's Socialist Libyan Arab Republic) is in North Africa, bounded by the Mediterranean Sea on the north, Egypt on the east, the Sudan on the southeast, Niger and Chad on the south, and Tunisia and Algeria on the west. Libya is largely composed of the Sahara, and the population is concentrated along the coast, where the de facto capital, Tripoli (Ṭarābulus), and Banghāzī (Benghazi), the de jure capital, are located.

"The virulent diarrheal disease is spreading quickly along waterways between and within countries, causing an "unacceptably high" rate of fatalities, the UN Children's Fund (UNICEF) said." "Cholera Epidemic Spreads in West, Central Africa: UN," October 11, 2011, http://www.worldbulletin.net/?aType=haber&ArticleID=80093; UNICEF, http://www.unicef.org/health/uganda_53862.html.

Horn of Africa (Somalia)
Lone (2009), Bennis
Democracy Now (Phyllis Bennis interviewed) "State of the Union 2005: Bush Pushes Aggressive Foreign Policy of Spreading Democracy," New York, accessed February 3, 2005, at http://www.democracynow.org/2005/2/3/state_of_the_union_2005_bush; Phyllis Bennis, *Before & After: U.S. Foreign Policy and the September 11th Crisis* (New York: Olive Branch Press, 2002); Bennis, *Calling the Shots: How Washington Dominates Today's UN*, (New York: Olive Branch Press/Interlink Publishing).

GlobalSecuritydotorg, "The Horn of Africa"; "Operation Enduring Freedom, Horn of Africa, Djibouti," Alexandria, Va., GlobalSecurity.org in the News: 27-04-2005 15:32:25 Zulu; http://www.globalsecurity.org/military/library/report/1984/GA.htm; http://www.globalsecurity.org/military/ops/oef-djibouti.htm

Democracy Now, "U.S. Launches Targeted Assassination Air Strikes in Somalia, Many Reported Killed" (includes an interview with Salim Lone and Amy Goodman), accessed January 9, 2007, http://www.democracynow.org/article.pl?sid=07/01/09/1454252.

Carolyn LaDelle Bennett, BREAKDOWN: Violence in Search of U (you)-Turn: Nature and Consequences of U.S. International and Domestic Affairs Geopolitics Occupation Human Rights Historical Contexts (Notes and Commentary) (2009), Chapter Two Part 1 Violence at the Heart of Relations Foreign and Domestic, pp. 73-74.

Encyclopædia Britannica Standard Edition, s.v. "United Nations."

Phyllis Bennis, *Calling the Shots: How Washington Dominates Today's UN* (Olive Branch Press).

David R. Hoffman, "America Is Still Dead," October 3, 2011, Pravda.Ru.

Background: Somalia

Region: Africa: Somali Republic

Religion: Islam (Sunni) with a small Christian minority in capital, Mogadishu

Official languages: Somali and Arabic; English, Italian and Swahili are spoken http://www.trust.org/alertnet/country-profiles/somalia/

Resting in the critical Horn of Africa at the Red Sea and Gulf of Aden waterways into Asia, Somalia (capital, Mogadishu; of Somaliland, Hargeysa) is a land (2006 est.) of 8,496,000 (including 3,700,000 in Somaliland) people spread over an area of 637,000 sq km (246,000 sq mi), including the 176,000-sq-km (68,000-sq-mi) area of the unilaterally declared (in 1991) and unrecognized Republic of Somaliland. At the beginning of 2011, more than 250,000 Somali refugees were in neighboring countries and 100,000 more resided in Europe or the United States.

"Somalis fleeing insecurity at home find more insecurity in Yemeni 'haven'—UN," October 21, 2011, http://www.un.org/apps/news/story.asp?NewsID=40146&Cr=somalia&Cr1

Refugees

"North African refugee deaths prompts UN agency to call for assistance—Thousands are fleeing north Africa for Europe by boat; the Italian coast guard saved another boat full of north African immigrants bound for Europe after NATO reportedly failed to intervene. The UN refugee agency has now called for rescue efforts to be redoubled," August 5, 2011, http://www.dw-world.de/dw/article/0,,15297933,00.html

Horn crossing Red Sea

Suffering Somalia

(U.S. Drone Strikes against Somalia and its People)

"U.S. Drone Strike Kills 44 in Somalia," October 21, 2011, http://www.presstv.ir/detail/205775.html.

"U.S. Drone Strike Kills 16 in Somalia," October 8, 2011, http://www.presstv.ir/detail/203413.html; "U.S. Drone Strike Kills Six in Somalia," October 5, 2011, http://www.presstv.ir/detail/202894.html.

Disease
"Cholera Kills 65 More Somali children," October 20, 2011, http://www.presstv.ir/detail/205690.html

Caption Somalia displaced hospital scene
A paramedic in a ward at Banadir hospital in Somalia's capital, Mogadishu, attends internally displaced children suffering cholera, August 18, 2011. (file photo)

Related: "Abductors Ask Cash for Dedieu's Body," October 20, 2011, http://www.presstv.ir/detail/205642.html

Lamu

Lamu is a port town, an island administered as part of Kenya in the Indian Ocean off the East African coast, 150 miles (241 kilometers) north-northeast of Mombasa. (*Britannica*).

Manda

Manda is near Lamu on the Kenyan coast, apparently established in the ninth century, distinguished for its seawalls of coral blocks. Trade, which seems to have been by barter, was considerable, with the main export probably of ivory. Manda had close trading connections with the Persian Gulf. It imported large quantities of Islamic pottery and, in the ninth and tenth centuries, Chinese porcelain. There is evidence of a considerable iron-smelting industry at Manda (*Encyclopædia Britannica*).

Somalia November

(U.S. Drone Strikes against Somalia and Its People)
November 18, 2011 (Friday), http://www.presstv.ir/section/3510205.html

November 17, 2011 (Thursday), http://www.presstv.ir/section/3510205.
html
November 16, 2011 (Wednesday), http://www.presstv.ir/section/3510205.html
November 15, 2011 (Tuesday), http://www.presstv.ir/section/3510205.
html
"U.S. Spy Drone Crashes in Somalia," November 8, 2011, http://www.
presstv.ir/detail/209011.html.

Pakistan flood victims
Zareen Khan, Sanghar District, Pakistan / emergency relief camp for
flood-affected communities / reported 300 deaths, 4.2 million destroyed
acres, 1.59 million destroyed crops. Photo UNHCR / S. Phelps

IV. Human costs—WAR-made Refugees:
Notes from Early 2011 Shelved Manuscript

Labeling migrants—UNHCR reports displaced people

Refugees, Asylum-seekers, Returnees, Internally Displaced, Stateless
Persons 2009 Global Trends Report released June 15, 2010: in the past
two decades, "2009 was the 'worst' year for voluntary repatriation,"
says UNHCR chief. UNHCR protects, assists, and seeks solutions for
refugees. These are the terms used and defined by UNHCR.

Glossary

The terms "refugees" and "asylum seekers" refer to people who flee across international borders.
Asylum Seeker is an individual seeking international protection.

Stateless people are persons not considered as nationals by any state under the operation of its law, including persons whose nationality is not established.

Refugee is a person who—owing to a well-founded fear of being persecuted for reasons of race, religion, nationality, membership in particular social groups, or holding a political opinion—is outside the country of his or her nationality and is unable or, owing to such fear, is unwilling to avail himself or herself of the protection of that country.

Also covered by the UNHCR are people outside their country of origin and unable to return there owing to serious and indiscriminate threats to life, physical integrity or freedom resulting from generalized violence or events seriously disturbing public order.

"U.S. enters murky legal waters as drone use increases," Deutsche Welle, October 22, 2010

Middle East and North Africa, 2010 UNHCR Regional Operations Profile (Middle East and North Africa), http://www.unhcr.org/4c162ed36.html

Trees Only Move in the Wind: a Study of Unaccompanied Afghan Children in Europe was released by UNHCR. The research involving interviews with 150 Afghan boys in France, Greece, Italy, the Netherlands, Norway, and the United Kingdom as well as experiences of several dozen other youth in Turkey was released shortly after the European Commission presented its "Action Plan on Unaccompanied Minors" concerned with promoting consistency in the treatment of unaccompanied children arriving in Europe from third countries (UNHCR research).

"Over 60 Percent of Afghans Suffer Mental Health Problems," Global Research (distinguished from the Centre for Research on Globalization viewpoint) reports, October 11, 2010 (AFP, October 10, 2010), www.globalresearch.ca/PrintArticle.php?articleId=21389

Afghanistan, Pakistan

"Nine Killed by Afghan Bomb En Route to Wedding" (© ANP/AFP), January 16, 2011, http://www.rnw.nl/Africa/bulletin/nine-killed-afghan-bomb-en-route-wedding
"Deaths in Afghan Roadside Blast—A car carrying nine people, including a child, destroyed by bomb that killed all its occupants in country's northeast," January 16, 2011, http://english.aljazeera.net/news/asia/2011/01/201111611526976374.html
"Suicide blast kills Afghan officers—Bomber on a motorbike struck a minibus full of intelligence officials, killing at least eight and wounding nearly 30," January 12, 2011, http://english.aljazeera.net/news/asia/2011/01/2011112524854151.html
"NATO Lorries Torched in Pakistan—Pakistani Taliban target tankers supplying conflict across the border in Afghanistan," January 15, 2011, http://english.aljazeera.net/news/asia/2011/01/201111517248680630.html
"Police Targeted in Pakistan Blasts—four officers dead in two attacks in northwestern Khyber-Pakhtunkhwa region, a day after deaths of 17 people in bombing," January 13, 2011, http://english.aljazeera.net/news/asia/2011/01/20111139533784926.html
"Foreign Envoys to Tour Iran Uranium Plant" (© ANP/AFP), January 16, 2011, http://www.rnw.nl/africa/bulletin/iran-opens-enrichment-plant-foreign-envoys
"Iraqi Soldier Shoots Dead U.S. Troops—Two U.S. troops killed and one injured after man opens fire during training exercise at a base in Mosul," January 15, 2011, http://english.aljazeera.net/news/middleeast/2011/01/2011115175756791495.html

Background Pakistan: Wazīristān

Under British political administration beginning in 1892 and the scene of large-scale British military operations against the tribes (Wazir in the north and Mahsud in the south) from the late 1800s until Pakistan's independence in 1947, Wazīristān is a mountainous land set in the geographic region of Pakistan's Northwest Frontier Province. Pashtun people inhabit the land.

Pashto-speaking people of southeastern Afghanistan and northwestern Pakistan constitute the majority of the population of Afghanistan and bore the exclusive name of Afghan before that name came to denote any native of the present land area of Afghanistan.

In Afghanistan are (est.) 7,500,000 Pashtun, in Pakistan 14,000,000 Pashtun. They comprise about 60 tribes of varying size and importance, each occupying a particular territory. In Afghanistan, where Pashtun are the predominant ethnic group, the main tribes—or, more accurately, federations of tribes—are the Durrānī south of Kābul and the Ghilzay east of Kābul. In Pakistan, Pashtun predominate north of Quetta between the Sulaimān Range and the Indus River. In the hill areas, the main tribes from south to north are: the Kākaṛ, Shērāni, and Ustarāna (south of the Gumal River); the Maḥsūd, Darwēsh Khēl, Wazīrī, and Biṭanī (between the Gumal River and Thal); the Tūrī, Bangash, Ōrakzay, Afrīdī, and Shinwārī (from Thal to the Khyber Pass); and the Mahmand, Utmān Khēl, Tarklānī, and Yūsufzay (north and northeast of the Khyber).

The Sulaimān Range occupies Wazīristān which is bounded on the north by the Kurram River, the south by the Gumal River, and on its west by Afghanistan. The region's rivers flowing toward the Indus River provide the main approaches to the interior of Wazīristān.

CIVIC (Campaign for Innocent Victims in Conflict) reports
Afghanistan, Pakistan, Drone Attacks

"Pakistan's IDP Crisis: Challenges and Opportunities" International Crisis Group, Campaign for Innocent Victims in Conflict (CIVIC), 2010, http://www.crisisgroup.org/en/regions/asia/south-asia/africar/B093-pakistans-idp-crisis-challenges-and-opportunities

Campaign for Innocent Victims in Conflict (CIVIC) reports cite critical problems with the use of remote-controlled bombs. Several key characteristics of the U.S. drone program increase the risk of harm to civilians.

- Other than small and secretive Special Forces units, there are no U.S. troops on the ground to assess civilian casualties and property damage nor is there any indication that the U.S. obtains such post-strike information from intelligence assets or Pakistani officials.

Without critical information feeding back into U.S. targeting practices and generating lessons learned, properly ensuring minimal 'collateral' damage is improbable.

- United States officials have not clarified who is a legal target—where U.S. government lawyers, intelligence officials or commanders and drone operators draw the line between combatant and noncombatant. This has real consequences for civilians on the ground. For example, people residing in areas where drones operate do not know what kind of conduct or relationships could put them at risk. Offering to 'militants' food or housing, political or ideological support (indirect support) would not formally qualify under international norms as 'direct participation in hostilities' but it is entirely possible that the U.S. considers many people to be 'combatants,' owing to their relationships to known 'militants,' when they are legally civilians.

U.S. definitions of combatant and civilian could thus heavily skew the presumed number of civilian casualties caused by drones and who is eligible to receive help should some source create an assistance program.

Whatever formal definition the U.S. is applying in distinguishing between combatants and noncombatants in practice is particularly difficult. For instance, in Pakistan many fighters live with their families—often 30 or 40 people in joint-family homes—and strong traditions of hospitality, tribal and familial allegiances mean food, water, and protection are given to guests. Some residents of North Waziristan told CIVIC they feel forced to provide food and shelter to militants.

- In the tribal areas, guns are omnipresent and have a distinct cultural importance. For military and intelligence personnel accustomed to identifying a threat by the weapon a person carries, it can be difficult to distinguish fighter from farmer. This is particularly true given that *drone operators work thousands of miles from Pakistan*, rely on a limited, "soda straw" view of the battlefield, and have little or no exposure to the areas or persons that they are observing and analyzing.

- Targeting intelligence provided by informants has proven faulty in the past and reliability of intelligence might be undermined by cash payments offered by the CIA and other U.S. operatives.
- 'Collateral' damage incidents in Afghanistan prove the potential for killing civilians in erred or miscalculated drone strikes or drone malfunctions.
- Secrecy surrounding the drone program prevents the accountability and transparency mechanisms needed to ensure civilians are being afforded adequate protection. The use of the CIA to conduct these attacks—a civilian intelligence organization whose personnel are not traditionally trained in the laws of war and not subject to military command, military law, or codes of conduct—might increase the risk that civilians are improperly targeted or disproportionately harmed.

Considering the estimated number of strikes conducted over the past two years (124) and the estimated number of persons killed (788-1,344), it is certain that the number of civilians killed in drone strikes far exceeds the figure put forward by U.S. officials. Given that one strike alone in June 2009 killed 45-60 people, including up to 18 civilians, it is unlikely that civilian casualties could be under 20 in total.

As whole communities are displaced and dispossessed, the CIVIC report shows, "traditional coping mechanisms are stretched to the brink." Civilians in these situations are trying to pick up the pieces of their lives while enduring emotional and psychological grief.

The CIVIC report was written by Christopher Rogers from Pakistan (October 2009-present) and was funded by the Harvard Law School Frederick Sheldon Traveling Fellowship and CIVIC, www. civicworldwide.org/africar_report_2010. All names in the report were changed to protect survivors' identity.

The Campaign for Innocent Victims in Conflict works on behalf of war victims by advocating that warring parties recognize and help the civilians they harm. CIVIC supports the principle that it is never acceptable for a warring party to ignore civilian suffering. In 2005,

CIVIC's founder, Marla Ruzicka, was killed in Iraq by a suicide bomb while advocating for families of victims. Campaign for Innocent Victims in Conflict (CIVIC) monitors news stories of civilian casualties from around the world and posts them online. The War Victims RSS feed provides updates. http://www.civicworldwide.org. Campaign for Innocent Victims in Conflict (CIVIC) is headquartered at 1210 18th Street NW, 4th Floor, Washington, D.C. 20036 USA; website: www. civicworldwide.org,

Related:

"Massive New Settlement Project in E. Jerusalem" (© ANP/AFP), January 16, 2011, Radio Netherlands, http://www.rnw.nl/africa/bulletin/ africa-eyes-huge-east-jerusalem-settlement-project.

"S. Africa Groups Seek Livni Arrest—Pro-Palestinian groups seek arrest warrant for Tzipi Livni, who heads Israel's Kadima party, for alleged war crimes," January 16, 2011, http://english.aljazeera.net/news/africa/ 2011/01/20111164466517708.html

Middle East, Southwest Asia

North Africa, Horn of Africa

Iraq, Yemen, Ethiopia, Somalia

Iraq

Today's Insight News (ed.), Monday, October 25, 2010, "High Crimes Logs"

Online whistleblower WikiLeaks founder Julian Assange's website "released close to 400,000 classified U.S. documents on the Iraq war, the largest intelligence leak in U.S. history and the largest internal account of any war on public record, a disclosure providing a trove of new evidence on the violence, torture and suffering that's befallen Iraq since the 2003 U.S. invasion." *Democracy Now*, October 25, 2010, http://www. democracynow.org/2010/10/25/wikileaks_iraq_war_logs_expose_us

"Iraq: The War Logs"—15,000 previously unknown civilian deaths contained in the Iraq War Logs released by WikiLeaks, *The Guardian* (UK), October 22, 2010, http://www.guardian.co.uk/world/fri-war-logs,

The UK-based independent NGO Iraq Body Count records violent civilian deaths resulting from the 2003 military intervention. This is some of what the NGO had to say about the WikiLeaks War Logs. The group commented on the war logs:

> It is totally unacceptable that for so many years the U.S. Government has withheld from the public these essential details about civilian casualties in Iraq. There is a vital public interest and an inalienable public right to know who died in this war and how they died, whether Iraqi or any other nationality.
>
> Every recoverable detail about the human death toll in Iraq, and in all other conflicts around the world, must be brought to light. Only such detailed and specific knowledge makes the full human consequences of war impossible to deny. http://www.iraqbodycount.org/analysis/reference/press-releases/18/

IBC's preliminary analysis of the Iraq War Logs released by WikiLeaks concludes that: "Most of the newly revealed deaths in the logs occurred in previously unreported violent incidents involving the deaths of one or two people. They include targeted assassinations, drive-by-shootings, torture, executions, and checkpoint killings. (http://www.iraqbodycount.org/analysis/numbers/warlogs)

64,000 civilian deaths recorded in these Logs are already represented in the IBC database. These were mainly gathered from press and media reports, as well as some NGO and official figures.

Even when the bare fact of a death is already known, the Logs frequently add important new detail including, for instance, the precise time and place of particular deaths only previously represented in numerical totals from morgues. Most significantly, the Logs contain many thousands of previously unreleased names of civilian victims. IBC has already been able to add over one hundred such names brought into the public domain for the first time (http://www.iraqbodycount.org/analysis/qa/warlogs/)

"Iraq Body Count Analyzes War Logs," *Today's Insight News* (ed.), Wednesday October 27, 2010.

> Early analysis by the independent NGO, Iraq Body Count (IBC), of the Iraq War Logs released by WikiLeaks suggests the logs contain 15,000 civilian deaths not previously reported.
>
> IBC calculates that over 150,000 violent deaths related to conflict have been recorded in Iraq since March 2003, with more than 122,000 (80 percent) of them civilian.
>
> IBC has fully analyzed all 360 of the Logs which account in total for over 17,000 deaths.
>
> "IBC plans to inspect all of the 390,000 Iraq War Logs for any casualty data they may contain, and then integrate them into the IBC database . . . . Three articles published on the IBC web site discuss what may be drawn from WikiLeaks' release: http://www.iraqbodycount.org/ http://www.iraqbodycount. org/analysis/numbers/warlogs/ http://www.iraqbodycount. org/analysis/beyond/warlogs/ http://www.iraqbodycount.org/ analysis/qa/warlogs//

Body count update posted at *Today's Insight News*, October 27, 2010, from IBC's worldwide update on civilians killed in the Iraq war and occupation: 98,585-107,594

Iraq Body Count (IBC), according to its website note for editors, is a UK-based independent NGO dedicated to recording the violent civilian deaths that have resulted from the 2003 military intervention in Iraq. Its public database includes deaths caused by U.S.-led coalition forces and paramilitary or criminal attacks by others. IBC's documentary evidence is drawn from crosschecked media reports of violent events leading to the death of civilians, or of bodies being found, and is supplemented by the careful review and integration of hospital, morgue, NGO and official figures. IBC figures are widely quoted as an authoritative source of information by governments, inter-governmental agencies and the worldwide media. IBC has been coordinating the publication of its own careful preliminary analyses with WikiLeaks and those press and media organizations listed at http://www.iraqwarlogs.com/

Iraqi Refugees

Refugees Middle East and North Africa, 2010 Regional Operations Profile (Middle East and North Africa), June 14, 2010, http://www.unhcr.org/4c162ed36.html

"Iraq: Toppling a Country: from Statue to Legality," Global Research Report presented to the 15th Session of the United Nations Human Rights Council in Geneva (Felicity Arbuthnot, September 13—October 1), Global Research posted October 21, 2010 at www.globalresearch.ca/PrintArticle.php?articleId=21545

In their report, "Testimonies of Crimes against Humanity in Fallujah: Towards a Fair International Criminal Trial," the researchers called on the United Nations Human Rights Council to investigate the crimes and violations cited in the study "and all that has been inflicted upon Iraq" including internal and external displacements, "savage corruption, child molestation, rape, rampant kidnapping."

"Iraqi Refugees Regret Returning Home" says UNHCR poll, October 19, 2010

"UN Slams European Governments for Deporting Iraqis," Deutsche Welle, September 3, 2010, http://www.dw-world.de/dw/article/0,,5972560,00.html

"Relatives Fear 97 Refugees Have Died at Sea," The Age (Melbourne, Australia), December 26, 2010, http://www.theage.com.au/national/relatives-fear-97-refugees-have-died-at-sea-20101225-197jw.html http://www.theage.com.au/national/relatives-fear-97-refugees-have-died-at-sea-20101225-197jw.html

"Govt. Urged to End 'War' on Refugees," December 22, 2010, *The Age,* http://news.theage.com.au/breaking-news-national/govt-urged-to-end-war-on-refugees-20101222-195li.html

Background: tied to Iraq references in body text

- Baghdad extends along both banks of the Tigris River. The east-bank settlement is Ruṣāfah, the west-bank settlement Al-Karkh.
- Christmas Island—Administered as an external territory of Australia, Christmas Island sits in the Indian Ocean, about 224 miles (360 kilometers) south of the island of Java, 870 miles (1,400 kilometers) northwest of Australia (*Britannica*)

"Mixed Migrations"

North African countries are a transit route and destination for displaced peoples, major mixed-migration movements, mostly from sub-Saharan African countries. Most of the people comprising these moving populations are searching for better economic opportunities but "many are in need of international protection (UNHCR/P. Taggart).

Middle East, North Africa
Somalia, Yemen
Africa Migrants
Refugees, IDPs

Somalia's neighbor across the Gulf of Aden, a Treacherous crossing

"Africa Migrants Drown off Yemen as Boats Sink," January 3, 2011, http://www.bbc.co.uk/news/world-africa-12108715

Sa'dah (also spelled "Saada") is a town of 51,870 people in northwestern Yemen in the mountainous Yemen Highlands, an administrative center of the northern part of Yemen.

"Three Found, Dozens Feared Drowned off Yemen," Agence France Presse, January 4, 2011, http://news.yahoo.com/s/afp/20110104/wl_africa_afp/yemenafricaethiopiaaccident_20110104122424

Refugees Middle East and North Africa, 2010 Regional Operations Profile (Middle East and North Africa), June 14, 2010, http://www.unhcr.org/4c162ed36.html

"To Whom It May Concern—Somali refugees write of their country's tragedy and ask the world for help," Macleod, Hugh and Annasofie Flamand from Kharaz Camp in south Yemen

Since 2005, the UN agency for refugees, UNHCR, has been receiving between 100 and 150 letters a month from Somali refugees; at the time of the 2010 report, nearly 10,000 letters, each of them explaining how and why its author ended up at Kharaz Camp and asking the world for help.

"Fierce fighting between rival militia groups in Somalia has forced an estimated 60,000 people from their homes," UNHCR, October 26, 2010.

Briefing journalists in Geneva, UNCHR representative Andrej Mahecic said some 40,000 people had sought safety in neighboring villages following recent clashes between the Al Shabaab militia and a rival group allied to the government in the town of Beled Hawo, near the border with Kenya. Many refugees were living in the open without access to food, water or sanitation.

Somalia/Kenya border: Health and security conditions have "worsened for thousands of others who have been camping out in the open at a makeshift settlement just inside the Kenyan border since mid-October."

The number of Somali refugees at the so-called Border Point One has been increasing daily and currently stands at more than five thousand. Most of those living in the settlement are women, children and the elderly. UNHCR staff on the ground report the site lacks shelter or sanitation. "The situation for the refugees there is truly deplorable," said the UNHCR representative.

"Tens of Thousands Displaced by Clashes in Somalia," October 26, 2010, Http://www.unhcr.org/4cc6f6d29.html. News Stories, © UNHCR/R. Gangale, http://www.unhcr.org/4cc6f6d29.html; http://www.unhcr.org/pages/49c3646c2.html. Further information can be found on the UNHCR websites, www.unhcr.org and www.unhcr.fr, which should also be checked for regular media updates on non-briefing days.) http://www.reliefweb.int/rw/rwb.nsf/db900SID/SKEA-8ALE5L?

Treacherous Crossing

"Africa Migrants Drown off Yemen as Boats Sink"—Up to 80 African migrants are feared to have drowned off the south coast of Yemen after their boats capsized, Yemeni officials say.

Yemen is seen as a gateway to a better life in the Middle East or Europe, but people smugglers often crowd the migrants onto old and unseaworthy vessels. Hundreds die before reaching their destination. BBC, January 3, 2011, http://www.bbc.co.uk/news/world-africa-12108715

Related:

"Yemen Separatists Kill Soldiers"—Southern secessionists in Lahaj kill at least three in an attack on army checkpoint, the latest in a wave of violence, BBC, January 9, 2011.

Far Reaching

"Thousands of People Flown Home from Tunisia as Evacuation Begins," News Stories, A. Duclos, March 3, 2011, http://www.unhcr.org/4d6fc2f99.html

"UNHCR seeks U.S. $32 million for Libya emergency operations," News Stories, F.Noy, March 7, 2011, http://www.unhcr.org/4d7513e49.html
"Sub-Saharan Africans Fleeing Libya Report Serious Intimidation, Violence," UN Refugee Agency News Stories, March 8, 2011, http://www.unhcr.org/4d7658719

Ann Jones, *The War Is Not Over when It's Over: Women Speak Out from the Ruins of War* (Metropolitan Books, 2010), pp. 220-239 (contains another view of the journey of migrants. The road is hard road for those who escape; many uprooted cannot go home again.

Why They Come, How to Respond

"European refugee policy has failed—as thousands of refugees flee Tunisia for Italy, cracks are appearing in the 'Fortress Europe' ideology. Isolationism is unworkable and only harms the continent," says opinion writer Stefan Troendle of Bavarian public broadcaster BR," Deutsche Welle, February 15, 2011, http://www.dw-world.de/dw/article/0,,14843208,00.html.

"Europe must create jobs for transforming Arab countries—Either European countries accept a greater influx from North Africans or they help improve the economic situation in the region," says opinion writer Juergen Wiemann.

Dr. Juergen Wiemann works for the department of Economic Development and Employment—Multilateral Trading System and Development Cooperation at the German Society for International Cooperation (GIZ) and is the former Deputy Director of the German Development Institute (DIE), Deutsche Welle, March 1, 2011, http://www.dw-world.de/dw/article/0,,14880529,00.html)

"Migrants from Morocco, Turkey, and Tunisia number in the several millions," says University of Lincoln (UK) journalism professor Richard Keeble, Euranet News Special aired on Network Europe Weekly March 9-11, 2011, http://www.euranet.eu/

Professor Richard Keeble is acting head of Lincoln School of Journalism and a director of the Institute of Communication Ethics where he co-edits the quarterly journal *Ethical Space*. He has written a number of articles on the journalism of George Orwell. Keeble writes for a number websites such as www.medialens.org, www.anti-spin.com, www.stateofnature.org, www.the-latest.com and www.fifth-estate-online.com.uk and is on the editorial boards of a number of international journals such as *Australian Journalism Review* (University of Queensland) and the *International Journal of Media and Cultural Politics*.

His books include *Secret State, Silent Press: New Militarism, the Gulf and the Modern Image of Warfare* (John Libbey Media, 1997); *Ethics for Journalists* (Routledge, 2001); and *Communicating War: Memory, Media and Military* (Arima Publishing, 2007).

V. Waste trumps want (price of presidency, costs in lives): Islanded in Criminal Excess as World's Majorities Languish

2012 Race for the White House

"Obama Campaign Raises $70 Million in Third Quarter—the total exceeds the campaign's goal, but it is less than what was raised in the previous quarter. New fundraising totals for his GOP challengers also are emerging," October 13, 2011, http://www.latimes.com/news/nationworld/nation/la-na-1014-campaign-finance-20111014,0,4966791.story?track=rss

"Maximizing the Incumbent Advantage—President Barack Obama continues to be a fund-raising juggernaut, practically exceeding the fund-raising total of the entire GOP field combined.

"During the third quarter, Obama raised $70.1 million, his campaign announced today. That sum includes $42.8 million that went directly into his own campaign war chest and $27.3 million raised for the Democratic National Committee," Center for Responsive Politics (Open Secrets), October 17, 2011, at *Today's Insight News*): Center for Responsive Politics Open secrets, http://www.opensecrets.org/news/2011/10/barack-obama-fundraising-juggernaut—OpenSecrets.org

Wellstone, Paul. *The Conscience of a Liberal: Reclaiming the Compassionate Agenda* (New York: Random House Trade Publishing, 2002; Ann Arbor, Michigan: first University of Minnesota Press edition 2002).

Paul David Wellstone (1944-2002) was a U.S. educator and politician. He was a member of the U.S. Senate representing the state of Minnesota and served from 1991 until his death in a plane crash in 2002. A biography published by the University of Michigan Press (Ann Arbor) in 2005 is *Paul Wellstone: The Life of a Passionate Progressive.*

Wellstone's career also included teaching political science at Carleton College, Northfield, Minnesota (1969-1990) and directing the Minnesota Community Energy Program (September 1983-September 1984). He took his academic credentials (B.A. and Ph.D.) at the University of North Carolina. Sources: Bibliography: Scribner Encyclopedia of American Lives: Wellstone, Paul D. *The Conscience of a Liberal: Reclaiming the Compassionate Agenda* (New York: Random House, 2001). Also at United States Congress Biographical Directory, Washington, D.C., http://bioguide.congress.gov/scripts/biodisplay.

Also

Carolyn LaDelle Bennett, *BREAKDOWN: Violence in Search of U (you)-Turn*: Nature and Consequences of U.S. International and Domestic Affairs Geopolitics Occupation Human Rights Historical Contexts (Notes and Commentary) (2009), pp. 155, 225-226, 310-311.

Rocky Anderson, Justice Party-U.S.

Ross C. (Rocky) Anderson is credited with being the only mayor of a major U.S. city (Salt Lake City, Utah) to advocate impeachment of U.S. President George W. Bush. He is also credited with championing such national and international causes as climate protection, immigration reform, restorative criminal justice, LGBT rights, and ending the "war on drugs.". Before and after the 2003 U.S. invasion of Iraq, Anderson was a leading opponent of invasion and occupation of Iraq and related human rights abuses.

 Rocky Anderson was a two-term mayor of Salt Lake City, Utah (2000-2008). Before that, he practiced law in Salt Lake City and during a 21-year law practice was listed by Martindale-Hubbell in *Best Lawyers in America* (rated A-V, highest rating) and was chair of the Utah State Bar Litigation Section. Anderson was also editor in chief of and a contributor to *Voir Dire* legal journal.

In 2011 when he launched his candidacy for the U.S. presidency and announced a new political party, Anderson was Executive director of High Road for Human Rights.

"I just hope we can be involved in the debate," Anderson said, "because if we don't, we're just going to be hearing a bunch of sound bites from people who, between their two parties, have colluded in so many ways in serving the interests of their campaign contributors, the wealthy and the powerful . . . .

> The middle class has been decimated . . . [In the past decade], outrageous, expensive wars have wasted lives and tax dollars . . . . The government has driven up the deficit while cutting taxes for those most capable of paying taxes. . . . Leaders have failed to provide affordable, essential health care for all Americans.

> [But if we] put together passion and organization, we can overcome any of these candidates who have all the money but really lack ideas." [dromboy@ksl.com]

"Rocky Creates Justice Party, Wants to Run for President—Rocky Anderson likely to run for president of the United States" (Dennis Romboy), November 30, 2011, KSL DOT COM—UTAH http://www.ksl.com/?nid=960&sid=18298937

Former UN Sectary-general Kofi Annan [2012 UN Envoy to Syria]
The state of world affairs and vital human sensibility of nations

The former United Nations Secretary-general urged meeting interconnected global challenges, "collectively," relinquishing "old mindset of national security/economic growth at the expense of other countries." In his 2006 final address as Secretary-general, Annan said he believed five principles to be "essential for the future conduct of international relations":

> *Collective responsibility*
> *Global solidarity*
> *Rule of law*
> *Mutual accountability*
> *Multilateralism*

"The Challenges for Leaders in a Multi-polar World" (speech by Kofi Annan, March 4, 2010 in Jakarta, Indonesia), http://kofiannanfoundation.org/newsroom/speeches/2010/03/challenges-leaders-multipolar-world

Excerpted in *Today's Insight News* "Kofi Annan comments on the world 2010," Sunday, March 21, 2010

While visiting Singapore in 2010, the former UN Secretary-general sat for an interview with Al Jazeera's Teymoor Nabili in discussions covering China-African relations, African land sales, eradication of poverty, the Millennium Development Goals, invasion of Iraq, Middle East peace process, the Goldstone report, Annan's role as mediator, and the future of Kenya. Annan had come to Singapore to lecture at the Lee Kuan Yew School of Public Policy at the National University of Singapore. The Al Jazeera program "Talk to Jazeera: Kofi Annan" began airing Wednesday, March 10, 2010. http://english.aljazeera.net/ programmes/talktojazeera/2010/03/201031163028606113.html

The Kofi Annan Foundation supports Kofi Annan's efforts to provide inspirational and catalytic leadership on critical global issues, particularly preserving and building peace and facilitating more equitable sharing of the benefits of globalization, by promoting poverty alleviation.

VI. Aggression-corruption-oppression Protests
(U. S. at war November 2011)

Iraq

Peter Van Buren, *We Meant Well: How I Helped Lose the Battle for the Hearts and Minds of the Iraqi People* (New York: Metropolitan Books Henry Holt and Company, 2011), pp. 253-254.

"Iraqi Women's Activist Rebuffs U.S. Claims of a Freer Iraq: 'This is not a Democratic Country,'" December 16, 2011, http://www.democracynow. org/2011/12/16/iraqi_womens_activist_rebuffs_us_claims

Background: Sharīah (also spelled "sharia"): the fundamental religious concept of Islam; its law, systematized during the second and third centuries of the Muslim era (eighth to ninth centuries AD).

"The Costs of War: Tens of Thousands Dead, Billions Spent, and a Country Torn Apart," December 16, 2011, http://www.democracynow. org/2011/12/16/iraqi_womens_activist_rebuffs_us_claims

"War without end, amen . . ." (Further excerpt from Chris Floyd's article):

In March 2003, the United States of America launched an entirely unprovoked act of military aggression against a nation that had not attacked it and posed no threat to it. This act led directly to the deaths of hundreds of thousands of innocent people. It drove millions more from their homes, and plunged the entire conquered nation into suffering, fear, hatred and deprivation.

This is the reality of what actually happened in Iraq: aggression, slaughter, atrocity, ruin. It is the only reality; there is no other. Moreover, it was done deliberately, knowingly, willingly . . . . [T]he bipartisan American power structure spent more than $1 trillion to make it happen. It is a record of unspeakable savagery, an abomination, an outpouring of the most profound and filthy moral evil.

Line up the bodies of the children, the thousands of children—the infants, the toddlers, the school kids—whose bodies were torn to pieces, burned alive or riddled with bullets during the American invasion and occupation of Iraq.

Line them up in the desert sand, walk past them, mile after mile, all those twisted corpses, those scraps of torn flesh and seeping viscera, those blank faces, those staring eyes fixed forever on nothingness.

This is the reality of what happened in Iraq; there is no other reality. . . . You cannot make it otherwise. It has already happened. It always will have happened.

You can of course ignore it. This is the path chosen by the overwhelming majority of Americans, and by the entirety of the bipartisan elite. This involves a pathological degree of disassociation from reality. Chris Floyd, "War without End, Amen: The Reality of America's Aggression against Iraq" (Chris Floyd), Friday December 16, 2011, http://www. chris-floyd.com/component/content/frontpage

"War without End, Amen: The Reality of America's Aggression against Iraq" (Chris Floyd, *Empire Burlesque*), December 17, 2011, http://www.presstv.ir/usdetail/216254.html

Chris Floyd is a U.S. journalist whose work has appeared in print and online: in The *Nation, Counterpunch, Columbia Journalism Review*, the *Christian Science Monitor, Il Manifesto*, the *Moscow Times* and many others. Floyd is *author* of *Empire Burlesque: High Crimes and Low Comedy in the Bush Imperium* and co-founder and editor of the 'Empire Burlesque' political blog.

"Divide Widening between U.S. Rich, Poor—the 'incredibly unequal top-down distribution of wealth' in the U.S. has formed an elite group who controls most aspects of the country's affluence, according to analysts" (Saul Landau interviewed), December 16, 2011, http://www.presstv.ir/detail/216090.html

Saul Landau is an internationally known scholar, author, commentator, and filmmaker on foreign and domestic policy issues. In 2008, the Chilean government presented him with the Bernardo O'Higgins Award for his human rights work. Landau has written fourteen books. He is Professor Emeritus at California State University (Pomona) and a senior Fellow at and vice chair of the Institute for Policy Studies (http://saullandau.com/).

Afghanistan, Pakistan
Iraq, Iran
Kashmir, India, Jammu and Kashmir
Encyclopædia Britannica Deluxe Edition

EARLY NOVEMBER

"Liberal Democracy Nearing End: Iran," November 4, 2011, http://www.presstv.ir/detail/208390.html

"As NATO Ends Libyan Bombing Campaign, Is the U.S. Seeking Greater Military Control of Africa?" November 1, 2011, http://www.democracynow.org/2011/11/1/as_nato_ends_libyan_bombing_campaign

Phyllis Bennis specializes in U.S. foreign policy issues, particularly involving Middle East and the United Nations. She worked as a journalist at the UN for ten years and currently serves as a special adviser to several top-level UN officials on Middle East and UN democratization issues. Bennis is a fellow at the Transnational Institute (a worldwide fellowship of scholar activists) and at the Institute for Policy Studies (Washington D.C.). At the latter, Bennis is director the New Internationalism Project.

Works by Bennis include *Understanding the U.S.-Iran crisis* (2008); *Ending the Iraq War: A Primer* (2008); *Understanding the Palestinian-Israeli Conflict: A Primer* (2007); *Challenging Empire: People, Governments and the UN Defy U.S. Power* (2005); *Before and After: U.S. Foreign Policy and the September 11th Crisis* (2002); *Understanding the Palestinian-Israeli Conflict: A Primer* (2003); *Calling the Shots. How Washington Dominates Today's UN* (2000); *Altered States. A Reader in the New World Order* (1993); *Beyond the Storm: A Gulf Crisis Reader* (1991); *From Stones to Statehood: The Palestinian Uprising* (1990) http://www.tni.org/sites/www.tni.org/files/bio_long/Nick%20Buxton/ phyllis%20long%20bio_0.pdf; http://www.tni.org/bio/phyllis-bennis

Under U.S./NATO hegemony

1. Afghanistan	2. Bahrain
3. Cuba	4. Djibouti
5. Eritrea	6. Ethiopia
7. Haiti	8. Honduras
9. Iran	10. Iraq
11. Japan (Okinawa)	12. Kenya
13. Libya	14. Mexico
15. Nigeria	16. North Korea
17. Pakistan	18. Palestine
19. Russia	20. Saudi Arabia
21. Somalia	22. South Korea

Syria	24. Uganda [dominoes The Sudan, South Sudan, Central African Republic, Republic of the Congo (Brazzaville), Democratic Republic of the Congo (Kinshasa)]
25. Yemen	26.

AFRICA	ASIA
Djibouti	Afghanistan
Eritrea	Bahrain
Ethiopia	Iran
Kenya	Iraq
Libya	Japan (Okinawa)
Nigeria	North Korea
Somalia	Pakistan
Uganda [dominoes South Sudan, Central African Republic, Republic of the Congo (Brazzaville), Democratic Republic of the Congo (Kinshasa)]	Palestine
	Saudi Arabia
AMERICAs	South Korea
Cuba	Syria
Haiti	Yemen
Honduras	
	EUROPE/ASIA
	Russian Federation

Background: Russia [Russian Federation]

Russia is the world's largest country, covering nearly twice the territory of the second largest country, Canada. Russia has a maximum east-west

DR. CAROLYN LADELLE BENNETT

extent of some 5,600 miles (9,000 kilometers) and a north-south width of 1,500 to 2,500 miles (2,500 to 4,000 kilometers).

Russia stretches over a vast expanse of Eastern Europe and northern Asia. It extends across the whole of northern Asia and the eastern third of Europe, spanning 11 time zones and incorporating a great range of environments and landforms, from deserts to semiarid steppes to deep forests and Arctic tundra. Russia contains Europe's longest river, the Volga, and its largest lake, Ladoga. Russia also is home to the world's deepest lake, Baikal, and the country recorded the world's lowest temperature outside the North and South poles.

- North and east—Russia is bounded to the north and east by the Arctic and Pacific oceans, and it has small frontages in the northwest on the Baltic Sea at St. Petersburg and at the detached Russian oblast (region) of Kaliningrad (a part of what was once East Prussia annexed in 1945), which also abuts Poland and Lithuania.
- South—Russia borders North Korea, China, Mongolia, and Kazakhstan, Azerbaijan, and Georgia.
- Southwest, west—Russia borders Ukraine, Belarus, Latvia, and Estonia, as well as Finland and Norway.
- Northern Hemisphere, Europe, Asia—Russia extends nearly halfway around the Northern Hemisphere and covers much of eastern and northeastern Europe and all of northern Asia

Once the preeminent republic of the Union of Soviet Socialist Republics (USSR, commonly known as the Soviet Union), Russia became an independent country after the dissolution of the Soviet Union in December 1991.

Kazakhstan (also spelled Kazakstan; officially Republic of Kazakhstan)

This is a country of Central Asia bounded on the northwest and north by Russia, on the east by China; and on the south by Kyrgyzstan, Uzbekistan, Turkmenistan, and the Aral Sea. The Caspian Sea bounds Kazakhstan to the southwest.

Kazakhstan (formerly a constituent union republic of the USSR, its independence declared December 16, 1991) is the largest country in

Central Asia and the ninth largest in the world. Between its most distant points, Kazakhstan measures about 1,820 miles (2,930 kilometers) east to west and 960 miles north to south. While Kazakhstan was not considered by authorities in the former Soviet Union to be a part of Central Asia, it does have physical and cultural geographic characteristics similar to those of the other Central Asian countries. Astana (formerly Tselinograd) is Kazakhstan's capital situated in the north-central part of the country.

Background: Africa Central

CONGO
Republic of the Congo
Democratic Republic of the Congo
Central African Republic

Congo (Brazzaville)
Officially known as the Republic of the Congo, this country is often called Congo (Brazzaville), its capital and most populous city added parenthetically to distinguish it from neighboring Democratic Republic of the Congo, the latter often called the DRC or Congo (Kinshasa). The Republic of the Congo straddled the Equator in west-central Africa.

Congo as a whole is sparsely inhabited with more than half of its population living in the cities—Brazzaville sits in the Republic of the Congo's southeastern corner and is a major inland port on the Congo River.

Congo (Kinshasa)
Democratic Republic of the Congo [DRC or Congo (Kinshasa)], the third largest country in Africa (only the Sudan and Algeria are larger), took its independence from Belgium in 1960 and from 1971 to 1997, its official name given by then-ruler General Mobutu Sese was the Republic of Zaire. The country boasts vast mineral wealth but suffers from mismanagement, corruption, incessant civil unrest, global recession, and insufficient investment.

A 2009 update on the Democratic Republic of the Congo reported internal conflict had left 800,000 civilians displaced. UN estimates said the number of internal refugees had reached two million and by 2009, the use of rape as a war tactic against women, children, and men by all armed forces had doubled or tripled in nine eastern conflict zones.

The DRC has a 25-mile (40-km) coastline on the Atlantic Ocean but is otherwise landlocked. Its capital, Kinshasa, located on the Congo River and serving as the country's official administrative, economic, and cultural center, is central Africa's largest city.

Central African Republic
Settled by an ancient people living in its western and southern forests 8,000 years ago, long before French colonialists descended (late 1800s) and its independence was retrieved (1960), the Central African Republic neighbors with Chad (north), The Sudan (north and east), the Democratic Republic of the Congo-Kinshasa and the Republic of the Congo-Brazzaville (south), and Cameroon (west). Its capital, Bangui, sits on the southern boundary, formed by the Ubangi River, a tributary of the Congo River.

WAR by direct action

AFRICA

"U.S. Terror Drones Kill 41 More in Somalia," November 3, 2011, http://www.presstv.ir/detail/208225.html
"U.S. Drone Raids Kill over 120 in 2 Days," November 3, 2011, http://www.presstv.ir/detail/208198.html
"11 Somali Soldiers Killed," November 4, 2011, http://www.presstv.ir/section/3510205.html

"'Oil Tanker Hijacked off Nigeria Coast.'" November 4, 2011, http://www.presstv.ir/detail/208279.html

ASIA

Pakistan
"Pakistan Holds Exhibit of Drone Attacks," November 1, 2011, http://www.presstv.ir/detail/207812.html

"U.S. Terror Drone Kills 3 in Pakistan"—at least three people died in U.S. assassination drone campaign in northwest Pakistan, November 3, 2011, http://www.presstv.ir/detail/208176.html.

"NATO Supply Truck Attacked in Pakistan," November 3, 2011, http://www.presstv.ir/detail/208130.html.

Press TV caption
NATO under attack in Pakistan
NATO's supply line has come under repeated attacks by "militants" opposing the U.S.-led terror drone strikes inside Pakistan's tribal belt.

Afghanistan
"Bomb Hits Afghan NATO Logistics Base," November 3, 2011, http://www.presstv.ir/detail/208152.html

Southeast Asia
In related news: Crimes of "Humanitarians"
Cambodia (U.S. occupied"

"A court in Cambodia sentenced New York physician James D'Agostino (age 56) to four years in prison." He had been found guilty of sexually abusing a 15-year-old boy.

D'Agostino had travelled to Cambodia two years earlier to volunteer at a children's hospital. The incident happened in February 2011. On November 4, judges at Phnom Penh Municipal Court ordered this man, who had previously worked as a pediatric emergency doctor in New York, to be deported after serving his jail term ("U.S. doctor jailed for abusing Cambodian boy," November 4, 2011, http://www.presstv.ir/detail/208385.html)

Background: Indochina

Indochina refers to the intermingling of Indian and Chinese influences in the culture of the region and is made up of three States: Vietnam, Laos, and **Cambodia**, formerly associated with France: first within its empire and later within the French Union.

Cambodia (on the Indochinese mainland of Southeast Asia) is largely a land of plains and great rivers, lying amid important overland and river trade routes linking China to India and Southeast Asia. Cambodia's are Thailand (to the west and northwest), Laos (to the northeast), Vietnam (to the east and southeast), and the Gulf of Thailand (to the southwest).

Asia Central

"Police Arrest More Minors in Kashmir," November 4, 2011, http://www.presstv.ir/detail/208417.html

Asia Middle East, South Central

"Foreigners Stir Trouble in Iraq: Maliki," November 4, 2011, http://www.presstv.ir/detail/208404.html

"Yemenis Hold Huge Anti-regime Rallies," November 4, 2011, http://www.presstv.ir/detail/208376.html

"Israel Intercepts Gaza-bound Aid Flotilla," November 4, 2011, http://www.presstv.ir/detail/208336.html

Caption Press TV
Greek coastguards stand in front of Canadian boat 'Tahrir' after forcing the Gaza-bound ship to return to the port of Agios Nikolaos, July 4, 2011.

"'Israeli Doctors Complicit in Torture,'" November 4, 2011, http://www.presstv.ir/detail/208305.html

"Jordanians Press New PM over Reforms," November 4, 2011, http://www.presstv.ir/detail/208429.html

"Police Clash with Bahraini Protesters," November 4, 2011, http://www.presstv.ir/detail/208329.html

VII. Despite Protests, Sound Advice . . .
(U.S. at war October/November/December 2011)

United States Heedlessly Terrorized Afghans and Pakistanis

In Kabul, Afghanistan, in 1977, a group of Afghan women intellectuals under the leadership of Meena (assassinated in 1987 in Quetta, Pakistan, by Afghan agents of the then KGB in connivance with the fundamentalist band of Gulbuddin Hekmatyar) established the Revolutionary Association of the Women of Afghanistan (RAWA). RAWA's objective was to involve increasing numbers of Afghan women in social and political activities aimed at acquiring women's human rights and contributing to the struggle for the establishment in Afghanistan of a government based on democratic and secular values, http://www.rawa.org/rawa.html.

"The U.S. government has never supported democratic organizations . . ." said Zoya in May 24, 2009 interview with Elsa Rassbach. Zoya is a leading activist with RAWA and represents it's the group's Foreign Committee. Zoya is a pseudonym that is necessary for security reasons.

The year before the interview, Zoya had testified before the Human Rights Commission of the German Parliament (Bundestag), trying to persuade the German government to withdraw its troops from Afghanistan. At that time of her interview with Elsa Rassbach in Berlin, Zoya and Rassbach believed the interview might be of interest to U.S. citizens as the U.S. House of Representatives had just approved tens of billions in further financing for the continued war and occupation in Afghanistan. "Women injected clarity into U.S. 'war on terror,'" Today's Insight News, Saturday, November 21, 2009

Carolyn LaDelle Bennett, *Same Ole or Something New: Uprooting power ENTRENCHMENT,* 2010, p. 221

Photo Caption

Afghan woman's body

Afghanistan

"U.S. Forces Kill Pregnant Afghan Woman," December 17, 2011, http://www.presstv.ir/detail/216210.html,http://www.presstv.ir/detail/216170.html.
"Police Station Bombed in Afghan Capital," December 16, 2011, http://www.presstv.ir/detail/216066.html.
"Bomb Blast Kills 2 Afghan Soldiers," December 15, 2011, http://www.presstv.ir/detail/215858.html.
"Roadside Bomb Kills 4 Afghan Civilians," December 15, 2011, http://www.presstv.ir/detail/215850.html.

Cluster Bombs

"Save Children from Cluster Bombs," *Today's Insight News*, November 12, 2011.

November 2011 conference

Convention on Prohibitions or Restrictions on the Use of Certain Conventional Weapons Which May Be Deemed to Be Excessively Injurious or to Have Indiscriminate Effects, 4th Review Conference of the High Contracting Parties (November 14-25, 2011) http://www.unog.ch/unog/website/calendar.nsf/(httpInternal~Conferences~Daily~en)/B6 1F08FB6901A36FC1257879001FE336?OpenDocument

Cluster Munition Coalition statement continued from book text

Strong existing legislation

> Since the negotiations began under the CCW, the international community [has] united under the Oslo Process to negotiate and adopt the 2008 Convention on Cluster Munitions.
>
> This Convention comprehensively bans cluster munitions and is the standard by which all states should be judged.
>
> The high number of states that have signed, ratified or acceded to the Convention on Cluster Munitions, now 111, is proof of

the strong commitment by the international community for this Convention to work.

Since entering into force in 2010, the Convention on Cluster Munitions is already producing significant results and has led to a global stigmatization of the use of cluster bombs.

Going back on their word

With a strong and comprehensive international ban in place, States that have joined the Convention on Cluster Munitions must not be complicit in the adoption of a new instrument of international humanitarian law that permits ongoing use of cluster munitions, contradicting their exiting commitments.

Furthermore, they must not risk weakening the international norm now established against cluster munition use, or provide an 'out' for countries that have not yet joined the Convention on Cluster Munitions by allowing them to adopt weak standards while claiming to be meaningfully addressing the humanitarian harm caused by cluster munitions. http://www. stopclustermunitions.org/ccw/

Cluster Munition Coalition

The Cluster Munition Coalition is an international civil society campaign working to eradicate cluster munitions, prevent further casualties from these weapons and put an end for all time to the suffering they cause. The Coalition works through its members to change the policy and practice of governments and organizations toward these aims and to raise public awareness to the problem. CMC's vision:

An end for all time to the suffering and casualties caused by cluster munitions http://www.stopclustermunitions.org/ the-coalition/ http://www.stopclustermunitions.org/news/

AVAAZ petition:

Send leaders a clear message: stand up for the cluster bombs ban and keep children safe. http://www.avaaz.org/en/ cluster_bombs_ii_b/?cl=1381876907&v=11085 http://www. avaaz.org/en/cluster_bombs_ii_b/?fp. http://www.avaaz.org/ en/index.php

In several European, Middle Eastern and Asian languages, Avaaz, means 'voice'. Avaaz is a global web movement bringing people-powered politics to decision-making everywhere. Launched in 2007, Avaaz claims the "democratic mission [of organizing] citizens of all nations to close the gap between the world we have and the world most people everywhere want." With a core team on four continents and thousands of volunteers, the Avaaz community campaigns in fourteen languages signing petitions, funding media campaigns and direct actions, emailing, calling and lobbying governments, organizing 'offline' protests and events—"to ensure that the views and values of the world's people inform the decisions that affect all people." http://www.avaaz.org/en/ about.php

Chemical Weapons

"U.S. Cluster Bomb Plan Fails—what of Chemical Weapons Plan," *Today's Insight News* (blog), November 27, 2011.

Conference

The Conference of the States Parties to the Chemical Weapons Convention began its sixteenth session at the World Forum Convention Center (WFCC) in The Hague November 28, 2011, and ended Friday December 2, 2011.

"UN Kills US Cluster Bombs Proposal," November 26, 2011, http:// www.presstv.ir/detail/212211.html.

"U.S. Rejects Destroying Chemical Weapons," November 23, 2011, http://www.presstv.ir/detail/211707.html.

"Sixteenth Session of the Conference of the States Parties," November 28-December 2, 2011, World Forum Convention Center, The Hague, http://www.opcw.org/csp16/

OPCW

The Organization for the Prohibition of Chemical Weapons (OPCW) is the implementing body of the Chemical Weapons Convention (CWC or Convention). Its mandate is to achieve the object and purpose of the Convention, to ensure the implementation of its provisions, including those for international verification of compliance with it and to provide a forum for consultation and cooperation among States Parties.

The OPCW States Parties represent about 98 percent of the global population and landmass, as well as 98 percent of the worldwide chemical industry. To all States not Party to the CWC, the OPCW provides support in preparing to join the CWC and effectively to implement the global ban on chemical weapons. http://www.opcw.org/about-opcw/

> OPCW is the fastest growing international disarmament organization in history.

> The United Nations has called on all States to join the CWC and to rid the world of the threat chemical weapons pose to international security.

Press TV captions
An unexploded cluster bomb revealing a large supply of cluster "bomblets" within (file photo)

An American B-1B Lancer dropping cluster bombs over Baghdad (file photo)

OPCW caption document
http://www.opcw.org/index.

"Stealth, Distance, Cover of Darkness—U.S. Reign of Terror," *Today's Insight News* (blog), November 24, 2011.

Night raids, drones 50 to 1, double standards

Pakistan
U.S. Drones on Pakistan

"22 Killed in NW Pakistan Clashes," November 24, 2011, http://www.presstv.ir/detail/211759.html.
"NATO Oil Tanker Torched in Pakistan," November 24, 2011, http://www.presstv.ir/detail/211827.html.
"Pakistan to Take U.S. Drone attacks to UN," November 24, 2011, http://www.presstv.ir/detail/211864.html.
"Pakistan: NATO Raids Were Deliberate," citing *Christian Science Monitor* report, December 16, 2011, http://www.presstv.ir/detail/215958.html.
"Pakistan: U.S. Must Heed Our Red Lines," December 16, 2011, http://www.presstv.ir/detail/216099.html.
"Pakistanis Protest Deadly NATO Attacks," December 16, 2011, http://www.presstv.ir/detail/215973.html,   http://www.presstv.ir/section/351020401.html.

Related:

Caption: Miami Workers Center
"Occupy Wall Street Evicted in Late Night Raid; Lawyers Secure Injunction to Reopen Zuccotti Park," November 15, 2011, http://www.miamiworkerscenter.org/index.php/en/news/7-national-news/108-occupy-wall-street-evicted-in-late-night-raid-lawyers-secure-injunction-to-reopen-zuccotti-park.

Afghanistan
U.S. Drones on Afghanistan

"U.S.-led forces Kill 7 Afghan Civilians," November 24, 2011, http://www.presstv.ir/detail/211898.html.
"Militant Attack Kills 12 in Afghanistan," November 24, 2011, http://www.presstv.ir/detail/211884.html.

"U.S. Terrorists Meet in Afghanistan," December 7, 2011, http://www.presstv.ir/detail/214408.html.

Somalia
U.S. Drones on Somalia

(U.S. Drone Strikes against Somalia and its people)
November 18, 2011 (Friday), http://www.presstv.ir/section/3510205.html
November 17, 2011 (Thursday), http://www.presstv.ir/section/3510205.html
November 16, 2011 (Wednesday), http://www.presstv.ir/section/3510205.html
November 15, 2011 (Tuesday), http://www.presstv.ir/section/3510205.html

"U.S. Spy Drone Crashes in Somalia," November 8, 2011, http://www.presstv.ir/detail/209011.html.

"U.S. Drone Strike Kills 44 in Somalia," October 21, 2011, http://www.presstv.ir/detail/205775.html.

"Cholera Kills 65 More Somali Children," October 20, 2011, http://www.presstv.ir/detail/205690.html.

Caption: Somalia displaced hospital scene
A paramedic attends to internally displaced children suffering from cholera inside a ward at Banadir hospital in Somalia's capital, Mogadishu, on August 18, 2011. (file photo)

"U.S. Drone Strike Kills 16 in Somalia," October 8, 2011, http://www.presstv.ir/detail/203413.html; "U.S. Drone Strike Kills Six in Somalia," October 5, 2011, http://www.presstv.ir/detail/202894.html.

Background: Somalia, Somaliland 2006
In June of 2006, Somaliland President Dahir Riyale Kahin paid official visits, for the first time, to Kenya, Tanzania, Rwanda, Zambia, and Uganda. This was a diplomatic breakthrough but it "was offset on the home front by economic stagnation and a political deadlock between an opposition-controlled House of Representatives and a pro-government Gurti (upper house)"

The year 2006, following a decade of stagnation, was a year of revolutionary upheaval in Somalia: the Council of Islamic Courts of Somalia (CSIC) rose and fell. Fears of renewed conflict triggered a humanitarian crisis in Kenya as thousands of Somalis poured across the border, seeking asylum. [These conditions preceded by a half decade the foreign drone strikes, epidemics health threats, and astounding displacements of peoples.]

The United Nations High Commissioner for Refugees in the fall of 2006 had counted more than 30,000 new arrivals and the flow continued at a rate of more than 1,000 a day. "In December, following Islamist attacks on government positions near the Somali town of Baidoa, Ethiopian forces intervened in support of the TFG [Transitional Federal Government], routing the CSIC militias and seizing control of Mogadishu and Kismayo."

The population of Somalia in 2006 was estimated at 8,496,000, including 3,700,000 in Somaliland; and at the beginning of that year, more than 250,000 refugees were in neighboring countries, and an additional 100,000 resided in Europe or the United States. The area of Somalia spans 637,000 square kilometers (246,000 square miles) including the 176,000-sq-km (68,000-sq-mi) area of the unilaterally declared (in 1991) and unrecognized Republic of Somaliland. The capital of Somalia is Mogadishu; the capital of Somaliland is Hargeysa. [Britannica 2006 update]

U.S.-UK collusion in Drone strikes probed

"Britain Questioned over CIA Drone Strike" ["'CIA drone strikes are killing hundreds—if not thousands—of civilians and destabilizing Pakistan'" (*and Somalia and Afghanistan*)], December 17, 2011, http://www.presstv.ir/detail/216274.html

Egypt

West's foreign relations in EGYPT
Geopolitics' Schizophrenia—U.S.-led West in Africa and Asia

"West Strikes Dangerous Balance in Dealings with Egypt's Military," Deutsche Welle, November 22, 2011, http://www.dw-world.de/dw/article/0,,15546334,00.html

Deutsche Welle reports:

> The latest street battles between demonstrators demanding the end of military rule and armed members of the security services under the command of the Supreme Council of Armed Forces (SCAF) have reopened barely healed wounds just 10 months since President Hosni Mubarak was forced out of power by similar protests.

> 'The SCAF represents the old military guard that propped up the Mubarak regime and its leadership is embedded within the networks of crony capitalists that are proving so hard to dislodge,' says Dr. Kristian Ulrichsen, a North Africa and Middle East expert at the London School of Economics.

"Two Protesters Killed in Cairo Violence," December 16, 2011, http://www.presstv.ir/detail/216089.html

Background: Muslim Countries

Muslims predominate in some 30 to 40 countries, from the Atlantic to the Pacific oceans and along a belt that stretches across northern Africa into Central Asia and south to the northern regions of the Indian subcontinent.

Arabs account for less than one-fifth of all Muslims, more than half of whom live east of Karachi, Pakistan. Despite the absence of large-scale Islamic political entities, the Islamic faith continues to expand, by some estimates faster than any other major religion. Some Muslim countries in Asia and Africa are Saudi Arabia, Yemen, Egypt, Syria, Jordan, Morocco, Algeria, Libya, and Tunisia, Turkey, Nigeria, Iran, Pakistan.

"Misguided Policies Eventually Unravel, Blow Back, Boomerang," *Today's Insight News*, October 28, 2011.

Alastair Crooke, "The 'great game' in Syria," *Asia Times Online*, October 22, 2011, http://conflictsforum.org/2011/the-%e2%80%98great-game%e2%80%99-in-syria/

Alastair Crooke is founder and director of Conflicts Forum and former adviser (1997-2003) to Javier Solana, the European Union Foreign Policy Chief.

David R. Hoffman, "America Is still Dead, October 3, 2011, Pravda.Ru.

VIII. Credibility loss—U.S.-International
(Reckless impunity, Global lawlessness)

Lawless

David R. Hoffman, "America Is Still Dead," October 3, 2011, Pravda.Ru.

"100s of Canadians Protest Bush's Visit," October 21, 2011, http://www. presstv.ir/detail/205798.html, http://www.presstv.ir/section/3510207.html.

Timothy Bancroft-Hinchney, "The Lesson from Sirte: NATO Protects Civilians from Terrorists by Murdering them," October 12, 2011, Pravda. Ru,   http://english.pravda.ru/opinion/columnists/12-10-2011/119311-sirte_nato-0/.

IX What's it to be—Stand with the dead or move constructively forward? Regress or Progress?

Bennett, Carolyn LaDelle, *Same Ole or Something New: Uprooting power ENTRENCHMENT* (Xlibris, 2010).

Mariam Claeson, public health specialist, World Bank, Washington DC; Roland Waldman, professor of clinical population and family health, Mailman School of Public Health, Columbia University.

Encyclopædia Britannica Deluxe Edition, s.v. "cholera."

Kevin Davis, journalist; author of *Defending the Damned: Inside Chicago's Cook County Public Defender's Office*; part-time journalism instructor, Loyola University, Chicago; adjunct faculty, Graham School of General Studies, University of Chicago.

Encyclopædia Britannica Deluxe Edition, s.v. "health and disease."

Appendix

Selective Chronology of U.S. Foreign Relations in Violence

TIMELINES

Post-World War II

1947 Britain, India, Pakistan

Without domestic or international support for continued colonization of India, Britain's Labor government in post-World War II (1946) decided to end British rule of India. In early 1947, Britain announced its intention to transfer power no later than June 1948. In June 1947, India's nationalist leaders agreed to a partition of the country along religious lines: predominantly Hindu and Sikh areas assigned to the new India, predominantly Muslim areas to the new nation of Pakistan. The plan included a partition of the provinces of Punjab and Bengal. (*Wikipedia*).

Cold War Era

1964-1975 U.S.-Vietnam War

When two American destroyers exchanged fire with a North Vietnamese torpedo boat eight miles off the North's coast in August 1964—an event whose occurrence was later disputed—the U.S. Congress passed the *Gulf of Tonkin Resolution* authorizing the President to take whatever measures he deemed necessary to protect American lives in Southeast Asia. President Lyndon Baines Johnson held off escalating the war during the 1964 electoral campaign but in February 1965 ordered sustained bombing of North Vietnam and sent the first U.S. combat units to the South. By June, U.S. troops in Vietnam numbered 74,000 . . .

U.S. forces reached a peak of 543,000 men in 1969. (Australia, New Zealand, Thailand, and the Philippines also sent small contingents and South Korea contributed 50,000.) The U.S. strategy was to employ mobility based on helicopters and firepower to wear down the enemy by attrition "at minimal cost in U.S. lives."

> . . . The world after the 1960s saw a proliferation of violence at every level except war among developed nations. A world financial structure was under tremendous strain, the worst economic downturn since the 1930s and reduced growth rates thereafter. [There were] recurrent fears of an energy crisis, depletion of resources and concurrent global pollution, famine and genocidal dictators in parts of Africa and Asia. There was a rise of an aggressive religious fundamentalism and widespread political terrorism in the Middle East and Europe.

> Superpowers never ceased to compete in the realms of strategic weapons and influence in the Third World and thus failed to sustain their brief experiment with détente. 'The factors that make for international instability are gaining the historical upper hand over the forces that work for more organized cooperation,'" President Jimmy Carter's national security adviser, Zbigniew Brzezinski, is quoted saying. 'The unavoidable conclusion of any detached analysis of global trends is that social turmoil, political unrest, economic crisis, and international friction are likely to become more widespread during the remainder of this century.' . . .

> After their 1975 victory, the North Vietnamese showed a natural strategic preference for the USSR [Union of Soviet Socialist Republics, the Soviet Union] and fell out with their historic enemy, neighboring China" (*Britannica*).

U.S. against South/Central Asia, Middle East

Iran (Islamic Republic of, the Heart of Persia)

Monarchy (the Shah of Iran) restored by a CIA-aided coup in 1953

Reza Shah Pahlavi had used Iran's oil revenues to finance rapid modernization of his country and the purchase of American arms.

President Richard M. Nixon had chosen Iran to be a U.S. surrogate in the vital Persian Gulf. As late as 1977, [President James (Jimmy) Earl] Carter praised the Shah for making Iran 'an island of stability.' Undetected or ignored by U.S. intelligence services was the widespread Iranian resentment of modernization (meaning, in this context, materialism, emancipation of women, and secularization), middle-class opposition to the autocracy, and the rising tide of Shiite fundamentalism that were undermining the Shah's legitimacy.

Fundamentalist movements and conflicts between Sunnite and Shīite Muslims have arisen periodically in the course of Islamic history but the outbreaks of the late 20th century were especially notable in light of the Western assumption that less developed countries would naturally secularize their politics and culture as they modernized their society and economy. Instead, rapidly developing Iran succumbed to a religious revolution led by Ayatollah Ruhollah Khomeini.

1978-1979 Iran

By November 1978, the beleaguered Shah saw his options reduced to democratization, military repression, or abdication. Despite the importance of Iran for U.S. interests, including the presence there of critical electronic listening posts used to monitor missile tests inside the USSR, President Carter was unable to choose between personal loyalty toward an old ally and the moral argument on behalf of reform or abdication. In January 1979, the Shah fled Iran.

1973-75, 1978 Afghanistan

Afghan government of Daud Khan worked to lessen Afghanistan's dependence on Soviet and U.S. aid and reportedly had a heated disagreement with Soviet leader Leonid Brezhnev during a 1977 visit to

Moscow. In April 1978, leftists in the Afghan officer corps killed Daud Khan and pledged friendly relations with the USSR.

Iran 1979: Iranian students seize U.S. Embassy in Tehran
Afghanistan 1979: The USSR (Soviet army) invades Afghanistan

Afghanistan is an ancient land at the heart of South Central Asia lying along important trade routes connecting southern and eastern Asia to Europe and the Middle East. It is a landlocked land whose neighbors are **Pakistan** *(including areas of Kashmir administered by Pakistan but claimed by India) to the east and south;* **Iran** *to the west; Central Asian states Turkmenistan, Uzbekistan and Tajikistan to the north ; and Xinjiang, China (a short border), at the end of the long, narrow Vākhān (Wakhan Corridor) in the extreme northeast.*

1979-89 Afghanistan

The Afghan regime loses authority with the people, Afghan soldiers defect in large numbers, and the Muslim and largely tribal resistance—armed with U.S. and Chinese weapons—hold out in the mountains against more than 100,000 Soviet troops and terror bombing of their villages. More than 2,000,000 Afghan refugees pour into Pakistan and Iran.

Old-country neighbors

> *Iran and Iraq connect significantly. The lands now comprising Iraq, the easternmost country of the Arab world, were, in ancient times, known as Mesopotamia ('Land between the rivers').*
>
> *Together with a 12-mile (19-kilometer) coastline along the northern end of the Persian Gulf giving Iraq a bit of sea territory, it neighbors with Turkey (north), Iran (east), Syria and Jordan (west), and Saudi Arabia and Kuwait (south).*

1980 Iraq-Iran War

Bolstered by arms purchased with oil revenues, the Iraqi government of Saddam Hussein unilaterally abrogates a 1975 accord on the waterway at the mouth of the Tigris-Euphrates river system and launches a full-scale invasion of Iran.

U.S.-Israeli Iraq war1981: The Israeli air force conducts surprise raid on Iraq.

1987 Persian Gulf War

The United States sharply increases its presence in the [Persian Gulf] by permitting Kuwaiti oil tankers to fly the U.S. flag and by deploying a naval task force to protect them in passage through the gulf. [Walter A. McDougall]

1987 U.S.-Iran-Central America War

Exposed: President Ronald Reagan's administration trades arms for hostages and against U.S. law funnels money through Swiss bank accounts to finance the Contras in Nicaragua.

1990-1991 U.S. Persian Gulf War

The George H. W. Bush administration sends a large military force to the Persian Gulf. The United States attacks Iraq in a month-long air assault culminating in a 100-hour ground war. An estimated 100,000 Iraqi died in that invasion.

1991, 2001 U.S. Haiti War

The majority of Haitian people elected Jean-Bertrand Aristide twice (1990 and later in 2000). During his tenure, he reportedly initiated a literacy program, dismantled a repressive system of rural section chiefs, oversaw a drastic reduction in human rights violations—found effective solutions to Haiti's economic problems and social inequalities. In response, Haiti's elite and its military ousted Jean-Bertrand Aristide from office and from his country.

U.S. Haiti War 1992: The United States denies political asylum to thousands of Haitian refugees.

1990s U.S. Iraq War

Western allies impose a no-fly zone over Iraq. The United Nations (UN) implements economic sanctions (held for 12 years) against Iraq.

1998 U.S. Iraq War

The William Jefferson (Bill) Clinton administration orders the bombing of several Iraqi military installations resulting in Iraq's refusal to allow reentry of weapons' inspectors and the erosion of sanctions as Iraq's neighbors sought to reopen trade with Iraq

Decade long U.S. terror Central America to Southwest/Central Asia

> 2001—Present (2011) Afghanistan war: U.S. invades and occupies Afghanistan
> 2003—Present (2011) U.S. Iraq war: U.S. invades and occupies Iraq
> 2009 U.S. Central America

Soldiers rousted Honduran President Manuel Zelaya from his bed at gunpoint and exiled him to Costa Rica . . . One of Latin America's poorest countries, Honduras was a staging area for the U.S.-backed Nicaraguan Contra rebels during the 1980s. The country of about eight million people subsists on exports of bananas, shrimp, coffee, apparel and remittances from Hondurans in the U.S. The United States has a controversial history of backing coups in Latin America. http://online. wsj.com/article/SB124619401378065339.html

2010 U.S. Pakistan War

Pakistan abandons its Independence Day (August 14) celebrations because of the flood disaster but the United States continued drone bombing attacks on defenseless Pakistani villages. http://mwcnews.net/ focus/editorial/4511-pakistan-independence-day.html

TIMELINE

Middle East and U.S.-funded Israel

Al Jazeera English News, January 27, 2009, english.aljazeera.net/news/middleeast/2009.

Gaza crisis: Key events in war on people of the Gaza Strip

- June 19: An Egyptian-brokered six-month ceasefire between Israel and Hamas comes into force.
- November 5: Israel closes all of its crossings with Gaza.
- December 14: Hamas political leader Khaled Meshaal announces the six-month ceasefire with Israel "will not be extended."
- December 19: Six-month ceasefire between Hamas and Israel officially expires.
- December 21: Israeli Foreign Minister Tzipi Livni says her primary goal if she wins Israeli elections "will be to overthrow Hamas."
- December 27: Israel launches air raids killing more than 225 Palestinians to begin its assault codenamed 'Operation Cast Lead' against Gaza. Palestinian fighters launch missile attacks resulting in one Israeli death and six others wounded.
- December 28: Israeli aircraft bomb the Islamic University in Gaza City and the length of the Gaza-Egypt border, taking out more than 40 tunnels used to smuggle vital goods to the Gaza Strip. Hundreds of Israeli infantry and armored forces mass on the border of the territory, and the Israeli government approves a call up of military reservists to bolster its fighting strength.
- December 29: Israeli air strikes hit the interior ministry in Gaza City as Israel declares a 'closed military zone' around the Gaza strip.
- December 30: Palestinian positions fire rockets resulting in the deaths of three Israelis, taking the death toll from Palestinian rocket attacks to four since the beginning of the Israeli offensive. The European Union calls for 'an unconditional halt to rocket attacks by Hamas on Israel and an end to Israeli military action.'

- December 31: Members of the UN Security Council end an emergency meeting on the crisis after failing to agree on the wording of a draft resolution.
- January 1: Israeli raid kills Hamas official Nizar Rayyan along with 14 members of his family
- January 2: Egypt begins talks with Hamas over a way to end the conflict. Around 25,000 Palestinians have fled the fighting [AFP].
- January 3: As Israel begins its ground offensive in Gaza, Israeli forces strike a mosque in the town of Beit Lahiya killing at least 11 Palestinians, including one child.
- January 4: As an Israeli soldier dies in the ongoing offensive, Israeli forces cut Gaza in half and ring Gaza City. The European Commission, the executive arm of the European Union, pledges an additional $4.2 million of emergency aid for Gaza and calls on Israel to respect international law. An Israeli air strike hits two ambulances in Gaza, killing four paramedics.
- January 5: Air and naval bombardments kill 45 Palestinians. French President Nicolas Sarkozy holds talks with Egyptian President Hosni Mubarak to push for a truce deal.
- January 6: An Israeli strike on a UN school in the northern town of Jabaliya leaves 43 Palestinians dead and at least 100 others injured who had taken refuge inside the school. Israeli strikes hit two other schools, killing two in the southern town of Khan Younis and three in the Shati refugee camp in Gaza City.
- January 7: 11 Palestinians die in air strikes and shelling in Gaza City and in the north of the Strip. Violence continues after Israel temporarily halts attacks in Gaza City for three hours to provide a 'humanitarian respite.' The Israeli military drops leaflets warning thousands of people in the Rafah zone on the Egyptian border to leave their houses or face air strikes. More than 4,300 Palestinians have suffered wounds in the fighting [AFP]
- January 8: The UN's refugee organization in Gaza suspends all aid deliveries after an Israeli tank attacks a UN convoy, killing one Palestinian driver and injuring two other people. Israeli bulldozers cross into Gaza and destroy a number of houses. At least three rockets fired from Lebanon hit the northern Israeli town of Nahariya. The UN Security Council passes a resolution—with 14 votes affirming *(only the U.S. abstaining)*—'stressing the urgency of and calling for an immediate, durable and fully

respected ceasefire, leading to the full withdrawal of Israeli forces from Gaza.'

- January 9: Soon after passage of the UN resolution, Israeli attacks continue in Gaza with a series of explosions and gunfire heard. Six Palestinians reportedly die in an air strike in the northern part of the Gaza Strip, raising the Palestinian death toll in Gaza to around 770, including more than 200 children, since the start of the Israeli offensive.
- January 10: Israel drops leaflets on Gaza City warning of a 'new phase' in its two-week-old offensive. An Israeli tank shell in Jabaliya kills eight family members, raising the Palestinian death toll in Gaza to 831 people. Khalid Meshaal, the exiled political leader of Hamas, says that Israel must halt the Gaza offensive and lift the blockade before Hamas agrees to a ceasefire deal.
- January 11: Israel is accused of firing white phosphorous bombs on Gaza's densely populated land in violation of international law. Israel reports to the UN that troops in the occupied Golan Heights came under small arms fire from Syria, but there were no injuries. *[The Golan Heights was part of extreme southwestern Syria until 1967 when it came under Israeli military occupation. In December 1981, Israel unilaterally annexed the part of the Golan it occupied.]* Israel began sending reservists into the Gaza Strip as the military offensive continued unabated for the 16th consecutive day. Israeli bombs hit a UN warehouse holding food and medicine as well as three hospitals [AFP].
- January 12: Israel continues its offensive and the UN Human Rights Council adopts a non-binding resolution condemning Israel's military offensive. The resolution calls for an international mission to be sent immediately to Gaza to investigate Israel's actions. The toll rises to 935 Palestinians killed and 4,300 wounded. At least 25,000 people in Gaza are internally displaced but are unable to flee because crossing points remain closed.
- January 13: Miguel d'Escoto Brockmann, the president of the UN General Assembly, condemns the offensive and says the killing of Palestinians in Gaza amounts to 'genocide.' Ban Ki-moon, the UN Secretary-general, arrives in Egypt to try to secure a ceasefire and end the war in Gaza.
- January 14: The number of Palestinians killed exceeds 1,000 as the UN's aid agency in Gaza urges an end to the fighting,

calling the war 'a test of our humanity.' Venezuela and Bolivia sever diplomatic ties with Israel, calling the onslaught on Gaza a 'holocaust.' Bolivia pledges to get Israeli officials charged in the International Criminal Court with committing 'genocide.'

- January 15: Israeli shells hit a UN warehouse setting fire to tons of food and medical supplies, as well as three hospitals as troops advance into Gaza City. An Israeli air raid in Jabaliya kills Said Siam, the Palestinian interior minister and one of Hamas's senior leaders in Gaza along with his brother and son. The UN General Assembly accuses Israel of violating international law and targeting civilians in Gaza, and rebukes member-states for the lack of action over the crisis. Hamas tells Egyptian negotiators it will agree to a yearlong truce on condition that Israeli forces withdraw within a week and that all border crossings are opened with international guarantees that it will remain so. Ban Ki-moon, the UN Secretary-general, says he feels optimistic the Israelis will accept a ceasefire deal with Hamas but not for a few days.

- January 16: The Strip experiences a relative lull in fighting as diplomatic efforts intensify. An emergency Arab summit in Doha, Qatar, highlights the split within the Arab world. Egypt and Saudi Arabia send delegates to a separate meeting of foreign ministers in Kuwait. Qatar and Mauritania suspend economic and political ties with Israel, following calls by Bashar al-Assad, the Syrian president, and Khaled Meshaal, the exiled leader of Hamas, for all Arab nations to do so. Tzipi Livni, the Israeli foreign minister and her U.S. counterpart, Condoleezza Rice, sign an agreement on stopping arms smuggling into Gaza. The UN general assembly demands an immediate ceasefire with the full withdrawal of Israeli forces. Recep Tayyip Erdogan, the Turkish prime minister, says Israel should be barred from the UN while it ignores UN demands to end the fighting. Talks continue in Cairo over an Egypt-sponsored truce. Amos Gilad, the Israeli chief negotiator, says Israel wants an open-ended ceasefire.

- January 17: Israel carries out more than 50 air strikes in Gaza; heavy explosions are heard south of Gaza City. Israel has been accused of using white phosphorus [Getty]. Israeli warships and tanks enter the outskirts of Gaza City and continue lobbing shells into the densely populated urban area. Fifteen Palestinians are killed in the Gaza Strip. The United Nations demands an

investigation into an Israeli strike on a UN school in the northern
town of Beit Lahiya. Two children (ages five and seven) died
in the attack. Chris Gunness, a UN representative, says an
investigation ought to be held 'to determine whether a war crime
has been committed.' Egypt says it will host an international
summit on the Gaza crisis that will be attended by several
European leaders as well as UN Secretary-general Ban Ki-moon.
Ahmed Abul Gheit, the Egyptian foreign minister, says Cairo is
'not bound' by a U.S.-Israeli agreement to stop arms smuggling
to the Hamas-ruled Gaza Strip. The Israeli security cabinet votes
in favor of a unilateral ceasefire in its 22-day-old war in the
Gaza Strip that has left 1,203 Palestinians dead and much of
the Gaza Strip in ruins. Ehud Olmert, the Israeli prime minister,
announces a unilateral end to military operations in the Gaza
Strip, beginning at 0000 GMT but says troops will remain in the
strip for the time being.

- January 18: Israeli attacks continue in the Gaza Strip, air raids
continue in the north, one Palestinian civilian is killed in Khan
Younis. The Israeli military says that they were responding to
at least 16 rockets being fired from the Gaza Strip into Israel
by morning. Palestinian factions Hamas, Islamic Jihad, al-Nidal,
the Popular Front for the Liberation of Palestine (PFLP)
and al-Saeqa announce an immediate one-week ceasefire at
1300GMT, with the condition that Israel's troops leave the Gaza
Strip within seven days. The Israeli military says it will not draw
up a timetable to leave until rocket fire ceases and will not have
a deadline dictated to them by Hamas. It says, 'The operation is
not over. This is only a holding of fire.' A summit of European
and Middle East leaders convenes in Egypt stressing the need
for humanitarian assistance.

- January 19: Palestinians living in the Gaza Strip venture out
to assess the damage caused by Israel's war on the territory, as
separate ceasefires called by Israel and Hamas take hold. Tens of
thousands of people have been made homeless by the offensive
[EPA]. Since the fighting ended, dozens of bodies have been
pulled from the rubble of buildings flattened during the Israeli
onslaught on Gaza. Some Israeli soldiers and tanks begin to
move from the centre of the Gaza Strip to the borders of the
territory, but Israeli military sources say that most of the troops

heading out of Gaza are reservists. Hamas, for its part, says that its ability to fight Israel remains intact despite 23 days of Israeli bombardment and attacks by ground forces.

- January 20: Amnesty International, the human rights group, accuses Israel of war crimes, saying its use of white phosphorus munitions in densely populated areas of the Gaza Strip was indiscriminate and illegal.
- January 21: Israel says that it has completed the withdrawal of its troops from the Gaza Strip, with forces being redeployed on the territory's outskirts, ending 'Operation Cast Lead.' However, Israeli naval vessels are still seen in Gaza's territorial waters and are heard firing throughout the morning. Ban Ki-moon, the UN secretary general, demands a 'full investigation' into Israel's bombing of a UN compound in Gaza City, calling the attack 'outrageous' and 'totally unacceptable.'
- January 27: A bomb planted by Palestinian fighters kills an Israeli soldier and wounds three other troops near the Kissufim border crossing. Palestinian medical workers say that a Palestinian farmer was killed when Israeli forces opened fire after the incident. Two Palestinians are wounded in an Israeli air raid, according to Hamas and Palestinian medical officials. http://english.aljazeera.net/news/middleeast/2009/01/2009172054186 65491.html Aljazeera-English News January 27, 2009, english. aljazeera.net/news/middleeast/2009

TIMELINE U.S. war on people of Somalia at Al Jazeera English

Somalia's civilians have taken the brunt of fierce fighting across the country [AFP]

Key events and developments in Somalia's recent history [latest update May 24, 2009]

- July 1, 1960: Somalia gains independence. British Somaliland Protectorate and Italian Somaliland merge forming the country.
- 1963: Somalia breaks diplomatic relations with Britain, amid border dispute with Kenya.
- 1964: Fighting breaks out over border dispute with Ethiopia.

- 1967: Abdi Rashid Ali Shermarke beats Aden Abdullah Osman Daar in elections for president.
- 1969: Shermake is assassinated.
- October 21, 1969: Major General Muhammad Siad Barre seizes presidency in a bloodless coup.
- 1970: Barre says Somalia is a socialist state and begins a process of nationalizing the country's economy.
- 1974-75: Somalia suffers severe drought causing widespread starvation.
- 1977: Somalia invades the Ethiopia's Ogaden region, home to hundreds of Somali people.
- 1978: Ethiopian forces backed by Cuban troops push Somali soldiers out of Ogaden. Barre turns to the United States after expelling Soviet advisers from Somalia.
- 1981: Barre prevents Mijertyn and Isaq clan members from holding posts in government and fills the vacant positions with people from the Marehan clan.
- 1988: Somalia reaches a peace accord with Ethiopia.
- January 1991: Barre's government is forced from power, promoting factional fighting.
- November 1991: A power struggle breaks out between rival clan regional commanders, Mohammed Farah Aideed and Ali Mahdi Mohammed. Soon the government collapses and fighting breaks out between rival leaders. Thousands of civilians die during the violence and thousands die of starvation because food aid cannot reach them due to the conflict. Somali government soldiers struggle to maintain order in the country [AFP]
- 1991: Somaliland declares unilateral independence from Somalia.
- February 1992: Rival commanders sign a United Nations-sponsored ceasefire but fail to agree on monitoring provisions. The UN deploys 500 soldiers in Mogadishu (Somalia's capital) as part of United Nations Operation in Somalia (Unosom) which is intended to observe the ceasefire. Fighting continues to escalate.
- December: A contingent of U.S. marines lands near Mogadishu, under a UN peacekeeping mandate to assist in the delivery of humanitarian aid. The soldiers' task is to restore order.
- 1993: U.S. forces target powerful Somali leader Muhammad Farah Aidid. About 2,000 people, many of them civilians, die in

clashes between the U.S. marines and Aidid's forces. Seventeen U.S. army rangers die when their helicopters are shot down in Mogadishu.

- March 1994: The U.S. ends its mission in Somalia.
- March 1995: UN peacekeepers leave Somalia, their mission a failure.
- 1996: Aidid dies and is succeeded by his son, Hussein.
- 1998: Puntland region declares that it is autonomous from Somalia.
- 2000: Abdulkassim Salat Hussein becomes president of Somalia. Ali Khalif Gelayadh, the country's prime minister, announces a new government.
- October 2004: Ethiopian-backed regional commander, Abdullahi Yusuf, is elected president of Somalia and head of a new transitional parliament.
- June 5, 2005: Fighters loyal to the Union of Islamic Courts (UIC) defeat U.S.-backed leaders and take control of Mogadishu.
- March-May 2006: Dozens of people are killed in fighting between rival armed groups in Mogadishu.
- September: Transitional government and the Union of Islamic Courts hold peace talks in the Sudanese capital, Khartoum.
- December: UIC loyalists flee Mogadishu in face of joint offensive by Ethiopian and Somali government forces. The joint force captures the city. Al-Shabab has led a campaign against the government in recent months [AFP]
- January 2007: Union of Islamic Courts loyalists flee Kismayo, their port stronghold. Interim government declares a state of emergency.
- April: The UN reports more than 320,000 Somalis have left their homes in Mogadishu since February amid fierce fighting.
- November: Nur Hassan Hussein is appointed as prime minister after his predecessor, Ali Mohamed Gedi, resigns.
- May 1, 2008: U.S. air raid kills Aden Hashi Ayro, leader of al-Shabab, an offshoot of the Union of Islamic Courts.
- August 18: Somalia formally signs a peace deal with some opposition figures but some groups reject the pact.
- August 22: Al-Shabab fighters seize Kismayo, a strategic southern port, after fighting that kills 70 people.

- November 14: President Yusuf admits that insurgents control most of the country, raising the prospect his government could completely collapse.
- December 14: Yusuf announces that he is sacking Nur Hassan Hussein, the prime minister, and the interim government.
- December 15: The parliament votes in a special session in favor of keeping Hussein and his cabinet in office.
- December 16: Yusuf appoints Mohamed Mohamoud Guled as prime minister, ignoring the parliament's vote in favor of keeping Hussein as prime minister.
- December 24: Mohamed Mohamoud Guled resigns.
- December 29: Yusuf resigns saying Sheikh Aden Madobe, the parliament speaker, will take over as interim president.
- January 2, 2009: Ethiopia says it has started pulling its troops out of Somalia.
- January 26: Ethiopia's remaining group of soldiers leave and fighters from al-Shabab move into Baidoa, the seat of the transitional government.
- January 30: Somali MPs elect Sharif Ahmed new president of Somalia in neighboring Djibouti.
- January 31: Ahmed is sworn in as Somalia's new president.
- February 14: Omar Abdirashid Ali Sharmarke is chosen by Ahmed to become Somalia's prime minister.
- April 18: Somalia's parliament approves draft law on implementation of sharia (Islamic law) across the country.

May: Fighters opposed to Somalia's government launch fresh attacks in Mogadishu, the Somali capital and government troops launch counter offensive. http://english.aljazeera.net/news/africa/2009/01/2009126212 443542421.html http://english.aljazeera.net/news/middleeast/2007/01/ 2008525184442319195.html

TIMELINE Middle East: U.S. in Iraq

United States military forces (update January 11, 2007) have been in Iraq for nearly three years and 10 months, fighting longer than they did in World War II

- March 20, 2003: After conducting an public relations and media campaign accusing Iraq of possessing weapons of mass destruction and seeking to portray the Iraqi government as a participant in the September 11, 2001, attacks in the United States, the U.S. administration of President George W. Bush mounts a bombing campaign followed by a land invasion on Iraq. The U.S.-led 'coalition of the willing' notably includes British and Spanish forces but the United Nations does not approve the attack on Iraq.
- April 9, 2003: U.S. forces enter central Baghdad and topple a large statue of Iraq's president, Saddam Hussein.
- May 1, 2003: Speaking from an aircraft carrier off the California coast, U.S. President Bush declares that major combat in Iraq is over.
- August 2003: A massive car bomb shatters the UN headquarters in Baghdad, Iraq's capital, killing the senior UN official in the country.
- December 2003: U.S. forces capture Iraq's president, Saddam Hussein, near Tikrit.
- March 2004: A series of devastating bomb attacks in Madrid lead Spain to pull its forces out of Iraq.
- April 2004: U.S. media show photographs taken by U.S. military in the Abu Ghraib prison near Baghdad of grinning Americans torturing Iraqi detainees.
- June 2004: U.S. officials set up an interim government in Iraq and U.S. authorities declare that Iraqis now enjoy sovereignty.
- November 2004: More than 10,000 U.S. soldiers backed by 2,000 Iraqi troops launch a massive attack on the Iraqi city of Fallujah.
- January 2005: The U.S. administration says it is giving up its search for weapons of mass destruction after having found none. Nationwide elections for a transitional government in Iraq give a large majority to Shia Muslim parties; many Sunnis refuse to vote. Kurdish parties make a strong showing.
- October 2005: A new constitution, approved by referendum, gives wide autonomy to the country's regions critics see as a recipe for partition. Saddam goes on trial for crimes committed during his rule.

- December 2005: Parliamentary elections attract wide participation and give victory to a Shia alliance.
- February 2006: A bomb attack destroys the dome of one of the world's most important Shia shrines (in Samarra), prompting widespread violence between Shia and Sunni Muslims.
- June 2006: A U.S. air strike kills Abu Musab al-Zarqawi, a-Qaeda's leader in Iraq.
- October 2006: British study concludes that about 655,000 Iraqi civilians have died during the U.S.-led invasion of Iraq.
- November 2006: The Bush administration suffers a major political setback as congressional elections deprive it of its parliamentary majority. A 'special tribunal' sentences Iraqi President Saddam Hussein to death after the first in a series of several trials. Amid widespread fighting, a single series of attacks kills more than 200 people in the Shia neighborhood of Sadr City, Baghdad.
- December 2006: Saddam Hussein is hanged and videos circulated via the Internet show him being taunted by Shia guards.
- January 2007: The number of U.S. military dead passes 3,000. Bush shakes up the military and political command of his Iraq operation before announcing a new strategy.

NUMBERS: The number of Iraqi deaths is unknown but estimates range from 50,000 to as high as 650,000. The Iraqi health ministry estimates that 100,000 to 150,000 Iraqis have been killed since the U.S. invasion in March 20, 2003. *[The figures are incomplete and inaccurate and the U.S. military presence with its accompanying violence and occupation remains in Iraq through 2011 and into 2012.]*

- U.S. military dead: 3,009 as of January 9, 2007.
- U.S. wounded in action: 22,834
- U.S. troops in Iraq: 132,000
- Iraqi security forces: 323,000
- Iraqi army: 134,700
- Iraqi ministry of interior: 188,300
- Average monthly war costs: $8.4bn
- Total cost of the war: $267.4 billion obligated through October 2006, according to the Pentagon.
- With additional appropriations in fiscal 2007 the Congressional total is about $350bn.

- http://english.aljazeera.net/news/middleeast/2007/01/20085251
  84442319195.html
- http://english.aljazeera.net/news/middleeast/2008/02/20085251
  85027407159.html

TIMELINE: Middle East—Palestine since 1915

Important events in Palestine since World War I (latest update February 23, 2008)

Palestinians say their nation has been occupied for the past 60 years [GALLO/GETTY]. No country in the Arab World conjures up as much anger and passion in Arab psyche than Palestine. Palestinians say it is nation of cultures and religions bound together by history and inalienable rights. Israelis say Palestine is a part of land that has been inherently bequeathed to them by [their] God. Religion and culture have often intermixed with colonial influence and the Cold War with deadly effect.

Since 1948 and again in 1967 millions of Palestinians have been driven from their homes and live in squalor in refugee camps throughout the Arab World. In Palestine and Israel, violence continues to drown any hopes of a negotiable peace deal to bring stability, security and a just peace to the region. Suicide attacks carried out by armed groups against Israeli military and civilian targets and the killing of thousands of Palestinians by the Israeli military in the past decade have embittered both sides and created nearly unwavering distrust. However, the roots of the conflict pre-date the UN mandate that led to the creation of Israel in 1948.

- 1915-1916: Husayn-McMahon correspondence.
  Exchange of letters between [Sharīf Ḥusayn ibn Alī], ruler of Mecca and the Hejaz, and Sir Henry McMahon, the British high commissioner in Egypt, regarding the future political status of the Arab lands of the Middle East, with Britain aiming to bring about an armed revolt against Ottoman rule. [sharifs were nobles; Sharif is an address of respect; Hejaz is in western Saudi Arabia along Red Sea coast of Arabian Peninsula; Mecca is in the same

area of western Saudi Arabia in the Ṣirāt Mountains inland from the Red Sea coast]

- Second letter October 24, 1915, McMahon writes: "'The districts of Mersin and Alexandretta, and portions of Syria lying to the west of the districts of Damascus, Homs, Hama and Aleppo, cannot be said to be purely Arab, and must on that account be excepted from the proposed delimitation. Subject to that modification, and without prejudice to the treaties concluded between us and certain Arab chiefs, we accept that delimitation. As for the regions lying within the proposed frontiers, in which Great Britain is free to act without detriment to interests of her ally France, I am authorized to give you the following pledges on behalf of the Government of Great Britain, and to reply as follows to your note: That subject to the modifications stated above, Great Britain is prepared to *recognize and uphold the independence of the Arabs* in all the regions lying within the frontiers proposed by the Sharif [nobleman] of Mecca.'"

- May 16, 1916: Sykes-Picot Agreement.
  Britain and France sign a secret pact outlining their spheres of control in the Middle East after the First World War. Palestine is designated for international administration pending consultations with Russia and other powers. The agreement is *seen by Arabs as a betrayal* of the Husayn-McMahon correspondence.

- November 2, 1917: Balfour Declaration.
  Arthur James Balfour, Britain's foreign secretary, sends a letter to Lord Rothschild, president of the Zionist federation, stating the government's support for the establishment of 'a national home for the Jewish people' in Palestine, the area consisting of today's Israel, the West Bank, Gaza Strip and Jordan. The declaration reads: 'His Majesty's Government view with favor the establishment in Palestine of a national home for the Jewish people, and will use their best endeavors to facilitate the achievement of this object, it being clearly understood that nothing shall be done which may prejudice the civil and religious rights of existing non-Jewish communities in Palestine, or the rights and political status enjoyed by Jews in any other country.'

- 1918: In the aftermath of the war, the sons of Husayn were made the kings of Transjordan (later Jordan), Syria and Iraq.

- July 24, 1922: The League of Nations gives Britain a mandate to administer Palestine. Britain expresses an interest in Zionism, and describes its intention to develop a Jewish state.
- 1929-1939: In large part because of the rise of fascism in Europe, about 250,000 Jews arrive in Palestine during this period.
- 1929: Arguments between Muslims and Jews over access to the Western Wall
  More than 130 Jews killed and 339 wounded (mainly by Arabs), 116 Arabs killed and 232 wounded (mainly by British-led personnel).
- August 23: Arab rioters kill 67 Jews in Hebron.
- 1930-35: Violent activities of Black Hand Islamist group led by Sheikh 'Izz al-Dīn al-Qassām against Jewish civilians and the British
- 1936-39: Arab revolt to protest against Jewish immigration to Palestine led by Haj Amin al-Husseini [al-Hajj Amīn (or Hajj Amīn) Husayni]. More than 5,000 Arabs are killed, mostly by the British. Several hundred Jews are killed by Arabs.
- July 22, 1946: Bombing of the King David Hotel in Jerusalem, which housed the British civil, military and police command in Palestine, by members of Irgun, a Zionist organization. Ninety-one people are killed, 28 British, 41 Arab, 17 Jewish and five from other countries. [Irgun Zvai Leumi is a Jewish right-wing underground movement in Palestine founded in 1931.]
- November 29, 1947: United Nations General Assembly passes a partition plan dividing the British Mandate of Palestine into two states. Accepted by the Jewish leadership; rejected by the Arab leadership.
- 1947-1949: The *Nakba* . . . (in Arabic)
  Up to 900,000 Palestinians flee their land or are expelled from their homes in that part of the land that becomes the state of Israel. [Wikipedia on *Nakba*: "During the 1948 Palestine War, an estimated 700,000 Palestinians were expelled or fled, and hundreds of Palestinian villages were depopulated and destroyed. The vast majority of Palestinian refugees, both those outside the 1949 armistice lines at the war's conclusion and those internally displaced, were barred by the newly declared state of Israel from returning to their homes or reclaiming their property . . . . That

displacement, dispossession and dispersal of the Palestinian people Palestinians term al-*Nakba* meaning 'the catastrophe,' or 'the disaster.'"]

- April 9/11, 1948: Deir Yassin massacre.
  Between 100 and 254 Palestinian villagers (mainly women, old people and children) are killed during and after an Irgun attack on the village of Deir Yassin near Jerusalem.
- May 15: Declaration of Israel as the Jewish state
  British withdraw from Palestine • Arab-Israeli war
  Egypt, Syria, Jordan, Saudi Arabia, Iraq and Lebanon declare war on Israel. Egypt, Jordan and Syria invade Israel.
- April 1949: Israel and Arab states agree to an armistice. Israel has taken about 50 percent more land than was originally allotted to it by the UN partition plan.
- 1956: Egypt nationalizes Suez Canal (July 26).
  France, Britain and Israel plan invasion of Egypt.
  Israel invades the Sinai Peninsula (October 29).
  Pressure from the United States and USSR force France, Britain and Israel to withdraw.
- May 1964: The Arab League establishes the Palestine Liberation Organization (PLO) in Cairo. The PLO states its goal as the destruction of the Israel through armed struggle, and the restoration of an 'independent Palestinian state' between the Jordan River and the Mediterranean Sea. Large numbers of Jews fleeing rising fascism in Europe migrated to Palestine.
- June 1967: Six-Day War
  Israel launches a preemptive attack on Egypt, Syria and Jordan. Israel captures Sinai Peninsula and Gaza Strip from Egypt, the Golan Heights from Syria, and the West Bank and East Jerusalem from Jordan. In this year, Israel begins settlement program in areas captured during the Six-Day War.
- 1968-1970: War of Attrition
  Limited war fought between Egypt and Israel in which Egypt attempts to regain the Sinai Peninsula lost in the Six-Day War. The war ends with a ceasefire in August 1970 with the same frontiers as at the start.
- February 2, 1969: Yasser Arafat is appointed PLO Chairman [Arafat led the Palestine Liberation Organization for 25 years].

[Yasir Arafat (byname of Muḥammad ʿAbd al-Raʾūf al-Qudwah al-Ḥusaynī , also known as Abū ʿAmmār)]

- 1972 September 5: Eleven members of the Israeli Olympic team and one German police officer are killed by Palestinian group Black September at the Munich Olympics.
- October 6, 1973: Yom Kippur war (October war)
  In a surprise attack on the Jewish Day of Atonement, Egypt and Syria retake the areas in Sinai and the Golan Heights that were lost in the Six-Day War. Despite initial gains, they are soon forced by Israeli forces to retreat.
- September 17, 1978: Israeli Prime Minister Menachem Begin and Egyptian President Anwar Sadat sign the 'Camp David Accord,' with Israel agreeing to withdraw from the Sinai Peninsula in exchange for peace and a framework for future negotiation over the West Bank and Gaza Strip.
- March 26, 1979: Peace deal between Egypt and Israel
  Egypt becomes the first Arab country to recognize Israel.
  Later in this year, following Egypt's peace agreement with Israel, the Arab League suspends Egypt's membership in the league and the organization moves its headquarters to Tunis [Tunisia's capital and largest city, situated on the northern African coast between the western and eastern basins of the Mediterranean Sea]
- October 6, 1981: Members of the Egyptian Islamic Jihad organization, in retaliation for his recognizing Israel, assassinate Anwar Sadat as he reviews a military parade.
- June 6, 1982: Israel invades Lebanon to remove PLO fighters who it says are threatening its border. In Israel's the six-month invasion of Lebanon, it also drives out the PLO. The PLO relocates to Tunis. Remains active in Lebanon but not to the same extent as before 1982.
- September 1982: Sabra and Shatila massacre.
  Lebanese Phalangists (members of a Christian paramilitary group) kill up to 2,750 Palestinians in the Palestinian refugee camps of Sabra and Shatila.
- August 1983: The Israeli army withdraws from most of Lebanon, maintaining a self-proclaimed 'security zone' in the south.

- September 25, 1985: Three Israelis are killed on their yacht off the coast of Larnaca, Cyprus, by Force 17, a commando group from Fatah, the largest organization in the PLO.
- October 1: Israel's 'Operation Wooden Leg' attempts to kill Arafat with an air raid on his headquarters in Tunis. He survives but 60 PLO members, including much of the leadership, are killed
- December 8, 1987: First *intifada* (uprising, 'shaking') starts. Palestinians begin general strikes, riots and civil disobedience campaigns across the West Bank and Gaza Strip. Israeli army replies with tear gas, plastic bullets, and live rounds. Sheikh Ahmed Yassin creates Hamas from the Gaza wing of the Egyptian Muslim Brotherhood.
- November 15, 1988: From its base in Tunis (Tunisia) the PLO unilaterally proclaims a State of Palestine.
- October 1991: Middle East peace conference opens in Madrid.
- September 13, 1993: Oslo declaration of principles
  PLO and Israel agree to recognize each other.
- February 25, 1994: American-Israeli settler Baruch Goldstein enters the Cave of the Patriarchs, a religious site in Hebron, and kills 29 Palestinians, injuring another 125.
- October 26: Israel and Jordan sign a peace treaty ending 45-years of hostility.
  Israel agrees to recognize the special role of Jordan over Muslim holy sites in Jerusalem.
- November 4, 1995: Israeli orthodox Jewish student, Yigal Amir, who is against the Middle East peace plan, assassinates Israeli Prime Minister Yitzhak Rabin. Shimon Peres assumes the office of prime minister.
- July 2000: The Camp David summit between Israeli Prime Minister Ehud Barak and Palestinian Authority Chairman Yasir Arafat aimed at reaching a 'final status' agreement ends after Arafat refuses to accept a proposal drafted by United States and Israeli negotiators.
- September: After Ariel Sharon of Israel's Likud Party visits the Temple Mount in Jerusalem, Palestinians riot. Second *intifada* begins.
- February 6, 2001: Sharon is elected the leader of Likud and refuses to continue negotiations with Arafat.

- June 1: A Hamas suicide bomber attacks a nightclub. Twenty-one Israelis are killed (mainly teenagers), more than 100 injured).
- October 17: Members of the Popular Front for the Liberation of Palestine shoot dead Israeli Tourism Minister Rehavam Zeevi in Jerusalem
- December: Sharon sends troops into Ramallah who shell and surround the Palestinian government's West Bank headquarters. Arafat is unable to leave.
- March 2002: Israeli army launches its largest military offensive ('Operation Defensive Shield') in the West Bank since the 1967 Six-Day War. Also in 2002, Israel begins construction of separation barrier (wall) between the West Bank and Israel and with the size of this construction annexes large areas of Palestinian land.
- March 27/28: Beirut, Lebanon, summit of heads of Arab nations to discuss plans to resolve the Palestinian-Israeli conflict. Israel refuses to guarantee his return to the West Bank, so Yasir Arafat is unable to attend the conference.

  Arab leaders collectively offer Israel peace, recognition and normal relations in return for Israel's withdrawal from Arab lands captured since 1967, the restoration of a Palestinian state with east Jerusalem as its capital, and a 'fair solution' for the 3.8 million Palestinian refugees.
- March 22, 2004: Israeli helicopter gunship assassinates Hamas founder Shaykh Aḥmad Yāsīn
- April 17: Israeli army kills Hamas co-founder and successor to Yasin, Abd al-Aziz al-Rantissi.
- July 9: International Court of Justice rules that the Israeli separation barrier (wall) violates international law and must be removed.
- November 11: Palestinian leader Yasir Arafat dies.
- January 9, 2005: Palestinian leader Mahmoud Abbas is elected president of the Palestinian National Authority.
- January 10: Sharon creates government of unity with Labor and United Torah Judaism parties. [A chief participant in the Arab-Israeli wars, Israeli military general and politician, Israeli prime minister (2001 until disabled by a stroke in 2006), Ariel Sharon (Arik Sharon) was born February 26, 1928 in Kefar Malal, Palestine (now in Israel) Britannica note].

- August: Completion of Israel's unilateral disengagement plan from Gaza and four West Bank settlements
- January 25, 2006: Hamas wins a majority of seats in the Palestinian legislative election. The United States, Israel and several European countries cut off their aid to the Palestinians as the party rejects Israel's right to exist.
- June 25: Palestinians cross the border from the Gaza Strip and capture Corporal Gilad Shalit, killing two Israeli soldiers and wounding four others.
- September: Violence erupts between Fatah and Hamas parties in the Gaza Strip. Abbas attempts to prevent civil war. Abbas's Fatah movement supports a Palestinian state alongside Israel; Hamas rejects Israel's right to exist.
- October 1: Eight people are killed in Gaza in factional infighting between Hamas and Fatah as a new wave of violence erupts.
- In October, a number of mediation conferences are held. Egypt and Qatar send their foreign ministers to meet with both sides. Other Palestinian groups such as the Islamic jihad and the Popular Front for the Liberation of Palestine mediate between the two sides to stop the clashes.
- November 13: Following talks between Hamas and Fatah, both sides agree to form a unity government unaligned with either movement. Gaza academic Muhammad Shbeir who is close to Hamas but not a party member accepts the offer to head the government.
- December 15: Hamas accuses Fatah of involvement in a gun attack on Palestinian Prime Minister Ismael Haniya as he crosses the border from Egypt into Gaza.
- December 16: Abbas calls for new elections as a solution to the ongoing crisis.
- January 21, 2007: Abbas meets Khaled Meshaal of Hamas in Damascus in response to an invitation by Syrian president Bashar Al-Assad
- January 30: Fatah and Hamas reach a ceasefire agreement mediated by Egypt after a series of clashes that leave 32 Palestinians dead. Both sides welcome a Saudi initiative to meet in Mecca.
- February 8: Hamas and Fatah agree on a deal in Mecca to end factional warfare that has killed scores of Palestinians and to

form a coalition, hoping this would lead Western powers to lift crippling sanctions imposed on the Hamas-led government.

- February 9: The Quartet welcomes the role of the Kingdom of Saudi Arabia in reaching the agreement to form a Palestinian National Unity government and later reaffirms requisite international demands to recognize Israel, renounce violence and abide by previous peace agreements.

  [The Quartet on the Middle East (sometimes called the Diplomatic Quartet or Madrid Quartet or simply the Quartet) is a foursome of nations and international and supranational entities involved in mediating the peace process in the Israeli-Palestinian conflict. Comprising Quartet are the United Nations, the United States, the European Union, and Russia (the Russian Federation). In light of escalating conflict in the Middle East, the Quartet formed in 2002 in Madrid, Spain. Wikipedia note]

- February 15: Ismail Haniya and his cabinet resign but he is re-appointed by President Abbas and begins the process of forming a new Palestinian unity government.
- March 15: Palestinians reach agreement on the formation of the government.
- March 17: The new Palestinian unity government holds its first cabinet meeting in Gaza City, with ministers in the West Bank participating from Ramallah via video link.
- Also in March: Israel refuses to talk to the coalition, saying it fails to meet international demands—renouncing violence, recognizing Israel and honoring past peace deals. In the first deadly clash between the two groups since the unity government was formed, Hamas-Fatah violence erupts in Gaza leaving one Fatah fighter dead and seven people wounded. Israeli Prime Minister Ehud Olmert labels his Palestinian counterpart and senior Hamas leader, Ismail Haniya, 'terrorist.'
- April: Israel plans Gaza invasion a day after Israeli Prime Minister Ehud Olmert calls for a regional peace conference with Arab states.
- Also in April: The United States gives military aid to Palestinian president Mahmoud Abbas, $60 million to boost the presidential guard, for other security expenses, for security expenses including improvements at Gaza's main commercial crossings with Israel, for logistics and communications equipment. Several U.S.

legislators had withheld funding against its reaching Hamas, which formed a unity government with Abbas's Fatah party after months of negotiation.

[Palestinian politician serving briefly as prime minister of the Palestinian Authority (2003) then elected Palestinian Authority president (2005) after the death of Yāsir ʿArafāt, Mahmoud Abbas (also known as Abu Mazen) was born (1935) in Zefat, Palestine (now in Israel). Britannica note]

- May: Israel presses ahead with air raids on Gaza, launching five attacks after dark. The strikes came after Prime Minister Ehud Olmert said Israel would continue its crackdown on Hamas following Qassam rocket attacks on [the small Negev town of] Sderot that killed one Israeli civilian and injured one.

- June: Hamas issues Gaza arms ultimatum and tightens its grip and control on the territory. President Mahmoud Abbas issues and swears in a new government, with Salam Fayyad, an economist, as head of the emergency government.

- June: Palestinian aid embargo lifted. The United States and the European Union resume aid to Palestine. Abbas announces it is time to resume peace talks with Israel.

- November: U.S. president George W. Bush hosts peace talks between Palestine and Israel at Annapolis, Maryland, while Hamas still holds control over Gaza.

January 2008: Israel steps up military actions on Gaza and Hamas, killing seven Palestinians. Olmert vows to hit back after Hamas rocket attacks in Israel. Israel continues powerful incursion on Gaza, leaving Palestinians in a humanitarian crisis without fuel, power, food and water. Palestinians blow up part of the border at Rafah going into Egypt. The border breach came several days after Israel had imposed a complete blockade on Gaza, with Egyptian backing, in response to a rocket barrage from Gaza on Israeli border towns. Hamas leader and one-time Prime Minister Ismail Haniya, meanwhile, said the group would not allow the border to be resealed. Egyptian President Hosni Mubarak had ordered the opening of the border crossing, allowing Palestinians trapped in Gaza to purchase important crucial necessities that were unavailable due to the Israeli blockade. Source: Al Jazeera and Agencies http://english.aljazeera.net/news/middleeast/2008/02/2008525185027407159.html http://english.aljazeera.net/focus/2010/01/201012855829544554.html

TIMELINE Afghanistan

Crisis and conflict major events in more than thirty years (update 2011)

- 1979: Then Soviet Union [Union of Soviet Socialist Republics] invades Afghanistan. In the years that follow, Moscow will rule Kabul by proxy while the United States, Pakistan, China, Iran and Saudi Arabia extend their support to anti-communist Muslim fighters, the *Mujahideen*, who oppose the Soviets.
- 1988-1989: The Soviet Union withdraws. More than 15,000 Soviet soldiers have died in the conflict.
- 1992: Led by Ahmed Shah Massoud, Mujahideen forces remove the Soviet-backed government, but in the years that follow rivalry between different groups of fighters reduce Kabul to rubble and effectively plunge Afghanistan into civil conflict.
- 1994: Muslim cleric Mullah Mohammed Omar sets up *Taliban* movement of Islamic students who take up arms to end the chaos in Afghanistan. They capture Kandahar and advance on Kabul.
- 1996: The Taliban takes Kabul and hangs then—President Mohammad Najibullah. The year also sees the return to Afghanistan of Osama bin Laden, al-Qaeda's leader who fought with [U.S.-allied] *Mujahideen* groups against the Soviet occupation.
- 1998: The United States launches missiles at suspected bin Laden bases in the country in retaliation for the bombing of U.S. embassies in Kenya and Tanzania.
- 1999: The UN imposes an air embargo and freezes Taliban assets in an attempt to force them to hand over bin Laden for trial. In depth reporting:
  McChrystal hopes for Taliban deal
  Taliban moderates taken off UN list
  Western donors '*back Taliban* plan'
  Video: Taliban groups continue to grow
  Taliban issues code of conduct
  Video: Taliban targets Afghan government
  Deadliest year for Afghan civilians
  Empire: The long war between the U.S. and al-Qaeda

- 2001: Taliban rule in Afghanistan based on their strict interpretation of *Sharia* (Islamic law) has become increasingly narrow: restricting women and religious minorities, banning satellite TV and destroying 2,000-year-old Buddhist statues in the cliffs above Bamiyan [central Afghanistan northwest of Kabul].

- September: Taliban rival Ahmed Shah Massoud, a senior commander of the *Northern Alliance* dies after suffering injuries in a suicide attack. Attacks on the United States on September 11, 2001, leads U.S. President George W. Bush to demand that the Taliban hand over bin Laden. They refuse pending U.S. show of evidence of bin Laden's involvement.

- In October, U.S. and British forces begin bombing Afghanistan and within weeks mount an invasion of the country. Later Afghan tribal leader Hamid Karzai will be chosen to head an interim administration.

- 2002: The first contingent of international peacekeeping forces takes up its duties. Months later Afghan Vice President Haji Abdul Qadir is assassinated in Kabul and Karzai escapes a separate assassination attempt in his hometown of Kandahar.

- 2003: Despite frequent incidents of violence, U.S. Defense Secretary Donald Rumsfeld claims that most of Afghanistan is secure and that U.S.-led forces had moved from major combat operations to stabilization and reconstruction projects. The year also sees NATO (the North Atlantic Treaty Organization)—in its first security operation outside of Europe—take control of security in Kabul.

- 2004: Afghanistan adopts a new constitution and Hamid Karzai is elected president; meanwhile, the Taliban begins regrouping and mounts sustained attacks.

- 2005: Afghanistan holds its first parliamentary elections in more than 30 years. Intensity of Taliban attacks continues to grow.

- 2006: Western forces and their Afghan allies mount 'Operation Mountain Thrust' against Taliban fighters. Scores of people die in the fighting. Later in the year, NATO takes over responsibility for security across the country. Civilian casualties are mounting and, when a U.S. military vehicle crashes and kills several civilians, widespread anti-U.S. protests erupt.

- 2007: NATO and Afghan forces launch 'Operation Achilles,' reported as their largest offensive to date. In May, the Taliban's chief military commander, Mullah Dadullah, is killed. The United Nations reports Afghanistan's opium production, much of which is thought to fund the Taliban, has reached record levels.
- 2008: A Taliban operation frees hundreds of its fighters from Kandahar prison. Weeks later a suicide attack on the Indian embassy in Kabul ramps up regional tensions as India accuses the Pakistani intelligence agency of involvement. Pakistan denies the allegations. Toward the end of the year, U.S. President George W. Bush sends 4,500 additional U.S. troops to Afghanistan. Germany boosts its troop numbers and extends its mission in the country.
- 2009: Afghans go to the polls to elect a new president and while the Taliban largely fails to act on its threats to attack voters, the election is beset by massive fraud. Karzai wins a runoff vote after his main rival, Abdullah Abdullah, withdraws. Afghanistan's 2009 presidential election was marred by allegations of fraud [Reuters]. T he presidential election of Barack Obama in the United States had prompted hopes of a new approach to Afghanistan but Taliban attacks made the year the bloodiest to that point for international troops. In December, U.S. Barack Obama agrees to a request from U.S. generals to boost U.S. troop levels in Afghanistan. The United States supplies 30,000 troops bringing the total number of U.S. troops in the country to 100,000; the president also announces that the United States will begin withdrawing U.S. forces by 2011.
- 2010: While Afghanistan President Karzai struggles to get his cabinet nominees approved by parliament, Taliban fighters carry out coordinated attacks in the country's capital and largest city, Kabul. Delegates gather in London for a conference on future strategy in Afghanistan including consideration of a proposal to negotiate with Taliban supporters and persuade them to lay down their arms in return for money and jobs.
- In February, U.S.-led NATO troops launch 'Operation Mushtarak' on the biggest Taliban-held town in the south of the country. [U.S. troops expected to begin withdrawing from Afghanistan in 2011 (GALLO/GETTY)] Source: Al Jazeera: http://english. aljazeera.net/focus/2010/01/201012855829544554.html http://

english.aljazeera.net/news/americas/2010/11/20101128201120
507943.html

Diplomatic Cables Release
November 28, 2010
Diplomatic files describe hazy geopolitical events; add color to military
interaction around the world.

Whistleblower website WikiLeaks on Sunday November 27, 2010, made public U.S. cables detailing a wide array of potentially explosive diplomatic episodes: from a tense nuclear standoff with Pakistan to North Korean missile sales to Iran.

The cables describe bargaining over the repatriation of Guantanamo Bay detainees, a Chinese government bid to hack into Google, and Saudi Arabia king urging Washington to 'cut off the head of the snake': appeals to the United States to strike Iran to halt its nuclear program. They detail plans to reunite the Korean peninsula after the North's eventual collapse. They also air suspicions about Saudi donors financing al-Qaeda and the U.S. failure to prevent Syria from providing a massive stockpile of weapons to the Lebanese Hezbollah militia since 2006. Most of the 251,287 cables—many of which are marked 'classified', none 'top secret—date back to 2007. The release also includes cables dated as far back as 1966. [New York Times reporting]

Highlights of WikiLeaks' leaked documents

Yemen covering up U.S. air strikes: Yemeni President Ali Abdullah Saleh admits covering up U.S. military strikes on al-Qaeda in Yemen, claiming Yemeni forces carried out the strikes. Cable content: 'We'll continue saying the bombs are ours, not yours,' Saleh says in January talks with then-commander of U.S. forces in the Middle East, General David Petraeus. Yemen's deputy prime minister tells his nation's Parliament, erroneously, that Yemeni forces had staged the strikes against al-Qaeda in the Arabian Peninsula, the Yemeni arm of al-Qaeda. U.S. Defense Secretary Robert Gates on November 16 said providing equipment and training to Yemeni security forces offered the best way to counter the threat posed by al-Qaeda.

Chinese cyber attacks: U.S. government officials believe Chinese authorities orchestrated a hacking campaign into computers of Google and Western governments. Cable content: U.S. embassy in Beijing cites 'a Chinese contact' saying 'Google hacking was part of a coordinated campaign of computer sabotage carried out by Chinese government operatives, private security experts and Internet outlaws recruited by the Chinese government'

North Korean aid to Iran

United States intelligence believes Iran has obtained advanced missiles from North Korea capable of striking Europe. Cable content: 'Secret American intelligence assessments have concluded that Iran has obtained a cache of advanced missiles, based on an improved version of Russia's R-27 . . . . Iran not only obtained the BM-25 but also saw the advanced technology as a way to learn how to design and build a new class of more powerful engines.' At the request of the Obama government, the New York Times said the paper had agreed not to publish the text of this cable. Source: Agencies and http://english.aljazeera.net/news/americas/2010/11/20101128201120507943.html

U.S. Wars and International Bodies

First post—Cold War crisis: Persian Gulf War

- ○ First post-Cold War crisis-Persian Gulf-1990
- ○ U.S. war on Afghanistan 2001-
- ○ U.S. war on Iraq 2003-
- ○ Geneva Conventions without U.S. compliance
- ○ International Criminal Court (ICC) without United States
- ○ North Atlantic Treaty Organization (NATO) and Member States
- ○ United Nations Security Council (five permanent-member dominance)
- ○ United Nations General Assembly and Member States
- ○ UNESCO Member States
- ○ United Nations High Commissioner for Refugees (UNHCR)

First post-Cold War crisis-Persian Gulf-1990

In the 1980s, U.S. policy had favored Iraq in its war against Iran and permitted the continued export of strategic materials to Saddam Hussein despite repeated indications of his fanaticism and ambition.

For nearly two years after the United Nations—brokered ceasefire in the Persian Gulf, the governments of Iraq and Iran failed to initiate conversations toward a permanent peace treaty but in July 1990 foreign ministers of the two states met in Geneva concerning the prospects for peace. Iraq's Saddam Hussein seemed willing to liquidate his decade-long conflict with Iran and give back the remaining land occupied at such cost by his armies. Two weeks later Hussein's motives became clearer. In an address that 'stunned the Arab world,' he accused neighboring Kuwait of siphoning off crude oil from the Ar-Rumaylah oil fields straddling their border. He also accused Persian Gulf states of conspiring to hold down oil prices, thereby damaging the interests of war-torn Iraq and catering to the wishes of the Western powers. Iraq's foreign minister insisted that Kuwait, Saudi Arabia, and the gulf emirates make partial compensation for these alleged 'crimes' by cancelling $30,000,000,000 of Iraq's foreign debt. Meanwhile, 100,000 of Iraq's best troops concentrated on the Kuwaiti border.

1990-991

- November 29, 1990: the United Nations Security Council authorized the use of force against Iraq if it did not withdraw from Kuwait by January 15, 1991.
- By January 1991: the allied coalition against Iraq had reached 700,000 troops including 540,000 U.S. personnel and smaller numbers of British, French, Egyptians, Saudis, Syrians, and several other national contingents.
- Saddam Hussein refused to withdraw Iraqi forces from Kuwait, which he maintained would remain a province of Iraq.
- January 16-17, 1991: the Persian Gulf War (also called 'Operation Desert Storm') began with a massive U.S.-led air offensive against Iraq that continued throughout the war. A sustained aerial bombardment destroyed Iraq's air defenses before attacking its

communications networks, government buildings, weapons plants, oil refineries, and bridges and roads.
- By mid February: the foreign troops had shifted their air attacks to Iraq's forward ground forces in Kuwait and southern Iraq, destroying their fortifications and tanks.

Source and notes: Edward C. Luck, Professor of Practice in International and Public Affairs and Director of the Center on International Organization at the School of International and Public Affairs at New York City's Columbia University and author of *Mixed Messages: American Politics and International Organization, 1919-1999* (1999). **Persian Gulf War.** (2011). Encyclopedia Britannica. *Encyclopedia Britannica Deluxe Edition.* Chicago: Encyclopedia Britannica.

U.S. war on Afghanistan 2001-2001 continuing through 2011 into 2012

In what the U.S. government labeled 'Operation Enduring Freedom', United States Armed Forces on October 7, 2001, invaded the sovereign country of Afghanistan. Joining U.S. forces in the invasion were the British Armed Forces and the Afghan United Front (or *Northern Alliance*) purportedly to dismantle Al-Qaeda and allied Taliban Islamic Emirate of Afghanistan, the U.S.-identified perpetrators of September 11, 2001, attacks on the New York City-based World Trade Center. The United Nations Security Council [*permanent* members China, France, Russian Federation, the United Kingdom and the United States] at the end of December 2001 established the International Security Assistance Force (ISAF) purportedly "to secure Kabul [the Afghanistan capital] and the surrounding areas." The North Atlantic Treaty Organization (NATO) assumed control of ISAF (troops from some 42 countries) in 2003; together with core forces from NATO member states, they have executed a endless war on Afghanistan from 2001 forward.

Sources and Notes Afghanistan, Iraq

Iraq Coalition Troops
For an updated listing as of late 2008, see "The Coalition of the willing: Numbers and News," http://www.globalsecurity.org/military/ops/iraq_orbat_coalition.htm

GlobalSecurity.org is neither affiliated nor connected with the private security/military company known as Global or Global Security, or variants thereof. GlobalSecurity.org does NOT provide security services and does NOT have their contact information.

Wikipedia Coalition Iraq: http://en.wikipedia.org/wiki/Multi-National_Force_%E2%80%93_Iraq

BBC News Online in Washington by Steve Schifferes [Source: U.S. State Department], March 18, 2003, http://news.bbc.co.uk/2/hi/americas/2862343.stm

Story from BBC NEWS: http://news.bbc.co.uk/go/pr/fr/-/2/hi/americas/2862343.stm

Published: 2003/03/18 21:38:10 GMT—© BBC 2011

Afghanistan: http://en.wikipedia.org/wiki/International_Security_Assistance_Force http://en.wikipedia.org/wiki/International_Security_Assistance_Force#NATO_nations

U.S. war on Iraq (and earlier) 2003-
Iraq war 2003 forward (also called Second Persian Gulf War)

Though public opinion in Europe and the Middle East overwhelmingly opposed this war—many in the Middle East saw it as a new brand of anti-Arab and anti-Islamic imperialism, most Arab leaders objected to foreign troops' occupation of a fellow Arab country—U. S. military forces combined mainly with British forces, invaded Iraq in 2003. In the years between the initial invasion and 2011, the United States and its agents destroyed vital institutions, displaced and killed thousands of people. The United States continued an unwanted occupation of this country through 2011 into 2012.

At the time of the November 2004 United States presidential election, U.S. troop deaths, according to some estimates, had increased to a thousand.

- By early 2007, three thousand and war coalition countries had lost several hundred soldiers.
- The number of Iraqi deaths was "uncertain."
- A late 2006 estimate only of the period between 2003 and October 2006 "put the total deaths at more than 650,000."
- Other estimates for this period put the figures at "40,000 to 50,000."

Sources and notes Afghanistan, Iraq
Iraq Coalition Troops
For an updated listing as of late 2008, see The Coalition of the willing: Numbers and News http://www.globalsecurity.org/military/ops/iraq_orbat_coalition.htm
Wikipedia   Coalition   Iraq,   http://en.wikipedia.org/wiki/Multi-National_Force_%E2%80%93_Iraq

Geneva Conventions without U.S. compliance

Convention for the Protection of Civilian Persons in Time of War Convention (IV); The conference developed four conventions approved in Geneva, August 12, 1949:

(1) Convention for the Amelioration of the Condition of the Wounded and Sick in Armed Forces in the Field
(2) Convention for the Amelioration of the Condition of the Wounded, Sick, and Shipwrecked Members of Armed Forces at Sea
(3) Convention Relative to the Treatment of Prisoners of War
(4) Convention Relative to the Protection of Civilian Persons in Time of War

More than 180 states have become parties to the 1949 conventions. Approximately 150 states are party to Protocol I. More than 145 states are party to Protocol II—though the United States is not. In addition, more than 50 states have made declarations accepting the competence of international fact-finding commissions to investigate allegations of grave breaches or other serious violations of the conventions or of Protocol I.

Protocol I supplementary to the Geneva Conventions of August 12, 1949

Proclaims to the High Contracting Parties' earnest wish to see peace prevail among peoples

- Recalling that every State has the duty, in conformity with the Charter of the United Nations, to refrain in its international relations from the threat or use of force against the sovereignty, territorial integrity or political independence of any State, or in any other manner inconsistent with the purposes of the United Nations
- Believing it necessary, nevertheless, to reaffirm and develop the provisions protecting the victims of armed conflicts and to supplement measures intended to reinforce their application
- Expressing their conviction that nothing in this Protocol or in the Geneva Conventions of 12 August 1949 can be construed as legitimizing or authorizing any act of aggression or any other use of force inconsistent with the Charter of the United Nations
- Reaffirming further that the provisions of the Geneva Conventions of 12 August 1949 and of this Protocol must be fully applied in all circumstances to all persons who are protected by those instruments, without any adverse distinction based on the nature or origin of the armed conflict or on the causes espoused by or attributed to the Parties to the conflict . . . *High Contracting Parties undertake to respect and to ensure respect for this Protocol in all circumstances.*
- In cases not covered by this Protocol or by other international agreements, civilians and combatants remain under the protection and authority of the principles of international law derived from established custom, from the principles of humanity and from dictates of public conscience.
- This Protocol, which supplements the Geneva Conventions of August 12, 1949 for the protection of war victims, shall apply in the situations referred to in Article 2 common to those Conventions.

This Convention IV establishes an international provision for the Protection of Civilian Persons in Time of War. Signing plenipotentiaries [persons, especially diplomatic agents invested with full power to transact business] of the Governments represented at the Diplomatic Conference held at Geneva, Switzerland, April 21 to August 12, 1949, agreed [excerpt] . . .

The High Contracting Parties undertake to respect and to ensure respect for the present Convention in all circumstances . . . .

Article 2: In addition to the provisions which shall be implemented in peace-time, the present Convention shall apply to all cases of declared war or of any other armed conflict which may arise between two or more of the High Contracting Parties, even if the state of war is not recognized by one of them.

The Convention shall also apply to all cases of partial or total occupation of the territory of a High Contracting Party, even if the said occupation meets with no armed resistance.

Although one of the Powers in conflict may not be a party to the present Convention, the Powers who are parties thereto shall remain bound by it in their mutual relations. They shall, furthermore, be bound by the Convention in relation to the said Power, if the latter accepts and applies the provisions thereof.

Article 3: In the case of armed conflict not of an international character occurring in the territory of one of the High Contracting Parties, each Party to the conflict shall be bound to apply, as a minimum, the following provisions:

(1) Persons taking no active part in the hostilities, including members of armed forces who have laid down their arms and those placed hors de combat [out of combat: disabled] by sickness, wounds, detention, or any other cause, shall in all circumstances be treated humanely, without any adverse distinction founded on race, color, religion or faith, sex, birth or wealth, or any other similar criteria

To this end the following acts are and shall remain prohibited at any time and in any place whatsoever with respect to the above-mentioned persons:

(2) The wounded and sick shall be collected and cared for. (a) Violence to life and person, in particular murder of all kinds, mutilation, cruel treatment and torture; (b) Taking of hostages; (c) Outrages upon personal dignity, in particular humiliating and degrading treatment; (d) The passing of sentences and the carrying out of executions without previous judgment pronounced by a regularly constituted court, affording all the judicial guarantees which are recognized as indispensable by civilized peoples.

An impartial humanitarian body, such as the International Committee of the Red Cross, may offer its services to the Parties to the conflict. • The Parties to the conflict should further endeavor to bring into force, by means of special agreements, all or part of the other provisions of the present Convention. • The application of the preceding provisions shall not affect the legal status of the Parties to the conflict.

Protocol II [excerpt]

Article 3 Non-intervention

(1) Nothing in this Protocol shall be invoked for the purpose of affecting the sovereignty of a State or the responsibility of the government, by all legitimate means, to maintain or re-establish law and order in the State or to defend the national unity and territorial integrity of the State.

(2) Nothing in this Protocol shall be invoked as a justification for intervening, directly or indirectly, for any reason whatever, in the armed conflict or in the internal or external affairs of the High Contracting Party in the territory of which that conflict occurs.

Article 13 Protection of the civilian population

(1) The civilian population and individual civilians shall enjoy general protection against the dangers arising from military operations. To give effect to this protection, the following rules shall be observed in all circumstances.

(2) The civilian population as such, as well as individual civilians, shall not be the object of attack. Acts or threats of violence the primary

purpose of which is to spread terror among the civilian population are prohibited.

(3) Civilians shall enjoy the protection afforded by this Part, unless and for such time as they take a direct part in hostilities.

Article 17 Prohibition of forced movement of civilians

(1) The displacement of the civilian population shall not be ordered for reasons related to the conflict unless the security of the civilians involved or imperative military reasons so demand. Should such displacements have to be carried out, all possible measures shall be taken in order that the civilian population may be received under satisfactory conditions of shelter, hygiene, health, safety and nutrition.

(2) Civilians shall not be compelled to leave their own territory for reasons connected with the conflict.

Geneva Conventions are a series of international treaties concluded in Geneva between 1864 and 1949 for the purpose of ameliorating the effects of war on soldiers and civilians. Two additional protocols to the 1949 agreement were approved in 1977.

Origins 1800s

The development of the Geneva Conventions was closely associated with the Red Cross, whose founder, Henri Dunant, initiated international negotiations that produced the Convention for the Amelioration of the Wounded in Time of War in 1864 . . . .

The 1864 convention was ratified within three years by all the major European powers as well as by many other states. It was amended and extended by the second Geneva Convention in 1906 and its provisions were applied to maritime warfare through the Hague conventions of 1899 and 1907. The third Geneva Convention, the Convention Relating to the Treatment of Prisoners of War (1929), required that belligerents treat prisoners of war humanely, furnish information about them, and permit official visits to prison camps by representatives of neutral states.

Because some belligerents in World War II had abused the principles contained in earlier conventions, an International Red Cross conference in Stockholm in 1948 extended and codified the existing provisions.

Sources and notes

Final Act of the Diplomatic Conference of Geneva, August 12, 1949, Conference convened by the Swiss Federal Council—

- for the purpose of revising the Geneva Convention of July 27, 1929
- for the Relief of the Wounded and Sick in Armies in the Field
- the tenth Hague Convention of October 18,1907, for the Adaptation to Maritime Warfare of the Principles of the Geneva Convention of July 6, 1906
- the Geneva Convention of July 27, 1929, relative to the Treatment of Prisoners of War
- for establishing a Convention for the Protection of Civilian Persons in Time of War

On the basis of the four Draft Conventions examined and approved by the 17th international Red Cross Conference held at Stockholm, deliberated from April 21 to August 12, 1949, at Geneva, the Conference established the texts of the following Four Conventions:

- Geneva Convention for the Amelioration of the Condition of the Wounded and Sick in Armed Forces in the Field •
- Geneva Convention for the Amelioration of the Condition of Wounded, Sick and Shipwrecked Members of Armed Forces at Sea •
- Geneva Convention relative to the Treatment of Prisoners of War •
- Geneva Convention relative to the Protection of Civilian Persons in Time of War Protocol Additional to the Geneva Conventions of August 12, 1949, and relating to the Protection of Victims of Non-International Armed Conflicts (Protocol II), June 8, 1977, http://www.icrc.org/ihl.nsf/WebART/475-760002?OpenDocumentProtocol
- Protocol Additional to the Geneva Conventions of August 12, 1949, and relating to the Protection of Victims of International

Armed Conflicts (Protocol I), June 8, 1977 http://www.
icrc.org/ihl.nsf/7c4d08d9b287a42141256739003e636b/
f6c8b9fee14a77fdc125641e0052b079

Geneva Conventions without U.S. compliance Why Geneva Conventions
Restrain State aggression, "The importance of the Geneva Conventions
and their additional protocols was reflected in the establishment of
war-crimes tribunals for Yugoslavia (1993) and Rwanda (1994) and
by the Rome Statute (1998) creating an International Criminal Court,"
compiled and edited by Carolyn Bennett, October 24, 2010

Convention signers

State Parties to
Geneva Conventions
of August 12, 1949
State Parties
Signature Ratification
/ Accession 1)
Reservation /
Declaration 2)
Unedited
(style of date:
day-month-year)

Afghanistan
08.12.1949
26.09.1956
Albania 12.12.1949
27.05.1957
27.05.1957 (text)
Algeria 20.06.1960
Andorra 17.09.1993
Angola 20.09.1984
20.09.1984 (text)
Antigua and Barbuda
06.10.1986
Argentina 08.12.1949
18.09.1956

Armenia 07.06.1993
Australia 04.01.1950.
14.10.1958
14.10.1958 (text)
Austria 12.08.1949
27.08.1953
Azerbaijan
01.06.1993
Bahamas 11.07.1975
Bahrain 30.11.1971
Bangladesh
04.04.1972
20.12.1988 (text)
Barbados 10.09.1968
10.09.1968 (text)
Belarus 12.12.1949
03.08.1954
Belgium 08.12.1949
03.09.1952
Belize 29.06.1984
Benin 14.12.1961
Bhutan 10.01.1991
Bolivia 08.12.1949
10.12.1976
Bosnia-Herzegovina
31.12.1992

Botswana 29.03.1968
Brazil 08.12.1949
29.06.1957
Brunei Darussalam
14.10.1991
Bulgaria 28.12.1949
22.07.1954
Burkina Faso
07.11.1961
Burundi 27.12.1971
Cambodia 08.12.1958
Cameroon
16.09.1963
Canada 08.12.1949
14.05.1965
Cape Verde
11.05.1984
Central African
Republic 01.08.1966
Chad 05.08.1970
Chile 12.08.1949
12.10.1950
China 10.12.1949
28.12.1956
28.12.1956 (text)

Colombia 12.08.1949
08.11.1961
Comoros 21.11.1985
Congo (Dem. Rep.)
24.02.1961
Congo 04.02.1967
Cook Islands
07.05.2002
Costa Rica
15.10.1969
Côte d'Ivoire
28.12.1961
Croatia 11.05.1992
Cuba 12.08.1949
15.04.1954
Cyprus 23.05.1962
Czech Republic
05.02.1993
Denmark 12.08.1949
27.06.1951
Djibouti 06.03.1978
Dominican Republic
22.01.1958
Dominica 28.09.1981
Ecuador   12.08.1949
11.08.1954
Egypt   08.12.1949
10.11.1952
El Salvador
08.12.1949
17.06.1953
Equatorial Guinea
24.07.1986
Eritrea 14.08.2000
Estonia 18.01.1993
Ethiopia 08.12.1949
02.10.1969
Fiji 09.08.1971

Finland 08.12.1949
22.02.1955
Former Yugoslav
Republic of
Macedonia
01.09.1993
18.10.1996. (text)
France 08.12.1949
28.06.1951
Gabon 26.02.1965
Gambia 20.10.1966
Georgia 14.09.1993
Germany 03.09.1954
03.12.1954. (text)
Ghana 02.08.1958
Greece 22.12.1949
05.06.1956
Grenada 13.04.1981
Guatemala
12.08.1949
14.05.1952
Guinea-Bissau
21.02.1974
21.02.1974. (text)
Guinea 11.07.1984
Guyana 22.07.1968
Haiti 11.04.1957
Holy See 08.12.1949
22.02.1951
Honduras 31.12.1965
Hungary 08.12.1949
03.08.1954
Iceland 10.08.1965
India 16.12.1949
09.11.1950
Indonesia 30.09.1958
Iran (Islamic Rep.
of) 08.12.1949

20.02.1957
20.02.1957 (text)
Iraq 14.02.1956
Ireland 19.12.1949
27.09.1962
Israel 08.12.1949
06.07.1951
08.12.1949 (text)
Italy 08.12.1949
17.12.1951
Jamaica 20.07.1964
Japan 21.04.1953
Jordan 29.05.1951
Kazakhstan
05.05.1992
Kenya 20.09.1966
Kiribati 05.01.1989
Korea (Dem.People's
Rep.) 27.08.1957
27.08.1957. (text)
Korea (Republic
of) 16.08.1966
16.08.1966. (text)
Kuwait 02.09.1967
02.09.1967. (text)
Kyrgyzstan
18.09.1992
Lao People's Dem.
Rep. 29.10.1956
Latvia 24.12.1991
Lebanon 08.12.1949
10.04.1951
Lesotho 20.05.1968
Liberia 29.03.1954
Libyan Arab
Jamahiriya
22.05.1956

Liechtenstein
12.08.1949
21.09.1950
Lithuania 03.10.1996
Luxembourg
08.12.1949
01.07.1953
Madagascar
18.07.1963
Malawi 05.01.1968
Malaysia 24.08.1962
Maldives 18.06.1991
Mali 24.05.1965
Malta 22.08.1968
Marshall Islands
01.06.2004
Mauritania
30.10.1962
Mauritius 18.08.1970
Mexico 08.12.1949
29.10.1952
Micronesia
19.09.1995
Moldova (Republic
of) 24.05.1993
Monaco 12.08.1949
05.07.1950
Mongolia 20.12.1958
Montenegro
(Republic of)
02.08.2006
Morocco 26.07.1956
Mozambique
14.03.1983
Myanmar 25.08.1992
Namibia 22.08.1991
Nauru 27.06.2006
Nepal 07.02.1964

Netherlands
08.12.1949
03.08.1954
New Zealand
11.02.1950.
02.05.1959
Nicaragua 12.08.1949
17.12.1953
Nigeria 20.06.1961
Niger 21.04.1964
Norway 12.08.1949
03.08.1951
Oman 31.01.1974
Pakistan 12.08.1949
12.06.1951
12.06.1951. (text)
Palau 25.06.1996
Panama 10.02.1956
Papua New Guinea
26.05.1976
Paraguay 10.12.1949
23.10.1961
Peru 12.08.1949
15.02.1956
Philippines
08.12.1949
06.10.1952
Poland 08.12.1949
26.11.1954
Portugal 11.02.1950.
14.03.1961
14.03.1961. (text)
Qatar 15.10.1975
Romania 10.02.1950.
01.06.1954
Russian Federation
12.12.1949
10.05.1954
12.12.1949 (text)

Rwanda 05.05.1964
Saint Kitts and Nevis
14.02.1986
Saint Lucia
18.09.1981
Saint Vincent
Grenadines
01.04.1981
Samoa 23.08.1984
San Marino
29.08.1953
Sao Tome and
Principe 21.05.1976
Saudi Arabia
18.05.1963
Senegal 18.05.1963
Serbia (Republic of)
16.10.2001
Seychelles
08.11.1984
Sierra Leone
10.06.1965
Singapore 27.04.1973
Slovakia 02.04.1993
Slovenia 26.03.1992
Solomon Islands
06.07.1981
Somalia 12.07.1962
South Africa
31.03.1952
Spain 08.12.1949
04.08.1952
Sri Lanka 08.12.1949
28.02.1959
Sudan 23.09.1957
Suriname 13.10.1976
13.10.1976. (text)
Swaziland
28.06.1973

Sweden 08.12.1949
28.12.1953
Switzerland
12.08.1949
31.03.1950
Syrian Arab
Republic 12.08.1949
02.11.1953
Tajikistan 13.01.1993
Tanzania (United
Rep.of) 12.12.1962
Thailand 29.12.1954
Timor-Leste
08.05.2003
Togo 06.01.1962
Tonga 13.04.1978
Trinidad and Tobago
24.09.1963
Tunisia 04.05.1957
Turkey 12.08.1949
10.02.1954
Turkmenistan
10.04.1992
Tuvalu 19.02.1981
Uganda 18.05.1964
Ukraine 12.12.1949
03.08.1954
United Arab Emirates
10.05.1972
United Kingdom
08.12.1949
23.09.1957
23.09.1957. (text)
United States of
America 12.08.1949
02.08.1955
02.08.1955. (text)

Uruguay 12.08.1949
05.03.1969
05.03.1969. (text)
Uzbekistan
08.10.1993
Vanuatu 27.10.1982
Venezuela
10.02.1950.
13.02.1956
Viet Nam 28.06.1957
28.06.1957. (text)
Yemen 16.07.1970
25.05.1977. (text)
Zambia 19.10.1966
Zimbabwe
07.03.1983

Terms related to conventions

Ratification: A treaty is generally open for signature for a certain time following the conference that has adopted it. However, a signature is not binding on a State unless it has been endorsed by ratification. The time limits having elapsed, the Conventions and the Protocols are no longer open for signature. The States which have not signed them may at any time accede or, in the appropriate circumstances, succeed to them.

Accession: Instead of signing and then ratifying a treaty, a State may become party to it by the single act called accession.

Reservation / Declaration: Unilateral statement, however phrased or named, made by a State when ratifying, acceding or succeeding to a treaty, whereby it purports to exclude or to modify the legal effect of certain provisions of the treaty in their application to that State (provided that such reservations are not incompatible with the object and purpose of the treaty).

Palestine—June 21, 1989:
The Swiss Federal Department of Foreign Affairs received a letter from the Permanent Observer of Palestine to the United Nations Office at Geneva informing the Swiss Federal Council that:

> The Executive Committee of the Palestine Liberation Organization, entrusted with the functions of the Government of the State of Palestine by decision of the Palestine National Council, decided, on May 4,1989, to adhere to the Four Geneva Conventions of August 12, 1949 and the two Protocols additional thereto

> September 13, 1989, the Swiss Federal Council informed the States that it was not in a position to decide whether the letter constituted an instrument of accession, 'due to the uncertainty within the international community as to the existence or non-existence of a State of Palestine.'" Copyright © 2005 International Committee of the Red Cross, International Humanitarian Law—Treaties and Documents, http://www.

icrc.org/ihl.nsf/FULL/380?OpenDocument   http://www.icrc.
org/ihl.nsf/WebART/360-560001?OpenDocument
Also Britannica notes

"Why Geneva Conventions: To Restrain State aggression," compiled and edited by Carolyn Bennett Posted by Bennett's Study Sunday, October 24, 2010, Labels: abuse of power, Convention for the Protection of Civilian Persons in Time of War, Geneva Conventions, Human Rights, International Committee of the Red Cross, International Law, war and conflict

International Criminal Court (ICC) without United States

The International Criminal Court (ICC), governed by the Rome Statute, is the first permanent, treaty based, international criminal court established to help end impunity for the perpetrators of the most serious crimes of concern to the international community. The ICC is an independent international organization, and is *not* part of the United Nations system. Its seat is at The Hague in the Netherlands. States Parties are the primary funders of the Court's expenses but the Court also receives voluntary contributions from governments, international organizations, individuals, corporations and other entities. ICC-Ataglance_en.pdf

As of June 1, 2008, 108 countries were States Parties to the Rome Statute of the International Criminal Court. Thirty are African States, 14 are Asian States, 16 are from Eastern Europe, 23 are from Latin American and Caribbean States, and 25 are from Western European and other States.

Rome Statute of the International Criminal Court [excerpt]

Preamble
The States Parties to this Statute—

> Conscious that all peoples are united by common bonds, their cultures pieced together in a shared heritage, and concerned that this delicate mosaic may be shattered at any time,

Mindful that, during this century millions of children, women and men have been victims of unimaginable atrocities that deeply shock the conscience of humanity,

Recognizing that such grave crimes threaten the peace, security and well-being of the world,

Affirming that the most serious crimes of concern to the international community as a whole must not go unpunished and that their effective prosecution must be ensured by taking measures at the national level and by enhancing international cooperation,

Determined to put an end to impunity for the perpetrators of these crimes and thus to contribute to the prevention of such crimes,

Recalling that it is the duty of every State to exercise its criminal jurisdiction over those responsible for international crimes,

Reaffirming the Purposes and Principles of the Charter of the United Nations, and in particular that all States shall refrain from the threat or use of force against the territorial integrity or political independence of any State, or in any other manner inconsistent with the Purposes of the United Nations,

Emphasizing in this connection that nothing in this Statute shall be taken as authorizing any State Party to intervene in an armed conflict or in the internal affairs of any State,

Determined to these ends and for the sake of present and future generations, to establish an independent permanent International Criminal Court in relationship with the United Nations system, with jurisdiction over the most serious crimes of concern to the international community as a whole,

Emphasizing that the International Criminal Court established under this Statute shall be complementary to national criminal jurisdictions,

Resolved to guarantee lasting respect for and the enforcement of international justice,

Have agreed as follows:

PART 1 Establishment of the Court
Article 1
The Court

An International Criminal Court ('the Court') is hereby established. It shall be a permanent institution and shall have the power to exercise its jurisdiction over persons for the most serious crimes of international concern, as referred to in this Statute, and shall be complementary to national criminal jurisdictions. The provisions of this Statute shall govern the jurisdiction and functioning of the Court.

Article 2
Relationship of the Court with the United Nations

The Court shall be brought into relationship with the United Nations through an agreement to be approved by the Assembly of States Parties to this Statute and thereafter concluded by the President of the Court on its behalf.

Article 3
Seat of the Court

1. The seat of the Court shall be established at The Hague in the Netherlands ('the host State').
2. The Court shall enter into a headquarters agreement with the host State, to be approved by the Assembly of States Parties and thereafter concluded by the President of the Court on its behalf.

3. The Court may sit elsewhere, whenever it considers it desirable, as provided in this Statute.

Article 4
Legal status and powers of the Court

1. The Court shall have international legal personality. It shall also have such legal capacity as may be necessary for the exercise of its functions and the fulfillment of its purposes.
2. The Court may exercise its functions and powers, as provided in this Statute, on the territory of any State Party and, by special agreement, on the territory of any other State.

Article 128
Authentic texts

The original of this Statute, of which the Arabic, Chinese, English, French, Russian and

Spanish texts are equally authentic, shall be deposited with the Secretary-General of the United Nations, who shall send certified copies thereof to all States.

IN WITNESS WHEREOF, the undersigned, being duly authorized thereto by their respective Governments, have signed this Statute.

DONE at Rome, this 17th day of July 1998.

Sources and notes

Rome Statute of the International Criminal Court (Text of the Rome Statute circulated as document A/CONF.183/9 of 17 July 1998 and corrected by procès-verbaux of November 10, 1998, July 12, 1999, November 30, 1999, May 8, 2000, January 17, 2001, and January 16, 2002. The Statute entered into force on July1, 2002). Produced by the

Public Information and Documentation Section Of the ICC Maanweg 174, 2516 AB The Hague, The Netherlands Tel.: +31 70 515 85 15 Fax: +31 70 515 85 55, http://www.icc-cpi.int

As of June 1, 2008, 108 countries were States Parties to the Rome Statute of the International Criminal Court. Thirty are African States, 14 are Asian States, 16 are from Eastern Europe, 23 are from Latin American and Caribbean States, and 25 are from Western European and other States.

States Parties

A

Afghanistan (Asian States)
Albania
Andorra
Antigua and Barbuda
Argentina
Australia
Austria

B

Barbados
Belgium
Belize
Benin
Bolivia
Bosnia and Herzegovina
Botswana
Brazil
Bulgaria
Burkina Faso
Burundi

C

Cambodia (Asian Sates)
Canada
Central African Republic
Chad
Colombia
Comoros
Congo
Cook Islands
Costa Rica
Croatia
Cyprus

D

Democratic Republic of the Congo
Denmark
Djibouti
Dominica
Dominican Republic

E

Ecuador
Estonia

F

Fiji
Finland
France

G

Gabon
Gambia
Georgia
Germany
Ghana
Greece
Guinea
Guyana

H

Honduras
Hungary

I

Iceland
Ireland
Italy

J

Japan
Jordan

K

Kenya

L

Latvia
Lesotho
Liberia
Liechtenstein
Lithuania
Luxembourg

M

Madagascar (African States)
Malawi
Mali
Malta
Marshall Islands
Mauritius
Mexico
Mongolia
Montenegro

N

Namibia
Nauru

Netherlands
New Zealand
Niger
Nigeria
Norway

P

Panama
Paraguay
Peru
Poland
Portugal

R

Republic of Korea
Romania

S

Saint Kitts and Nevis
Saint Vincent and the Grenadines
Samoa
San Marino
Senegal
Serbia
Sierra Leone
Slovakia
Slovenia
South Africa
Spain
Surinam

Sweden
Switzerland

T

Tajikistan
The Former Yugoslav Republic of Macedonia
Timor-Leste
Trinidad and Tobago

U

Uganda
United Kingdom
United Republic of Tanzania
Uruguay

V

Venezuela

Z

Zambia

North Atlantic Treaty Organization (NATO) and Member States

Belgium, Bulgaria, Canada, Czech Republic, Denmark, Estonia, France, Germany, Greece, Hungary, Iceland, Italy, Latvia, Lithuania, Luxembourg, Netherlands, Norway, Poland, Portugal, Romania, Slovakia, Slovenia, Spain, Turkey, United Kingdom, United States of America

The North Atlantic Treaty Organization is a military alliance established by the North Atlantic Treaty (also called the Washington Treaty) of April 4, 1949, which, after World War II, sought to create a counterweight to Soviet armies stationed in central and Eastern Europe.

Its original members were Belgium, Canada, Denmark, France, Iceland, Italy, Luxembourg, The Netherlands, Norway, Portugal, the United Kingdom, and the United States. Joining the original signatories were Greece and Turkey (1952); West Germany (1955; from 1990 as Germany); Spain (1982); the Czech Republic, Hungary, and Poland (1999); Bulgaria, Estonia, Latvia, Lithuania, Romania, Slovakia, and Slovenia (2004); and Albania and Croatia (2009). France withdrew from the integrated military command of NATO in 1966 but remained a member of the organization; and in 2009, French President Nicolas Sarkozy announced that the country would resume its position in NATO's military command.

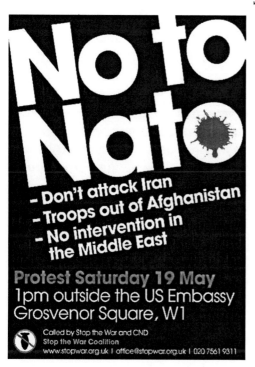

Stop the War Coalition UK 2012 protest

NATO post-Cold War

The end of the Cold War brought a revamping of the North Atlantic Treaty Organization's military structure, strategy and membership while seeking to define its new role in a changed Europe.

A summit in April 1999, a couple of years before the War on Afghanistan, in Washington, D.C., to celebrate NATO's 50th anniversary (founded April 4, 1949) reportedly resembled "a council of war because of the ongoing conflict in the Balkans and NATO's extraordinary involvement in it."

Strategic Concept

The summit set a new basic agenda, the NATO Strategic Concept, to guide a transformed alliance into the 21st century next century. The NATO leaders endorsed a plan to deepen military cooperation with partnership nations and to give them a larger political voice in the oversight and planning of future operations.

NATO's efforts to build a convincing and positive partnership with Russia had failed. Russian President Boris Yeltsin boycotted the Washington summit to underline Russia's unhappiness with the NATO bombing campaign against Serbia. Despite a high-sounding 'Founding Act' between NATO and Russia and the joint consultative council it created, the Russians knew they were helpless to influence NATO behavior.

NATO's new Strategic Concept represented a significant expansion of the alliance's mission. NATO retained the traditional security task of collective self-defense, its original raison d'être, but advanced its role in crisis management throughout the 'Euro Atlantic' area. It described ethnic conflict and human rights abuses as two of the threats to the stability of this region and reaffirmed NATO's readiness to intervene militarily to counter them—as it had done in Kosovo and in Bosnia and Herzegovina.

In NATO jargon, both of the Balkan operations were 'out of area'—that is, not on NATO soil. As NATO sought to define its role in this new era, many had argued that the alliance had to get 'out of area or out of business.' Some went so far as to project a global role for NATO, suggesting involvement in such crisis spots as Rwanda or Algeria. The

Washington summit's communiqué, however, made it clear that for the time being the alliance's efforts would be restricted to the Euro Atlantic area.

War without international mandate

The bombing campaign against Serbia was a watershed event for NATO. It had brushed aside traditional regard for national sovereignty [as later in Afghanistan, Iraq, Pakistan, Libya, Somalia] by, in effect, declaring war on Serbia for actions it was taking against its own citizens within its own borders.

NATO went to war for 'humanitarian and moral' rather than security reasons. Because both Russia and China had threatened to veto any enabling resolution, NATO acted against Serbia *without a mandate from the United Nations Security Council*. This troubled many people. Writing in NATO's own magazine, former West German chancellor Helmut Schmidt warned that neither the U.S. government nor any other member of the alliance should think that the Kosovo intervention, conducted without specific UN authorization, set a precedent [but it did].

Yugoslavia

The NATO bombing campaign in Yugoslavia once again highlighted the imbalance between the United States and European pillars of the alliance. While many nations participated in the effort, U.S. aircraft flew the bulk of the strike sorties.

The U.S. had a clear and growing lead over Europe in such important military capabilities as stealth technology, precision-guided munitions, airlift, electronic warfare, and intelligence.

The NATO leaders who gathered in Washington pledged anew to strengthen the European pillar, but similar past declarations had had few practical consequences. The decision of the European Union to implement a common foreign-and-security policy and the choice of NATO Secretary-general Javier Solana to supervise the effort suggested that the Europeans were determined to right the balance.

"If George Kennan is proved correct and NATO undermines European security by alienating Russia," Douglas L. Clarke concludes his article on NATO, "the cause may turn out to have been . . . the latest expansion of NATO's mission."

> The respected historian and former U.S. diplomat George F. Kennan called 'NATO's expansion a *fateful error*, [arguing] 'that European security in the long run depended on a stable, democratic, and friendly Russia and . . . that NATO's eastward expansion would turn Russia onto another course.'

Sources and notes

David G. Haglund is Director, Center for International Relations, Queen's University, Kingston, Ontario, Canada; and author of Alliance Within the Alliance?: Franco-German Military Cooperation and the European Pillar of Defense, Pondering NATO's Nuclear Options: Gambits for a Post-Westphalian World, The North Atlantic Triangle Revisited: Canadian Grand Strategy at Century's End, and others.

Douglas L. Clarke is a retired captain in the U.S. Navy, a military analyst and author of *The Missing Man: Politics and the MIA*. In: North Atlantic Treaty Organization (NATO). (2011). Encyclopedia Britannica. Encyclopedia Britannica Deluxe Edition. Chicago: Encyclopedia Britannica.

United Nations Security Council (Five Permanent-member Dominance)

There are 193 member states of the United Nations General Assembly; on the UNSC 5 permanent, 10 non-permanent

United Nations Conference on International Organization (UNCIO) convened in San Francisco on April 25, 1945, and produced the final Charter of the United Nations. Attending the San Francisco conference were representatives of 50 countries from all geographic areas of the world:

9 from Europe, 21 from the Americas, 7 from the Middle East, 2 from East Asia, and 3 from Africa, as well as 1 each from the Ukrainian Soviet Socialist Republic and the Belorussian Soviet Socialist Republic (in addition to the Soviet Union itself) and 5 from British Commonwealth countries. Poland, not present at the conference, received permission to become an original member of the United Nations.

UN Security Council veto power (*among the permanent members*) was affirmed, though any member of the General Assembly was able to raise issues for discussion. Other political issues resolved by compromise were the role of the organization in the promotion of economic and social welfare; the status of colonial areas and the distribution of trusteeships; the status of regional and defense arrangements; and Great Power dominance versus the equality of states. The UN Charter was unanimously adopted and signed on June 26 and promulgated on October 24, 1945. [Britannica note]

UN Security Council Members 2012
Council's five *permanent* members:

1. People's Republic of China
2. France
3. Russian Federation
4. United Kingdom
5. United States

Council's ten *non-permanent* members (with year of term's end):

Azerbaijan (2013)	India (2012)	South Africa (2012)
Colombia (2012)	Morocco (2013)	Togo (2013)
Germany (2012)	Pakistan (2013)	
Guatemala (2013)	Portugal (2012)	

A wide view of the Security Council as Members unanimously adopt resolution 1969 (2011), extending the UN Integrated Mission in Timor-Leste (UNMIT) for one year, until 26 February 2012, UN Photo/JC McIlwaine|

Security Council

The United Nations Charter assigns to the Security Council primary responsibility for the maintenance of international peace and security. The Security Council originally consisted of 11 members—five permanent and six nonpermanent—elected by the General Assembly for two year terms. From the beginning, nonpermanent members of the Security Council were elected to give representation to certain regions or groups of states. As membership increased, however, this practice ran into difficulty. An amendment to the UN Charter in 1965 increased the council's membership to 15, including the original 5 permanent members plus 10 nonpermanent members. Among the permanent members, the People's Republic of China replaced the Republic of China (Taiwan) in 1971, and the Russian Federation succeeded the Soviet Union in 1991. After the unification of Germany, debate over the council's composition resurfaced arose, and Germany, India, and Japan each applied for permanent council seats.

The nonpermanent members are chosen to achieve equitable regional representation, five members coming from Africa or Asia, one from eastern Europe, two from Latin America, and two from western Europe or other areas. The General Assembly elects five of the 10 nonpermanent members each year for two-year terms; five retire each year. Each member in rotation for a period of one month holds the presidency.

Veto power

Each Security Council member is entitled to one vote. On all "procedural" matters—the definition of which is sometimes in dispute—decisions by the council are made by an affirmative vote of any nine of its members. Substantive matters, such as the investigation of a dispute or the application of sanctions, also require nine affirmative votes, including those of the five permanent members *holding veto power*. In practice, however, a permanent member may abstain without impairing the validity of the decision.

A vote on whether a matter is procedural or substantive is itself a substantive question. Because the Security Council is required to function continuously, each member is represented at all times at the United Nations headquarters in New York City.

During the Cold War, continual disagreement between the United States and the Soviet Union coupled with the veto power of the Security Council's permanent members made the Security Council an ineffective institution.

Since the late 1980s, however, the council's power and prestige have grown. Between 1987 and 2000, the UNSC authorized more peacekeeping operations than at any previous time. The use of the veto has declined dramatically, though disagreements among permanent members of the Security Council—most notably in 2003 over the use of military force against Iraq—have occasionally undermined the council's effectiveness.

To achieve consensus, comparatively informal meetings are held in private among the council's permanent members, a practice that has been criticized by nonpermanent members of the Security Council.

On the other hand, the charter granted the leaders of the victorious World War II coalition—the United States, the Soviet Union, the United Kingdom, China, and France—veto power over the Council's substantive decisions. This was seen as a way to both protect their individual interests and help perpetuate the wartime alliance, a key goal. These provisions were soon put to a severe test.

When the alliance gave way or yielded place to the Cold War just a few years after the UN's founding conference in San Francisco, Moscow began to cast veto after veto, and the Council was paralyzed for much of the next four decades. Critics, particularly from the U.S. Congress, questioned the utility of a Council that was so fundamentally divided.

Many called for the elimination of the veto, which did not happen for reasons concerning charter and structure. As large numbers of newly independent states from Africa and Asia joined the world body—the United States was the country that came to rely on its right to block Council actions.

U.S. outside law, convention

In the United Nations first quarter century, the United States on the Security Council did not exercise a single veto. However, after 1970, it exercised its veto power substantially more often than did any other of the four permanent members. Following the end of the Cold War, the United Nations Security Council rediscovered Chapter VII and "began to act more decisively to protect world security."

During the 1990s, the UNSC passed a record number of enforcement, peacekeeping, and nation-building measures among these was its authorization in 1991 of a U.S.-led military coalition to expel Iraqi forces that had invaded Kuwait; its damaging economic sanctions imposed on Baghdad, and its unusually intrusive inspections mandate of Iraq's weapons development. Because Iraqi President Saddam Hussein for more than a decade had responded with cooperation amid defiance, UNSC members in 1991 were divided as to how to proceed concerning Iraq. In 2002-2003, despite U.S. President George W. Bush's repeated contention that the credibility of the Council was at stake, the Council members refused to endorse the use of force against Iraq.

The United States had never accepted that it [the United States] could use force *only* with the Council's approval and the actions of other countries over the decades had made clear that they too reserved this prerogative. . . . The U.S.-UK's military intervention in Iraq in 2003 "without the explicit authorization of the Council represented what [UN Secretary-General Kofi] Annan called 'a fundamental challenge to the principles on which, however imperfectly, world peace and stability have rested for the last 58 years.'"

Sources and notes (references)

Edward C. Luck is Professor of Practice in International and Public Affairs and Director of the Center on International Organization at the School of International and Public Affairs at Columbia University, New York City, and author of Mixed Messages: American Politics and International Organization, 1919-1999 (1999).

Cecelia M. Lynch is Associate Professor of Political Science, University of California at Irvine and author of Beyond Appeasement: Interpreting Interwar Peace Movements in World Politics and others.

Karen Mingst is Professor of Political Science, University of Kentucky, Lexington, author of Essentials of International Relations, coauthor of The United Nations in the Post-Cold War Era.

Jacques Fomerand is Director, United Nations University, New York and coauthor of Higher Education in Western Europe and North America: A Selected and Annotated Bibliography. In United Nations (UN). (2011). Encyclopedia Britannica. Encyclopedia Britannica Deluxe Edition. Chicago: Encyclopedia Britannica.

UN General Assembly and Member States
The UN General Assembly is the main deliberative organ of the UN. Decisions on important questions, such as those on peace and security, admission of new members and budgetary matters, require a two-thirds majority. Decisions on other questions are by simple majority. http://www.un.org/en/ga/about/index.shtml

How does a country become a Member of the United Nations?

Membership in the Organization, in accordance with the Charter of the United Nations, "is open to all peace-loving States that accept the obligations contained in the United Nations Charter and, in the judgment of the Organization, are able to carry out these obligations". States are admitted to membership in the United Nations by decision of the General Assembly upon the recommendation of the Security Council.

How does a new State or Government obtain recognition by the United Nations?

The recognition of a new State or Government is an act that only other States and Governments may grant or withhold. It generally implies readiness to assume diplomatic relations. The United Nations is neither a State nor a Government, and therefore does not possess any authority to recognize either a State or a Government. As an organization of independent States, it may admit a new State to its membership or accept the credentials of the representatives of a new Government.

Membership in the Organization, in accordance with the Charter of the United Nations, 'is open to all peace-loving States which accept the obligations contained in the [United Nations Charter] and, in the judgment of the Organization, are able to carry out these obligations.' States are admitted to membership in the United Nations by decision of the General Assembly upon the recommendation of the Security Council. The procedure is briefly as follows:

The State submits an application to the Secretary-General and a letter formally stating that it accepts the obligations under the Charter.

The Security Council considers the application. Any recommendation for admission must receive the affirmative votes of 9 of the 15 members of the Council, provided that none of its five permanent members—China, France, the Russian Federation, the United Kingdom of Great Britain and Northern Ireland and the United States of America—have voted against the application.

If the Council recommends admission, the recommendation is presented to the General Assembly for consideration. A two-thirds majority vote is necessary in the Assembly for admission of a new State.

Membership becomes effective the date the resolution for admission is adopted. http://www.un.org/en/members/about.shtml

UNITED NATIONS (UN) Member States

Data: Member State, Date of Admission

A

Afghanistan 19-11-1946—

Albania 14-12-1955—

Algeria 08-10-1962—

Andorra 28-07-1993—

Angola 01-12-1976—

Antigua and Barbuda
11-11-1981—

Argentina 24-10-1945—

Armenia 02-03-1992—

Australia 01-11-1945—

Austria 14-12-1955—

Azerbaijan 02-03-1992—

B

Bahamas 18-09-1973—

Bahrain 21-09-1971—

Bangladesh 17-09-1974—

Barbados 09-12-1966—

Belarus* 24-10-1945—
*On 19 September 1991, the
Byelorussian Soviet Socialist
Republic informed the
United Nations that it had
changed its name to Belarus.

Belgium 27-12-1945—

Belize 25-09-1981—

Benin 20-09-1960—

Bhutan 21-09-1971—

Bolivia (Plurinational State of)
14-11-1945—

Bosnia and Herzegovina*
22-05-1992—
* The Socialist Federal Republic
of Yugoslavia was an original
Member of the United
Nations, the Charter having
been signed on its behalf on
26 June 1945 and ratified
19 October 1945, until its
dissolution following the
establishment and subsequent
admission as new Members
of Bosnia and Herzegovina,
the Republic of Croatia, the
Republic of Slovenia, The
former Yugoslav Republic of

Macedonia, and the Federal Republic of Yugoslavia.

The Republic of Croatia was admitted as a Member of the United Nations by General Assembly resolution A/RES/46/238 of 22 May 1992.

The Republic of Bosnia and Herzegovina was admitted as a Member of the United Nations by General Assembly resolution A/RES/46/237 of 22 May 1992.

The Republic of Slovenia was admitted as a Member of the United Nations by General Assembly resolution A/RES/46/236 of 22 May 1992.

By resolution A/RES/47/225 of 8 April 1993, the General Assembly decided to admit as a Member of the United Nations the State being provisionally referred to for all purposes within the United Nations as "The former Yugoslav Republic of Macedonia" pending settlement of the difference that had arisen over its name.

The Federal Republic of Yugoslavia was admitted as a Member of the United Nations by General Assembly resolution A/RES/55/12 of 1 November 2000.

On 4 February 2003, following the adoption and promulgation of the Constitutional Charter of Serbia and Montenegro by the Assembly of the Federal Republic of Yugoslavia, the official name of "Federal Republic of Yugoslavia" was changed to Serbia and Montenegro.

In a letter dated 3 June 2006, the President of the Republic of Serbia informed the Secretary-General that the membership of Serbia and Montenegro was being continued by the Republic of Serbia, following Montenegro's declaration of independence.

Montenegro held a 21 May 2006 referendum and declared itself independent from Serbia on 3 June.

On 28 June 2006 it was accepted as a United Nations Member State by General Assembly resolution A/RES/60/264.

Botswana 17-10-1966—

Brazil 24-10-1945—

Brunei Darussalam 21-09-1984—

Bulgaria 14-12-1955—

Burkina Faso 20-09-1960—

Burundi 18-09-1962—

C

Cambodia 14-12-1955—

Cameroon 20-09-1960—

Canada 09-11-1945—

Cape Verde 16-09-1975—

Central African Republic
20-09-1960—

Chad 20-09-1960—

Chile 24-10-1945—

China 24-10-1945—

Colombia 05-11-1945—

Comoros 12-11-1975—

Congo 20-09-1960—

Costa Rica 02-11-1945—

Côte D'Ivoire 20-09-1960—

Croatia* 22-05-1992—
*The Socialist Federal Republic
   of Yugoslavia was an original
   Member of the United
   Nations, the Charter having
   been signed on its behalf on
   26 June 1945 and ratified
   19 October 1945, until its
   dissolution following the
   establishment and subsequent
admission as new Members
of Bosnia and Herzegovina,
the Republic of Croatia, the
Republic of Slovenia, The
former Yugoslav Republic of
Macedonia, and the Federal
Republic of Yugoslavia.
The Republic of Bosnia and
   Herzegovina was admitted
   as a Member of the United
   Nations by General Assembly
   resolution A/RES/46/237 of
   22 May 1992.
The Republic of Croatia was
   admitted as a Member of the
   United Nations by General
   Assembly resolution A/
   RES/46/238 of 22 May 1992.
The Republic of Slovenia was
   admitted as a Member of the
   United Nations by General
   Assembly resolution A/
   RES/46/236 of 22 May 1992.
By resolution A/RES/47/225 of
   8 April 1993, the General
   Assembly decided to admit
   as a Member of the United
   Nations the State being
   provisionally referred to
   for all purposes within the
   United Nations as "The
   former Yugoslav Republic
   of Macedonia" pending
   settlement of the difference
   that had arisen over its name.
The Federal Republic of
   Yugoslavia was admitted
   as a Member of the United
   Nations by General Assembly

resolution A/RES/55/12 of 1 November 2000.

On 4 February 2003, following the adoption and promulgation of the Constitutional Charter of Serbia and Montenegro by the Assembly of the Federal Republic of Yugoslavia, the official name of "Federal Republic of Yugoslavia" was changed to Serbia and Montenegro.

In a letter dated 3 June 2006, the President of the Republic of Serbia informed the Secretary-General that the membership of Serbia and Montenegro was being continued by the Republic of Serbia, following Montenegro's declaration of independence.

Montenegro held a 21 May 2006 referendum and declared itself independent from Serbia on 3 June.

On 28 June 2006 it was accepted as a United Nations Member State by General Assembly resolution A/RES/60/264.

Cuba 24-10-1945—

Cyprus 20-09-1960—

Czech Republic* 19-01-1993—
* Czechoslovakia was an original Member of the United Nations from 24 October 1945.

In a letter dated 10 December 1992, its Permanent Representative informed the Secretary-General that the Czech and Slovak Federal Republic would cease to exist on 31 December 1992 and that the Czech Republic and the Slovak Republic, as successor States, would apply for membership in the United Nations.

Following the receipt of their application, the Security Council, on 8 January 1993, recommended to the General Assembly that the Czech Republic and the Slovak Republic be both admitted to United Nations membership. Both the Czech Republic and the Slovak Republic were thus admitted on 19 January of that year as Member States.

D

Democratic People's Republic of Korea 17-09-1991—

Democratic Republic of the Congo * 20-09-1960—
*Zaire joined the United Nations on 20 September 1960.
On 17 May 1997, its name was changed to the Democratic Republic of the Congo.

Denmark 24-10-1945—

Djibouti 20-09-1977—

Dominica 18-12-1978—

Dominican Republic
    24-10-1945—

E

Ecuador 21-12-1945—

Egypt* 24-10-1945—
*Egypt and Syria were original
    Members of the United
    Nations from 24 October 1945.
Following a plebiscite on
    21 February 1958, the
    United Arab Republic was
    established by a union
    of Egypt and Syria and
    continued as a single Member.
On 13 October 1961, Syria,
    having resumed its status as
    an independent State, resumed
    its separate membership in the
    United Nations.
On 2 September 1971, the United
    Arab Republic changed its
    name to the Arab
Republic of Egypt.

El Salvador 24-10-1945—

Equatorial Guinea 12-11-1968—

Eritrea 28-05-1993—

Estonia 17-09-1991—

Ethiopia 13-11-1945—

F

Fiji 13-10-1970—

Finland 14-12-1955—

France 24-10-1945—

G

Gabon 20-09-1960—

Gambia 21-09-1965—

Georgia 31-07-1992—

Germany* 18-09-1973—
*The Federal Republic of
    Germany and the German
    Democratic Republic were
    admitted to membership in
    the United Nations on 18
    September 1973.
Through the accession of the
    German Democratic Republic
    to the Federal
Republic of Germany, effective
    from 3 October 1990, the two
    German States united to form
    one sovereign State.

Ghana 08-03-1957—

Greece 25-10-1945—

Grenada 17-09-1974—

Guatemala 21-11-1945—

Guinea 12-12-1958—

Guinea Bissau 17-09-1974—

Guyana 20-09-1966—

H

Haiti 24-10-1945—

Honduras 17-12-1945—

Hungary 14-12-1955—

I

Iceland 19-11-1946—

India 30-10-1945—

Indonesia* 28-09-1950—
*By letter of 20 January 1965,
    Indonesia announced its
    decision to withdraw from
    the United Nations "at this
    stage and under the present
    circumstances".
By telegram of 19 September
    1966, it announced its
    decision "to resume full
    cooperation with the United
    Nations and to resume
    participation in its activities".
On 28 September 1966, the
    General Assembly took

note of this decision and
the President invited
representatives of Indonesia
to take seats in the
Assembly.

Iran (Islamic Republic of)
    24-10-1945—

Iraq 21-12-1945—

Ireland 14-12-1955—

Israel 11-05-1949—

Italy 14-12-1955—

J

Jamaica 18-09-1962—

Japan 18-12-1956—

Jordan 14-12-1955—

K

Kazakhstan 02-03-1992—

Kenya 16-12-1963—

Kiribati 14-09-1999—
At this time, Kiribati does not
    have a Permanent Mission
    at the United Nations
    Headquarters in New York.

Kuwait 14-05-1963—

Kyrgyzstan 02-03-1992—

L

Lao People's Democratic
    Republic 14-12-1955—

Latvia 17-09-1991—

Lebanon 24-10-1945—

Lesotho 17-10-1966—

Liberia 02-11-1945—

Libyan Arab Jamahiriya
    14-12-1955—

Liechtenstein 18-09-1990—

Lithuania 17-09-1991—

Luxembourg 24-10-1945—

M

Madagascar 20-09-1960—

Malawi 01-12-1964—

Malaysia* 17-09-1957—
*The Federation of Malaya joined
    the United Nations on 17
    September 1957.
On 16 September 1963, its name
    was changed to Malaysia,
    following the admission to the
    new federation of Singapore,

Sabah (North Borneo) and
    Sarawak.
Singapore became an independent
    State on 9 August 1965 and a
    Member of the
United Nations on 21 September
    1965.

Maldives 21-09-1965—

Mali 28-09-1960—

Malta 01-12-1964—

Marshall Islands 17-09-1991—

Mauritania 27-10-1961—

Mauritius 24-04-1968—

Mexico 07-11-1945—

Micronesia (Federated States of)
    17-09-1991—

Monaco 28-05-1993—

Mongolia 27-10-1961—

Montenegro* 28-06-2006—
*The Socialist Federal Republic
    of Yugoslavia was an original
    Member of the
United Nations, the Charter
    having been signed on its
    behalf on 26 June 1945 and
    ratified 19 October 1945, until
    its dissolution following the
    establishment and subsequent

admission as new Members of Bosnia and Herzegovina, the Republic of Croatia, the Republic of Slovenia, The former Yugoslav Republic of Macedonia, and the Federal Republic of Yugoslavia.

The Republic of Bosnia and Herzegovina was admitted as a Member of the United Nations by General Assembly resolution A/RES/46/237 of 22 May 1992.

The Republic of Croatia was admitted as a Member of the United Nations by General Assembly resolution A/RES/46/238 of 22 May 1992.

The Republic of Slovenia was admitted as a Member of the United Nations by General Assembly resolution A/RES/46/236 of 22 May 1992.

By resolution A/RES/47/225 of 8 April 1993, the General Assembly decided to admit as a Member of the United Nations the State being provisionally referred to for all purposes within the United Nations as "The former Yugoslav Republic of Macedonia" pending settlement of the difference that had arisen over its name.

The Federal Republic of Yugoslavia was admitted as a Member of the United Nations by General Assembly resolution A/RES/55/12 of 1 November 2000.

On 4 February 2003, following the adoption and promulgation of the Constitutional Charter of Serbia and Montenegro by the Assembly of the Federal Republic of Yugoslavia, the official name of "Federal Republic of Yugoslavia" was changed to Serbia and Montenegro.

In a letter dated 3 June 2006, the President of the Republic of Serbia informed the Secretary-General that the membership of Serbia and Montenegro was being continued by the Republic of Serbia, following Montenegro's declaration of independence.

Montenegro held a 21 May 2006 referendum and declared itself independent from Serbia on 3 June.

On 28 June 2006 it was accepted as a United Nations Member State by General Assembly resolution A/RES/60/264.

Morocco 12-11-1956—

Mozambique 16-09-1975—

Myanmar 19-04-1948—

N

Namibia 23-04-1990—

Nauru 14-09-1999—

Nepal 14-12-1955—

Netherlands 10-12-1945—

New Zealand 24-10-1945—

Nicaragua 24-10-1945—

Niger 20-09-1960—

Nigeria 07-10-1960—

Norway 27-11-1945—

O

Oman 07-10-1971—

P

Pakistan 30-09-1947—

Palau 15-12-1994—

Panama 13-11-1945—

Papua New Guinea
    10-10-1975—

Paraguay 24-10-1945—

Peru 31-10-1945—

Philippines 24-10-1945—

Poland 24-10-1945—

Portugal 14-12-1955—

Q

Qatar 21-09-1971—

R

Republic of Korea 17-09-1991—

Republic of Moldova
    02-03-1992—

Romania 14-12-1955—

Russian Federation*
    24-10-1945—
*The Union of Soviet Socialist
    Republics was an original
    Member of the United
    Nations from 24 October
    1945.
In a letter dated 24 December
    1991, Boris Yeltsin, the
    President of the Russian
    Federation, informed the
    Secretary-General that the
    membership of the Soviet
    Union in the Security
    Council and all other United
    Nations organs was being
    continued by the Russian
    Federation with the support
    of the 11 member countries

of the Commonwealth of Independent States.

Rwanda 18-09-1962—

S

Saint Kitts and Nevis 23-09-1983—

Saint Lucia 18-09-1979—

Saint Vincent and the Grenadines 16-09-1980—

Samoa 15-12-1976—

San Marino 02-03-1992—

Sao Tome and Principe 16-09-1975—

Saudi Arabia 24-10-1945—

Senegal 28-09-1960—

Serbia* 01-11-2000—
*The Socialist Federal Republic of Yugoslavia was an original Member of the United Nations, the Charter having been signed on its behalf on 26 June 1945 and ratified 19 October 1945, until its dissolution following the establishment and subsequent admission as new Members of Bosnia and Herzegovina, the Republic of Croatia, the Republic of Slovenia, The former Yugoslav Republic of Macedonia, and the Federal Republic of Yugoslavia.

The Republic of Bosnia and Herzegovina was admitted as a Member of the United Nations by General Assembly resolution A/RES/46/237 of 22 May 1992.

The Republic of Croatia was admitted as a Member of the United Nations by General Assembly resolution A/RES/46/238 of 22 May 1992.

The Republic of Slovenia was admitted as a Member of the United Nations by General Assembly resolution A/RES/46/236 of 22 May 1992.

By resolution A/RES/47/225 of 8 April 1993, the General Assembly decided to admit as a Member of the United Nations the State being provisionally referred to for all purposes within the United Nations as "The former Yugoslav Republic of Macedonia" pending settlement of the difference that had arisen over its name.

The Federal Republic of Yugoslavia was admitted as a Member of the United Nations by General Assembly resolution A/RES/55/12 of 1 November 2000.

On 4 February 2003, following the adoption and promulgation of the Constitutional Charter of Serbia and Montenegro by the Assembly of the Federal Republic of Yugoslavia, the official name of "Federal Republic of Yugoslavia" was changed to Serbia and Montenegro.
In a letter dated 3 June 2006, the President of the Republic of Serbia informed the Secretary-General that the membership of Serbia and Montenegro was being continued by the Republic of Serbia, following Montenegro's declaration of independence.

Seychelles 21-09-1976—

Sierra Leone 27-09-1961—

Singapore* 21-09-1965—
*The Federation of Malaya joined the United Nations on 17 September 1957.
On 16 September 1963, its name was changed to Malaysia, following the admission to the new federation of Singapore, Sabah (North Borneo) and Sarawak.
Singapore became an independent State on 9 August 1965 and a Member of the United Nations on 21 September 1965.

Slovakia* 19-01-1993—
*Czechoslovakia was an original Member of the United Nations from 24 October 1945.
In a letter dated 10 December 1992, its Permanent Representative informed the Secretary-General that the Czech and Slovak Federal Republic would cease to exist on 31 December 1992 and that the Czech Republic and the Slovak Republic, as successor States, would apply for membership in the United Nations.
Following the receipt of their application, the Security Council, on 8 January 1993, recommended to the General Assembly that the Czech Republic and the Slovak Republic be both admitted to United Nations membership. Both the Czech Republic and the Slovak Republic were thus admitted on 19 January of that year as Member States.

Slovenia* 22-05-1992—
*The Socialist Federal Republic of Yugoslavia was an original Member of the United Nations, the Charter having been signed on its behalf on 26 June 1945 and ratified

19 October 1945, until its dissolution following the establishment and subsequent admission as new Members of Bosnia and Herzegovina, the Republic of Croatia, the Republic of Slovenia, The former Yugoslav Republic of Macedonia, and the Federal Republic of Yugoslavia.

The Republic of Bosnia and Herzegovina was admitted as a Member of the United Nations by General Assembly resolution A/RES/46/237 of 22 May 1992.

The Republic of Croatia was admitted as a Member of the United Nations by General Assembly resolution A/RES/46/238 of 22 May 1992.

The Republic of Slovenia was admitted as a Member of the United Nations by General Assembly resolution A/RES/46/236 of 22 May 1992.

By resolution A/RES/47/225 of 8 April 1993, the General Assembly decided to admit as a Member of the United Nations the State being provisionally referred to for all purposes within the United Nations as "The former Yugoslav Republic of Macedonia" pending settlement of the difference that had arisen over its name.

The Federal Republic of Yugoslavia was admitted as a Member of the United Nations by General Assembly resolution A/RES/55/12 of 1 November 2000.

On 4 February 2003, following the adoption and promulgation of the Constitutional Charter of Serbia and Montenegro by the Assembly of the Federal Republic of Yugoslavia, the official name of "Federal Republic of Yugoslavia" was changed to Serbia and Montenegro.

In a letter dated 3 June 2006, the President of the Republic of Serbia informed the Secretary-General that the membership of Serbia and Montenegro was being continued by the Republic of Serbia, following Montenegro's declaration of independence.

Montenegro held a 21 May 2006 referendum and declared itself independent from Serbia on 3 June.

On 28 June 2006 it was accepted as a United Nations Member State by General Assembly resolution A/RES/60/264.

Solomon Islands 19-09-1978—

Somalia 20-09-1960—

South Africa 07-11-1945—

South ‎Sudan*
14-07-2011—
*The Republic of South Sudan
formally seceded from Sudan
on 9 July 2011 as a result of
an internationally monitored
referendum held in January
2011, and ‎was
admitted as a new Member
State ‎by the United
Nations General Assembly on
14 ‎July 2011.

Spain 14-12-1955—

Sri Lanka 14-12-1955—

Sudan 12-11-1956—

Suriname 04-12-1975—

Swaziland 24-09-1968—

Sweden 19-11-1946—

Switzerland 10-09-2002—

Syrian Arab Republic*
24-10-1945—
*Egypt and Syria were original
Members of the United
Nations from 24 October
1945.
Following a plebiscite on
21 February 1958, the
United Arab Republic was
established by a union

of Egypt and Syria and
continued as a single Member.
On 13 October 1961, Syria,
having resumed its status as
an independent State, resumed
its separate membership in the
United Nations.
On 2 September 1971, the United
Arab Republic changed its
name to the Arab Republic of
Egypt.

T

Tajikistan 02-03-1992—

Thailand 16-12-1946—

The former Yugoslav Republic of
Macedonia* 08-04-1993—
*The Socialist Federal Republic
of Yugoslavia was an original
Member of the United
Nations, the Charter having
been signed on its behalf on
26 June 1945 and ratified
19 October 1945, until its
dissolution following the
establishment and subsequent
admission as new Members
of Bosnia and Herzegovina,
the Republic of Croatia, the
Republic of Slovenia, The
former Yugoslav Republic of
Macedonia, and the Federal
Republic of Yugoslavia.
The Republic of Bosnia and
Herzegovina was admitted
as a Member of the United

Nations by General Assembly resolution A/RES/46/237 of 22 May 1992.

The Republic of Croatia was admitted as a Member of the United Nations by General Assembly resolution A/RES/46/238 of 22 May 1992.

The Republic of Slovenia was admitted as a Member of the United Nations by General Assembly resolution A/RES/46/236 of 22 May 1992.

By resolution A/RES/47/225 of 8 April 1993, the General Assembly decided to admit as a Member of the United Nations the State being provisionally referred to for all purposes within the United Nations as "The former Yugoslav Republic of Macedonia" pending settlement of the difference that had arisen over its name.

The Federal Republic of Yugoslavia was admitted as a Member of the United Nations by General Assembly resolution A/RES/55/12 of 1 November 2000.

On 4 February 2003, following the adoption and promulgation of the Constitutional Charter of Serbia and Montenegro by the Assembly of the Federal Republic of Yugoslavia, the official name of "Federal Republic of Yugoslavia" was changed to Serbia and Montenegro.

In a letter dated 3 June 2006, the President of the Republic of Serbia informed the Secretary-General that the membership of Serbia and Montenegro was being continued by the Republic of Serbia, following Montenegro's declaration of independence.

Montenegro held a 21 May 2006 referendum and declared itself independent from Serbia on 3 June.

On 28 June 2006 it was accepted as a United Nations Member State by General Assembly resolution A/RES/60/264.

Timor-Leste 27-09-2002—

Togo 20-09-1960—

Tonga 14-09-1999—

Trinidad and Tobago 18-09-1962—

Tunisia 12-11-1956—

Turkey 24-10-1945—

Turkmenistan 02-03-1992—

Tuvalu 05-09-2000—

U

Uganda 25-10-1962—

Ukraine 24-10-1945—

United Arab Emirates
    09-12-1971—

United Kingdom of Great
    Britain and Northern
    Ireland 24-10-1945 More
    information

United Republic of Tanzania*
    14-12-1961—
*Tanganyika was a Member of
    the United Nations from 14
    December 1961 and Zanzibar
    was a Member from 16
    December 1963.
Following the ratification on
    26 April 1964 of Articles of
    Union between Tanganyika
    and Zanzibar, the United
    Republic of Tanganyika
    and Zanzibar continued as a
    single Member, changing its
    name to the United Republic
    of Tanzania on 1 November
    1964.

United States of America
    24-10-1945—

Uruguay 18-12-1945—

Uzbekistan 02-03-1992—

V

Vanuatu 15-09-1981—

Venezuela (Bolivarian Republic
    of) 15-11-1945—

Viet Nam 20-09-1977—

Y

Yemen* 30-09-1947—
*Yemen was admitted to
    membership in the United
    Nations on 30 September
    1947 and Democratic Yemen
    on 14 December 1967.
On 22 May 1990, the two
    countries merged and have
    since been represented as
    one Member with the name
    "Yemen".

Z

Zambia 01-12-1964—

Zimbabwe 25-08-1980—

Source: Press Release ORG/1469
of 3 July 2006

A wide view of the Security Council as Members unanimously adopt resolution 1969 (2011), extending the UN Integrated Mission in Timor-Leste (UNMIT) for one year, until 26 February 2012, UN Photo/JC McIlwaine|

United Nations Educational, Scientific and Cultural Organization (UNESCO) and Member States

UNESCO has 193 Member States and 7 Associate Member States. It is governed by the General Conference and the Executive Board; the Secretariat, headed by the Director-General, implements the decisions of these two bodies.

The General Conference establishes the Organization's goals and priorities every two years and sets the budget. The Executive Board meets twice a year to follow program implementation.

UNESCO has its headquarters in Paris. It is housed in an outstanding, Modernist building inaugurated in 1958 and recently renovated. The Organization also has more than 50 field offices around the world.

The United States provides about 22 percent of UNESCO's budget.

UNESCOMemberStateshttp://www.unesco.org/new/en/member-states/countries/

List of the 194 Member States (and the 8 Associate Members) of UNESCO and the date on which they became members (or Associate Members) of the Organization, as of 27 October 2011

Member States

Flag	Country	Date (yyyy/mm/dd)
	Afghanistan	1948-5-4
	Albania	1958-10-16
	Algeria	1962-10-15
	Andorra	1993-10-20
	Angola	1977-3-11
	Antigua and Barbuda	1982-7-15
	Argentina	1948-9-15
	Armenia	1992-6-9
	Australia	1946-11-4
	Austria	1948-8-13
	Azerbaijan	1992-6-3
	Bahamas	1981-4-23
	Bahrain	1972-1-18
	Bangladesh	1972-10-27
	Barbados	1968-10-24
	Belarus	1954-5-12
	Belgium	1946-11-29
	Belize	1982-5-10
	Benin	1960-10-18
	Bhutan	1982-4-13
	Bolivia (Plurinational State of) (1)	1946-11-13
	Bosnia and Herzegovina	1993-6-2
	Botswana	1980-1-16
	Brazil	1946-11-4
	Brunei Darussalam	2005-3-17
	Bulgaria	1956-5-17

Flag	Country	Date (yyyy/mm/dd)
	Burkina Faso	1960-11-14
	Burundi	1962-11-16
	Cambodia	1951-7-3
	Cameroon	1960-11-11
	Canada	1946-11-4
	Cape Verde	1978-2-15
	Central African Republic	1960-11-11
	Chad	1960-12-19
	Chile	1953-7-7
	China	1946-11-4
	Colombia	1947-10-31
	Comoros	1977-3-22
	Congo	1960-10-24
	Cook Islands	1989-10-25
	Costa Rica	1950-5-19
	Côte d'Ivoire	1960-10-27
	Croatia	1992-6-1
	Cuba	1947-8-29
	Cyprus	1961-2-6
	Czech Republic	1993-2-22
	Democratic People's Republic of Korea	1974-10-18
	Democratic Republic of the Congo	1960-11-25
	Denmark	1946-11-4
	Djibouti	1989-8-31
	Dominica	1979-1-9
	Dominican Republic	1946-11-4
	Ecuador	1947-1-22

Flag	Country	Date (yyyy/mm/dd)
	Egypt	1946-11-4
	El Salvador	1948-4-28
	Equatorial Guinea	1979-11-29
	Eritrea	1993-9-2
	Estonia	1991-10-14
	Ethiopia	1955-7-1
	Fiji	1983-7-14
	Finland	1956-10-10
	France	1946-11-4
	Gabon	1960-11-16
	Gambia	1973-8-1
	Georgia	1992-10-7
	Germany	1951-7-11
	Ghana	1958-4-11
	Greece	1946-11-4
	Grenada	1975-2-17
	Guatemala	1950-1-2
	Guinea	1960-2-2
	Guinea-Bissau	1974-11-1
	Guyana	1967-3-21
	Haiti	1946-11-18
	Honduras	1947-12-16
	Hungary	1948-9-14
	Iceland	1964-6-8
	India	1946-11-4
	Indonesia	1950-5-27
	Iran, Islamic Republic of	1948-9-6

Flag	Country	Date (yyyy/mm/dd)
	Iraq	1948-10-21
	Ireland	1961-10-3
	Israel	1949-9-16
	Italy	1948-1-27
	Jamaica	1962-11-7
	Japan	1951-7-2
	Jordan	1950-6-14
	Kazakhstan	1992-5-22
	Kenya	1964-4-7
	Kiribati	1989-10-24
	Kuwait	1960-11-18
	Kyrgyzstan	1992-6-2
	Lao People's Democratic Republic	1951-7-9
	Latvia	1991-10-14
	Lebanon	1946-11-4
	Lesotho	1967-9-29
	Liberia	1947-3-6
	Libya (2)	1953-6-27
	Lithuania	1991-10-7
	Luxembourg	1947-10-27
	Madagascar	1960-11-10
	Malawi	1964-10-27
	Malaysia	1958-6-16
	Maldives	1980-7-18
	Mali	1960-11-7
	Malta	1965-2-10
	Marshall Islands	1995-6-30

Flag	Country	Date (yyyy/mm/dd)
	Mauritania	1962-1-10
	Mauritius	1968-10-25
	Mexico	1946-11-4
	Micronesia (Federated States of)	1999-10-19
	Monaco	1949-7-6
	Mongolia	1962-11-1
	Montenegro (3)	2007-3-1
	Morocco	1956-11-7
	Mozambique	1976-10-11
	Myanmar	1949-6-27
	Namibia	1978-11-2
	Nauru	1996-10-17
	Nepal (4)	1953-5-1
	Netherlands	1947-1-1
	New Zealand	1946-11-4
	Nicaragua	1952-2-22
	Niger	1960-11-10
	Nigeria	1960-11-14
	Niue	1993-10-26
	Norway	1946-11-4
	Oman	1972-2-10
	Pakistan	1949-9-14
	Palau	1999-9-20
	Panama	1950-1-10
	Papua New Guinea	1976-10-4
	Paraguay	1955-6-20
	Peru	1946-11-21

Flag	Country	Date (yyyy/mm/dd)
	Philippines	1946-11-21
	Poland	1946-11-6
	Portugal (5)	1974-9-11
	Qatar	1972-1-27
	Republic of Korea	1950-6-14
	Republic of Moldova	1992-5-27
	Romania	1956-7-27
	Russian Federation	1954-4-21
	Rwanda	1962-11-7
	Saint Kitts and Nevis	1983-10-26
	Saint Lucia	1980-3-6
	Saint Vincent and the Grenadines	1983-1-14
	Samoa	1981-4-3
	San Marino	1974-11-12
	Sao Tome and Principe	1980-1-22
	Saudi Arabia	1946-11-4
	Senegal	1960-11-10
	Serbia (6)	2000-12-20
	Seychelles	1976-10-18
	Sierra Leone	1962-3-28
	Singapore	2007-10-8
	Slovakia	1993-2-9
	Slovenia	1992-5-27
	Solomon Islands	1993-9-7
	Somalia	1960-11-15
	South Africa (7)	1994-12-12
	South Sudan	2011-10-27

Flag	Country	Date (yyyy/mm/dd)
	Spain	1953-1-30
	Sri Lanka	1949-11-14
	Sudan	1956-11-26
	Suriname	1976-7-16
	Swaziland	1978-1-25
	Sweden	1950-1-23
	Switzerland	1949-1-28
	Syrian Arab Republic	1946-11-16
	Tajikistan	1993-4-6
	Thailand	1949-1-1
	The former Yugoslav Republic of Macedonia	1993-6-28
	Timor-Leste	2003-6-5
	Togo	1960-11-17
	Tonga	1980-9-29
	Trinidad and Tobago	1962-11-2
	Tunisia	1956-11-8
	Turkey	1946-11-4
	Turkmenistan	1993-8-17
	Tuvalu	1991-10-21
	Uganda	1962-11-9
	Ukraine	1954-5-12
	United Arab Emirates	1972-4-20
	United Kingdom of Great Britain and Northern Ireland (8)	1997-7-1
	United Republic of Tanzania	1962-3-6
	United States of America (9)	2003-10-1
	Uruguay	1947-11-8
	Uzbekistan	1993-10-26

Flag	Country	Date (yyyy/mm/dd)
	Vanuatu	1994-2-10
	Venezuela (Bolivarian Republic of)	1946-11-25
	Viet Nam	1951-7-6
	Yemen	1962-4-2
	Zambia	1964-11-9
	Zimbabwe	1980-9-22

Associate Members

Flag	Country	Date (yyyy/mm/dd)
	Aruba	1987-10-20
	British Virgin Islands	1983-11-24
	Cayman Islands	1999-10-30
	Curaçao	2011-10-25
	Faroes	2009-10-12
	Macao, China	1995-10-25
	Sint Maarten	2011-10-25
	Tokelau	2001-10-15

Today's Insight News Monday, October 31, 2011: UNESCO's 194 "yes," U.S. "no" to Palestine

Today the UNESCO General Conference admitted Palestine as Member State. Palestine's entry brings the number of UNESCO's Member States to 195.

The vote garnered cheers in the UNESCO hall but since U.S. officials know better than the majority of nations in the world, they announced that the United States will punish the United Nations Educational, Scientific and Cultural Organization for its vote to admit Palestine as a member.

For its membership to take effect, Palestine must sign and ratify UNESCO's Constitution which is open for signature in the archives of the Government of the United Kingdom in London. The vote was carried by 107 votes in favor of admission and 14 votes against with 52 abstentions.

Admission to UNESCO for states that are not members of the United Nations requires a recommendation by the Organization's Executive Board and a two thirds majority vote in favor by the General Conference of Member States present and voting (abstentions are not considered as votes).

The General Conference consists of the representatives of the States Members of the Organization. It meets every two years and is attended by Member States and Associate Members together with observers for non-Member States, intergovernmental organizations and non-governmental organizations (NGOs). Each Member State has one vote, regardless to its size or the extent of its contribution to the budget.

The General Conference determines the policies and the main lines of work of the Organization. Its duty is to set the programs and the budget of UNESCO. It also elects the Members of the Executive Board and appoints, every four years, the Director-General.

UN General Secretary Ban Ki-moon urged member states not to cut UNESCO's funding.

European Union Foreign Policy Chief Catherine Ashton said in her call on states to maintain funding, "'This is about peace, identity, culture, heritage and freedom of expression'; therefore, "'The EU urges all parties to pause for reflection before taking precipitate actions.'"

Sources and notes

"UNESCO's General Conference today voted to admit Palestine as a Member State of the Organization" (© UNESCO/Dou Matar, c.f UNESCO Constitution, Article XV, on 'Entry into force'), October 31,

2011, http://www.unesco.org/new/en/media-services/single-view/news/general_conference_admits_palestine_as_unesco_member_state/

"U.S. pulls UNESCO funding after Palestine admitted as member—The United States has announced it will withhold funding for UNESCO after the UN's cultural body admitted Palestine as a member. The US sees UNESCO's decision as counterproductive to the Middle East peace process," http://www.dw-world.de/dw/article/0,,15500946,00.html

United Nations High Commissioner for Refugees (UNHCR)

Established on December 14, 1950, by the United Nations General Assembly, the Office of the United Nations High Commissioner for Refugees' mandate is to lead and coordinate international action to protect refugees and resolve refugee problems worldwide. Its primary purpose is to safeguard the rights and wellbeing of refugees. It strives to ensure that everyone can exercise the right to seek asylum and find safe refuge in another State, with the option to return home voluntarily, integrate locally or to resettle in a third country. It also has a mandate to help stateless people. In more than six decades, the agency has helped tens of millions of people restart their lives. Under its mandate, the UNHCR staff of some 7,685 people in more than 125 countries helps an estimated 33.9 million people. http://www.unhcr.org/pages/49c3646c2.html

Geopolitics and Waterways

- o   Arabian Sea
- o   Atlantic Ocean
- o   Bay of Bengal
- o   Gulf of Aden
- o   Gulf of Iskenderun-Turkey
- o   Indian Ocean
- o   Mediterranean Sea
- o   Persian Gulf
- o   Red Sea

Arabian Sea
Lies in the northwestern part of the Indian Ocean covering about
1,491,000 square miles
(3,862,000 square kilometers) and
Forming part of the principal sea route between Europe and India
Bounded to the west by the **Horn of Africa** and the Arabian Peninsula
To the west, the Gulf of Aden connects it with
Red Sea via the Bab el-Mandeb Strait
To the north by Iran and **Pakistan**
To the north, the Gulf of Oman connects
Arabian Sea with the Persian Gulf via the Strait of Hormuz
To the east by **India**
To the south by the remainder of the Indian Ocean
The Arabian Sea has a mean depth of 8,970 feet (2,734 meters)

Petroleum and natural-gas deposits have been discovered in the Arabian
Sea on the continental shelf off the coast of India to the west and
northwest of Mumbai (Bombay) and have been intensively exploited.
High levels of inorganic nutrients, such as phosphate concentrate, which
produce a rich fish life, have been observed in the western Arabian Sea
and off the southeastern coast of the Arabian Peninsula. Occurring in the
euphotic zone (zone of light, which is found in the upper 450 feet [140
meters] of the sea), this fertilizing effect undoubtedly is attributable in
part to coastal upwelling, which circulates settled nutrients from the
seafloor.

Atlantic Ocean
'Sea of Atlas' (salt water, second in size to the Pacific Ocean) covering
approximately a fifth of the Earth's surface **separating continents** of
Europe and Africa to the east
North and South America to the west

Without its dependent seas, the S-shaped Atlantic is approximately
31,830,000 square miles (82,440,000 square kilometers); with them,
41,100,000 square miles (106,460,000 square kilometers). Average
depth (with its seas) of 10,925 feet (3,300 meters); maximum depth of
27,493 feet (8,380 meters) in the Puerto Rico Trench, north of the island
of Puerto Rico.

From east to west, the ocean's breadth varies considerably: between Newfoundland and Ireland, it is about 2,060 miles; farther south, it widens to more than 3,000 miles before narrowing again so that the distance from Cape São Roque, Brazil, to Cape Palmas, **Liberia**, is only some 1,770 miles.

Southward it again becomes broader and is bordered by simple coasts almost without islands; between Cape Horn and the Cape of Good Hope, the ocean approaches Antarctica on a broad front nearly 4,000 miles wide. [Britannica]

Bay of Bengal

The Bay of Bengal is large but relatively shallow embayment of the northeastern Indian Ocean, occupying an area of about 839,000 square miles (2,173,000 square km). It lies roughly between latitudes 5° and 22° N and longitudes 80° and 90° E. It is bordered by Sri Lanka and India to the west, Bangladesh to the north, and Myanmar (Burma) and the northern part of the Malay Peninsula to the east. According to the definition of the International Hydrographic Bureau, the southern boundary extends from Dondra Head at the southern end of Sri Lanka in the west to the northern tip of the Indonesian island of Sumatra in the east. The bay is about 1,000 miles (1,600 km) wide, with an average depth of more than 8,500 feet (2,600 meters). The maximum depth is 15,400 feet (4,694 meters). A number of large rivers—the Mahanadi, Godavari, Krishna, and Kaveri (Cauvery) on the west and the Ganges (Ganga) and Brahmaputra on the north—flow into the Bay of Bengal. The Andaman and Nicobar groups, which are the only islands, separate the bay from the Andaman Sea.

Petroleum and natural-gas discoveries have been made in the Bay of Bengal, notably offshore of the Godavari and Manandi deltas. The bay has a geologic setting similar to that of the Indus River basin and the western margin of the Indian Peninsula. Hydrocarbon resources in the Bay of Bengal generally are located in deep areas, as compared to those in the Arabian Sea. There are placer deposits of titanium off northeastern Sri Lanka and rare earths off northeastern India. Heavy mineral sands occur around Nagapatnam (in Tamil Nadu state) on the southeastern Indian coast, near Chennai (Madras), and in coastal areas around Vishakhapatnam. They consist of ilmenite, garnet, sillimanite, zircon, rutile, and manganite. [Joseph R. Morgan Philomene A. Verlaan Ed.]

Gulf of Aden
A deepwater basin that forms a natural sea link between the
Red Sea and the Arabian Sea
Named after the seaport of Aden, in southern **Yemen**,
The gulf lies between the coasts of Arabia and the Horn of Africa

Gulf of Iskenderun-Turkey
Seaport and chief city of İskenderun ilçe, formerly Alexandretta
(district), Hatay il (province) in southern Turkey, located on the eastern
shore of the Gulf of Iskenderun.

The port (on or near the site of Alexandria ad Issum) was an outlet for the medieval and early modern overland trade from Iran, India, and eastern Asia, before the development of alternate shipping routes around the Cape of Good Hope and later through the Suez Canal.

Traditionally, it was the port for the Ottoman province of Aleppo (now in Syria). In 1918 to1937, it served as the capital of the autonomous sancak (subdivision of an Ottoman province) of Alexandretta under French mandate.

Indian Ocean
The Indian Ocean's marginal waterways are: the inland Red Sea and
Persian Gulf (north), the Arabian Sea (northwest), the Andaman Sea
(northeast); the large gulfs of Aden and Oman (northwest), the Bay of
Bengal (northeast), and the Great Australian Bight (off the southern
coast of Australia).

The most valuable mineral resource is oil, and the Persian Gulf is the largest oil-producing region in the world. Exploration for offshore petroleum and natural gas also has been under way in the Arabian Sea and the Bay of Bengal, both of which are believed to have large reserves. Other sites of exploration activity are off the northwestern coast of Australia, in the Andaman Sea, off the coast of Africa south of the Equator, and off the southwestern coast of Madagascar. Other than the countries of the Persian Gulf, only India produces commercial quantities of oil from offshore areas, with a large proportion of its total production coming from fields off the coast of Mumbai. Some natural gas also is produced from fields off the northwestern coast of Australia.

This salt water body covering approximately one-fifth of the total ocean area of the world is bounded by Iran, Pakistan, India, and Bangladesh (north); the Malay Peninsula, the Sunda Islands of Indonesia, and Australia (east); Antarctica (south); and Africa and the Arabian Peninsula (west). In the southwest, this waterway joins the Atlantic Ocean south of the southern tip of Africa; to the east and southeast its waters mingle with those of the Pacific.

Related: The Pacific Ocean lies between the continents of Asia and Australia on the west, and North and South America on the east; and extends from the Antarctic region in the south to the Arctic in the north.

There is no universal agreement on the southern limit of the Indian Ocean. The general definition includes its extending southward to the coast of Antarctica. However, many—notably in Australia—consider the portion closest to Antarctica (along with the corresponding southern extensions of the Atlantic and Pacific) to be part of the Southern (or Antarctic) Ocean. Australians often call the entire expanse south of that continent's south coast the Southern Ocean. [Britannica note]

Mediterranean Sea
Intercontinental sea stretching from the Atlantic Ocean on the west to Asia on the east, and separating Europe from Africa—ancient 'sea between the lands.' often called the incubator of Western civilization

From the Strait of Gibraltar between Spain and Morocco (west-east extent) to the shores of the Gulf of Iskenderun [seaport/chief city Iskenderun in southern Turkey on the eastern shore of the Gulf of Iskenderun] on the southwestern coast of **Turkey**—is approximately 2,500 miles (4,000 kilometers).

Between the shores of Yugoslavia and **Libya** (its average north-south extent), about 500 miles The Mediterranean Sea, including the Sea of Marmara, occupies an area of approximately 970,000 square miles (2,510,000 square kilometers). [Britannica]

Persian Gulf (Arabian Gulf)
A shallow marginal sea of the Indian Ocean that
Lies between the Arabian Peninsula and southwestern Iran
Bordered on the north, northeast and east by **Iran**;
On the southeast and south by part of Oman and by the **United Arab Emirates**;
On the southwest and west by Qatar, **Bahrain**, and **Saudi Arabia**; and
On the northwest by Kuwait and **Iraq**
The term Persian Gulf sometimes refers not only to Persian Gulf proper but
Also to its outlets—
The **Strait of Hormuz** and the Gulf of Oman, which open into the Arabian Sea

Since World War II the Persian Gulf and the surrounding countries have come to account for a significant proportion of the world's oil production. In addition, the area has approximately two-thirds of the world's estimated proven oil reserves and one-third of the world's estimated proven natural gas reserves. The region thus has acquired considerable strategic significance for the world's industrialized countries. Exploration has remained active, and new reserves are continually being discovered, both on land and offshore. Control of these reserves has led to numerous legal wrangles among states about exact territorial limits and has been at least partially responsible for major conflicts in the region: the Iran-Iraq War of the 1980s, the Persian Gulf War of the early 1990s, and the Iraq War of the early 21st century. Large amounts of oil are refined locally, but most is exported to northwestern Europe, East Asia, and other areas of the world. Petrochemical and other petroleum-based industries, as well as consumer industries, have been developing rapidly in the gulf region.

Red Sea
The Red Sea separates the coasts of Egypt, The Sudan, and Eritrea (Africa) to the west from those of Saudi Arabia and Yemen (Asia) to the east; and with its connection to the Mediterranean Sea via the Suez

Canal, the Red Sea is one of the most heavily traveled waterways in the world, carrying maritime traffic between Europe and Asia.

This narrow strip of water—maximum width 190 miles, greatest depth 9,974 feet (3,040 meters), area approximately 174,000 square miles (450,000 square km)—extends southeastward from Suez, Egypt, for about 1,200 miles (1,930 km) to the Bab el-Mandeb Strait, which connects with the Gulf of Aden and then with the Arabian Sea. Geologically, the Gulfs of Suez and Aqaba (Elat) are considered the northern extension of the same structure. Red Sea name derives from the color changes observed in its waters (*Britannica rev.*).

War defined and Weapons of Mass Destruction (Nuclear) Issues

War Defined

War is a phenomenon of organized violent conflict typified by extreme aggression, societal disruption and adaptation, and high mortality. The objective of warfare differs in accord with a group's role in a conflict: Offensive warfare's goals are typically the submission, assimilation or destruction of another group.

> Defensive warfare's goals are the repulsion of the offensive force and, often, survival itself.

> The terms military, militant, and militarism each refer to fundamental aspects of war: the organized group, the combative individual, and the supportive ethos (respectively). http://en.wikipedia.org/wiki/Armed_conflict

Weapons of Mass Destruction (Nuclear) Issues

Treaty on the Non-proliferation of Nuclear Weapons (also called Nuclear Non-proliferation Treaty or NPT), the agreement of July 1, 1968, signed by the United Kingdom, the United States, the Soviet Union, and 59 other states. Under the Treaty, the three major signatories that possessed nuclear weapons agreed not to assist other states in obtaining or producing nuclear weapons. The treaty became effective in March 1970 and was to remain so for a 25-year period; in 1995 by a consensus vote of 174 countries at the United Nations headquarters in New York City, extended the treaty without conditions indefinitely. Additional countries ratified the treaty. As of 2007 only three countries—India, Israel, and Pakistan—had refused to sign the treaty. One country, North Korea, signed then withdrew from the treaty.

The Non-proliferation Treaty is uniquely unequal, as it obliges nonnuclear states to forgo development of nuclear weapons while allowing the established nuclear states to keep theirs.

In the 2005 Review Conference of the Parties to the Treaty on Non-proliferation of Nuclear Weapons, this inequality was a major complaint against the established nuclear powers. [Britannica: Lawrence D. Freedman, Professor and Head, Department of War Studies, King's College, University of London; author of *The Evolution of Nuclear Strategy* and others.

Major initiatives aimed at controlling the spread of nuclear weapons materials and technologies are the Treaty on the Non-Proliferation of Nuclear Weapons (NPT) (close to 200 member states in 2003) and the Comprehensive Nuclear-Test-Ban Treaty (CTBT), the latter still unsigned by India, Pakistan, and North Korea. Nine more countries including the United States must ratify the CTBT before it can come into force. The International Atomic Energy Agency (IAEA), established in 1957 under the auspices of the United Nations, was supposed to ensure that states live up to their NPT obligations.

United Nations

The second multipurpose international organization established in the 20th century (October 24, 1945) that was worldwide in scope and membership. Aims sent out in its post-World War II Charter:

> To save succeeding generations from the scourge of war, . . .
> to reaffirm faith in fundamental human rights, . . . to establish

conditions under which justice and respect for the obligations arising from treaties and other sources of international law can be maintained, and to promote social progress and better standards of life in larger freedom.

Facing the United Nations in the post-Cold War (1989—) period is widespread, uncontrolled, careless disparity and suffering (amidst conspicuous waster) and discontent because of this state of affairs: Northern economic and political domination, economic development, the proliferation of nuclear weapons, and support for Israel. The North prospers, the South hungers: countries on either side of the North-South divide—more prosperous, industrialized countries of the Northern Hemisphere; the poorer, less industrialized developing countries of the Southern Hemisphere—are in constant disagreement.

U.S. arms the world: Arms without Borders 2006 Report Excerpt

U.S. Arms the World

Arms without Borders 2006 report [Excerpt]

> There are other huge costs associated with the arms trade. Government arms purchases can exceed legitimate security needs, diverting substantial amounts of money from health and education. The U.S. Congressional Research Service estimated that, collectively, countries in Asia, the Middle East, Latin America and Africa spent $22.5 billion on arms during 2004—8 percent more than they did in 2003. This sum would have enabled those countries to put every child in school and to reduce child mortality by two-thirds by 2015 thus fulfilling two of the United Nations Millennium Development Goals.

These are edited excerpts from a paper written for the Control Arms campaign by Edmund Cairns of Oxfam GB with support from Robert Parker, Oliver Sprague, Simon Gray and Michael Bailey of OGB and Brian Wood and Helen Hughes of Amnesty International. The Omega Research Foundation contributed research on arms production and transfers. Amnesty International and IANSA contributed further material.

Despite a drop in the number of conflicts following the end of the Cold War, at least 30 conflicts are currently ongoing. The global trade maintains arms supplies to all of them, despite the serious and widespread violation of human rights and international humanitarian law by many belligerents. While weapons do not cause these conflicts, the continuing supply and misuse of easily available arms and ammunition fuels their continuation, and makes them more deadly.

> In Sri Lanka, for example, the steady international supply of weapons to both sides has significantly prolonged the country's internal conflict, which has claimed the lives of an estimated 65,000 people.

Estimates of the annual number of deaths caused by armed violence range from 280,000 up to 378,000. This takes into account non-conflict deaths caused by the use of arms by state security forces, as well as firearm homicide, firearm suicide and accidental shootings . . . .

The estimated figures for people killed directly in armed conflict vary widely, but may be less than half the total number of those killed by armed violence overall. Massive numbers of people—men, women, older people, and children—die indirectly from the effects of armed conflict. The human suffering caused by collapsing economies, devastated health and security infrastructures, disease and famine is horrifying. Many more people are made refugees or internally displaced, injured, abused and bereaved, and lose the chance to lead prosperous and peaceful lives in a safe and secure environment.

> The global trade in weapons supplies arms to many of those who commit serious violations of human rights, such as extrajudicial executions, torture, rape and sexual violence, and enforced displacement. Human rights standards including those binding in treaties and in international customary law apply both during armed conflict and during peacetime, but the proliferation and poor regulation of arms contributes

to serious human rights violations by armed forces, police, security services, militias and other armed groups in many countries both before and after conflict. These violations often occur widely where small arms are readily available.

Large numbers of women and girls suffer directly and indirectly from armed violence. Women are particularly at risk of certain crimes because of their gender—crimes such as violence in the home and rape. . . .

The time for an effective international Arms Trade Treaty is now. Every year at least a third of a million people die as the direct result of conventional weapons use. Many more die, are injured, abused, forcibly displaced and bereaved because of armed violence . . . .

Military spending has risen steadily since 1999 and is expected to overtake peak Cold War levels by the end of 2006 and the arms trade has become more 'Globalized', with weapons assembled using components from around the world. This has exposed major loopholes in existing arms regulations that allow the supply of weapons and weapon components . . . to parties in breach of international law in armed conflict and to those who use these lethal instruments flagrantly to violate human rights . . . .

Instruments of violence Globalized

This paper shows how the changing pattern of ownership and production since the early 1990s means that national regulations are insufficient to prevent arms from reaching the hands of abusers. Weapons are now commonly assembled from components sourced from across the globe, with no single company or country responsible for the production of all the different components. Companies themselves are increasingly globalized: setting up offshore production facilities, foreign subsidiaries and other collaborative ventures, sometimes in countries with few controls over where the weapons go, or to what ends they are used.

Faced with an arms industry that operates globally, governments cannot rely solely on traditional national or regional export control systems;

effective control of a global arms trade requires new international standards and regulations based on international law. This paper concludes that existing arms regulations are dangerously out of date and that states must agree a legally binding international Arms Trade Treaty to address the problem . . . .

Leading arms producing and distributing countries and companies

The Group of Eight (G8) countries—four of them Permanent Members of the United Nations Security Council—continue to be among the most substantial distributors of the weapons and other military equipment used in conflicts and the violation of human rights worldwide. In 2005, the traditional big five arms-exporting countries—Russia, the USA, France, Germany and the UK [insufficient data available for China companies]—still dominated global sales of major conventional weapons, with an estimated 82 per cent of the market.

Eighty-five of the world's top 100 arms companies in 2003 were headquartered in the industrialized world. This paper shows how many of them (including Canada's Pratt and Whitney, Germany's Mercedes-Benz and the UK's BAE Systems) have been involved in exports of weapon systems from China, Egypt, India and South Africa to sensitive destinations including Indonesia, Sudan and Uganda. In all those destinations, those or similar weapons and military equipment have been used to commit serious abuses. For example, Arms Without Borders, Control Arms Campaign, October 2006 armored vehicles originally manufactured by Land Systems (OMC), a South African subsidiary of BAE Systems, have been exported to Uganda and Indonesia despite concerns that armored vehicles have been used to commit or facilitate human rights violations in both countries.

. . . It is difficult to determine whether some companies are transferring production overseas precisely to avoid relatively strict controls over direct exports at home . . . . All governments have a duty to ensure that arms and security equipment manufactured, assembled or supplied by companies within their jurisdiction do not facilitate violations of international human rights law or international humanitarian law.

Human costs

The scale of human suffering caused by uncontrolled arms transfers makes political action by the world's governments imperative. On average, up to one thousand people die every day as a direct result of armed violence. Countless more are injured, bereaved, abused and displaced by state security forces, armed groups, criminal gangs, and other armed individuals. Between a third and three fourths of all grave violations of human rights and 85 percent of killings Amnesty International reported over the past decade have involved the use of small arms and light weapons. Massive numbers of people—men, women, older people, and children—die from the indirect effects of armed conflict: collapsing economies, devastated health and security infrastructures, disease and famine.

> Attack helicopters, combat aircraft and air-to-surface missiles for example supplied to Israel primarily by the USA, often incorporating components supplied by other countries, have been used in the Occupied Territories, resulting in hundreds of deaths and thousands of injuries in apparent violation of international humanitarian law. . . . Palestinian armed groups have used rockets, explosive belts and other bombs to kill and injure hundreds of Israelis . . . [T]he Lebanese armed group Hezbollah has fired rockets at civilian areas in northern Israel.

. . . Easy access to weapons not only contributes to violations of human rights and humanitarian law, it also increases the threat from armed groups and organized crime. This is especially the case with small arms and light weapons. . . .

Weapons availability contributes greatly to the scale of killing, suffering and fear; however, in that weapons themselves do not create violence, governments must take measures to address the causes of conflict. Control of arms transfers is an indispensable element in the effort to make a more peaceful world . . . .

> 'My country has suffered appallingly from the effects of the uncontrolled arms trade—and continues to suffer . . . We

don't manufacture these guns, yet they end up in our country, erode our security and have terrible consequences for our development' [Florella Hazeley, Sierra Leone Action Network on Small Arms, July 9, 2006].

Need for action

. . . In June 2006, 42 governments, ranging from Brazil to Indonesia, Japan and Nigeria to South Africa, signed up to the 'Geneva Declaration on Armed Violence and Development', resolving to 'promote sustainable security and a culture of peace by taking action to reduce armed violence and its negative impact on socio-economic and human development'. The Declaration summed up what goes wrong when the arms trade is out of control:

> . . . 'Armed violence destroys lives and livelihoods, breeds insecurity, fear and terror, and has a profoundly negative impact on human development. Whether in situations of conflict or crime, it imposes enormous costs on states, communities and individuals.
>
> '[It] closes schools, empties markets, burdens health services, destroys families, weakens the rule of law, and prevents humanitarian assistance from reaching people in need . . . It threatens permanently the respect of human rights.'

The signatories resolved to 'take further action to deal effectively both with the supply of, and demand for, small arms and light weapons [. . .] promoting the development of further international instruments, including legally binding ones.' Many developing country governments such as Bangladesh, Costa Rica and Kenya are now saying that one such instrument is an international Arms Trade Treaty.

An Arms Trade Treaty—if based upon existing international human rights and humanitarian law—will prevent arms transfers into conflict zones where they are likely to be used to facilitate serious violations of those laws, including torture, enforced disappearances, war crimes, crimes against humanity or genocide. It will also help prevent the supply of arms to law enforcement agencies that use them to commit grave and persistent violations of human rights, including extrajudicial executions, enforced disappearances and torture. The Treaty will also help to prevent violations of key economic, social and cultural rights, reduce the diversion of human and economic resources from sustainable development and poverty reduction efforts, and reduce the flow of weapons to criminals and terrorists.

Sources and notes

© Amnesty International, the International Action Network on Small Arms, and Oxfam International, October 2006

This paper was written for the Control Arms campaign by Edmund Cairns of Oxfam GB with support from Robert Parker, Oliver Sprague, Simon Gray and Michael Bailey of OGB and Brian Wood and Helen Hughes of Amnesty International. The Omega Research Foundation contributed much of the research on arms production and transfers. Amnesty International and IANSA contributed further material.

The text may be used free of charge for the purposes of advocacy, campaigning, education, and research, provided that the source is acknowledged in full. The copyright holders request that all such use be registered with them for impact assessment purposes. For copying in any other circumstances, or for re-use in other publications, or for translation or adaptation, permission must be secured and a fee may be charged.

Copies are available to download from www.controlarms.org
AI Index—POL 34/006 /2006

Amnesty International is an independent worldwide voluntary activist movement working for human rights, with more than 1.5 million members, supporters and subscribers in over 150 countries and territories. It has national sections in 54 countries in every region of the world. Email: info@amnesty.org.uk

The International Action Network on Small Arms is the global movement against gun violence—'more than 500 civil society organizations

working in 100 countries to stop the proliferation and misuse of small arms and light weapons. IANSA seeks to reduce the impact of small arms through advocacy, promoting the development of regional and thematic networks, supporting capacity building and raising awareness.
Email: contact@iansa.org

Oxfam International is a confederation of twelve organizations working together in more than 100 countries to find lasting solutions to poverty and injustice: Oxfam America, Oxfam Australia, Oxfam-in-Belgium, Oxfam Canada, Oxfam Germany, Oxfam Great Britain, Oxfam Hong Kong, Intermón Oxfam (Spain), Oxfam Ireland, Oxfam New Zealand, Oxfam Novib, and Oxfam Quebec. www.oxfam.org.
Email: advocacy@oxfaminternational.org

Arms without Borders: Why a Globalized trade needs global controls

> Arms are out of control: Arms kill up to a third of a million men, women, and children on average each year. Many thousands more are maimed, or tortured, or forced to flee their homes.

> The uncontrolled proliferation of arms fuels human rights violations, escalates conflicts, and intensifies poverty. The time for world leaders to act is now.

To confront this crisis, Oxfam, Amnesty International, and the International Action Network on Small Arms (IANSA) have together launched an international campaign calling for effective arms controls to make people genuinely safer from the threat of armed violence. You can help us to put an end to this horrific abuse. Log on to the control arms website and become part of the largest, most effective visual petition in the world. www.controlarms.org

U.S. Global Military Deployment—Global Research et al

Dufour on U.S. global military bases

The United States views the Earth surface as a vast territory to conquer, occupy and exploit. That the U.S. Military splits the World up into geographic command units vividly illustrates this underlying geopolitical reality. Worldwide control of humanity's economic, social and political activities is under the helm of U.S. corporate and military power. Underlying this process are various schemes of direct and indirect military intervention. These U.S. sponsored strategies ultimately consist in a process of global subordination. The Network of U.S. military bases controls and enslaves humanity.

Twenty years after the Global Report published in 1980 outlining 'the State of the World' by focusing on so-called 'level of threats' which might negatively influence or undermine U.S. interests—U.S. strategists attempting to justify their military interventions in different parts of the World conceptualized the greatest fraud in U.S. history, namely, 'the Global War on Terrorism' (GWOT). . . . "Using a fabricated pretext, this ['Global War on Terrorism'] constitutes a global war against all those who oppose U.S. hegemony. A modern form of slavery, instrumented through militarization and the 'free market' has unfolded."

The conquest, occupation and (or) otherwise supervision of various regions of the World is supported by an integrated network of military bases and installations that covers the entire Planet (Continents, Oceans and Outer Space). Major elements of the U.S. conquest and world domination strategy refer to—

(1) Control of the world economy and its financial markets
(2) Taking over of all natural resources (primary resources and nonrenewable sources of energy), this constitutes the cornerstone of U.S. power through the activities of its multinational corporations.

The 'Global War on Terrorism' (GWOT) Washington launched in the wake of the September 11, 2001, events—first in a war on Afghanistan, then a second Persian Gulf War on Iraq—punishes countries that do not faithfully obey Washington's directives. Among these are Iran, North Korea, Syria and Venezuela whom the U.S. has "earmarked for possible U.S. military intervention . . . . The ongoing re-deployment of U.S. troops and military bases must analyzed in a thorough manner to obtain an understanding of the nature of U.S. interventionism in different regions of the World."

Quoting Iraklis Tsavdaridis, Secretary of the World Peace Council (WPC), Professor Jules Dufour explains—

> 'The establishment of U.S. military bases should not be seen simply in terms of direct military ends. These deployments are always used to promote the economic and political objectives of U.S. capitalism: for some time, U.S. corporations and the U.S. government have been eager to build a secure corridor for U.S.-controlled oil and natural gas pipelines from the Caspian Sea in Central Asia through Afghanistan and Pakistan to the Arabian Sea. This region has more than 6 percent of the world's proven oil reserves and almost 40 percent of its gas reserves. The war in Afghanistan and the creation of U.S. military bases in Central Asia are viewed as a key opportunity to make such pipelines a reality.

Global U.S. Military Deployment

Wikipedia reports in data updated October 20, 2010: The United States deploys its military in more than 150 countries around the world, with more than 369,000 of its 1,479,551 active-duty personnel serving outside the United States and its territories. Many of these personnel are still located at installations activated during the Cold War, by which the U.S. government sought to counter the Soviet Union in the aftermath of World War II. Since 2001, the United States has redeployed some of its forces as part of its 'War on Terror.'

U.S. personnel are seeing active combat in several countries, most notably but not exclusively Afghanistan and Iraq. The United States deploys other of its personnel in several "peacekeeping missions."

Listed by region, the United States deploys personnel in these places (omitted are countries in which there are fewer than 100 deployed U.S. personnel).

Combat Zones

HOTSPOT South Central Asia/Middle East—Lands around the southern and eastern shores of the Mediterranean Sea, extending from Morocco to the Arabian Peninsula and Iran and sometimes beyond. The central part of this general area was formerly 'Near East' . . .

Near East applying to the region nearest Europe, extending from the Mediterranean Sea to the Persian Gulf; Middle East, from the Gulf to Southeast Asia; and Far East, those regions facing the Pacific Ocean.

Iraq—Approximately 50,000 U.S. personnel (advisors) as of 19 August 2010

Afghanistan—Approximately 98,000 U.S. personnel as of 25 August 2010

AFRICA
Kenya—42
Cairo, Egypt—52
Sinai Desert,
Egypt—Approximately 500 personnel [excluding multinational force]

ASIA

Middle (Near) East
Qatar—411
Bahrain—1,495 [U.S. Fifth Fleet]
Kuwait—10,548
Oman—36
United Arab Emirates—96

East
South Korea—27,014
Japan—32,803

Philippines—95
Diego Garcia—311
Jakarta, Indonesia—27
Singapore—125
Thailand—96
Malaysia—15

OCEANIA
Australia—140
Marshall Islands [In the central Pacific Ocean, the Republic of the Marshall Islands consists of some of the easternmost islands of Micronesia: the Marshalls are composed of more than 1,200 islands and islets in 2 parallel chains of coral atolls—the Ratak (or Sunrise) to the east and the Ralik (or Sunset) to the west. The chains lie about 125 miles (200 km) apart and extend some 800 miles northwest to southeast.

[From 1947 to 1986, when the Trust Territory was dissolved by the U.S. government, the Marshall Islands were administered by the United States as part of the Trust Territory of the Pacific Islands]—17
New Zealand—5

EUROPE
U.S. military bases in Germany in
2009:
Germany—57,080
Souda Bay, Greece—386
Italy—9,855
United Kingdom—9,825
Spain—1,286
Norway—81
Sweden—12
Belgium—1,328
Portugal—826
Netherlands—579
Greece—363
Greenland—126
Poland—100
Turkey—1,594

WESTERN HEMISPHERE
Antigua [eastern Caribbean]—2
Colombia [Republic of Colombia,
northwestern South America:
1,000 miles (1,600 km) coastline
north the Caribbean Sea, 800
miles (1,300 km) coastline west
the Pacific Ocean; northwest
borders Panama dividing the
two bodies of water, east borders
Venezuela and Brazil, south
borders Peru and Ecuador]—123
Saint Helena [South Atlantic
Ocean 1,200 miles (1,950 km)
west of southwestern coast of
Africa]—3
Guantanamo Bay, Cuba
[waterways: Atlantic Ocean,
Caribbean Sea, Gulf of
Mexico]—932

Netherlands Antilles [Caribbean
Sea]—10

UNITED STATES
Active duty personnel in the
United States and its territories:
1,084,548

Contiguous United States:
882,201
Transients: 52,527
Hawaii—34,838
Guam—2,836
Puerto Rico—137
Alaska—19,408

Sources and notes

"The Worldwide Network of U.S. Military Bases: The Global Deployment of U.S. Military Personnel" by Professor Jules Dufour, Global Research, July 1, 2007

Jules Dufour is President of the United Nations Association of Canada (UNA-C)—Saguenay-Lac-Saint-Jean branch and Research Associate at the Center for Research on Globalization (CRG); and Emeritus Professor of Geography at the University of Quebec, Chicoutimi.

In 2007, Dufour became Chevalier de l'Ordre national du Québec, a distinction conferred by the Quebec government, for contributions to World peace and human rights: Dufour's numerous scholarly writings and the work he accomplished in the context of national and international commissions on issues pertaining to regional development, human rights and the protection of the environment. His article at Global Research was translated from the French, first published in French [April] 10, 2007, on Global Research's French language website: www.mondialisation.ca www.globalresearch.ca contains copyrighted material the use of which specifically authorized by the copyright owner is made available under provisions of 'fair use' in an effort to advance a better understanding of political, economic and social issues. The material is distributed without profit to those who have expressed a prior interest in receiving it for research and educational purposes. © Copyright Jules Dufour, Global Research, 2007, Global Research ca www.globalresearch.ca/index. php?context=va&aid=5564

The deployment data on these pages offer a sense of the scope of global U. S. military deployment. However, the information falls far short of a complete and updated picture of and precise data on the countries under U.S. threat, invasion and occupation or the numbers of deployed U.S. official military, related private contractors and mercenaries, and civilian governmental and nongovernmental personnel and agents.

Many of the numbers, *Wikipedia* notes, are out of date as they are based on Department of Defense statistics from June 2005.

Wikipedia, s.v. "Deployment of the U.S. military," last modified October 20, 2010; http://siadapp.dmdc.osd.mil/personnel/MILITARY/history/hst0712.pdf.   http://siadapp.dmdc.osd.mil/personnel/MILITARY/history/hst0709.pdf

U.S. DOD 2005 stats http://www.telegraph.co.uk/news/worldnews/asia/afghanistan/7762893/U.S.-troops-in-Afghanistan-surpass-number-in-Iraq.html

Country background information in chart and sources and notes by *Britannica* (excerpted and revised)

West Indies NOTE

From the peninsula of Florida on the mainland of the United States, the islands stretch 1,200 miles (1,900 km) southeastward, then 500 miles (800 km) south, then west along the north coast of Venezuela on the South American mainland.

The West Indies are a crescent-shaped group of islands more than 2,000 miles (3,200 km) long separating the Gulf of Mexico and the Caribbean Sea, to the west and south, from the Atlantic Ocean, to the east and north.

Three major physiographic divisions constitute the West Indies: the Greater Antilles, comprising the islands of **Cuba**, Jamaica, Hispaniola (Haiti and the Dominican Republic), and Puerto Rico; the Lesser Antilles, including the Virgin Islands, Anguilla, Saint Kitts and Nevis, **Antigua and Barbuda**, Montserrat, Guadeloupe, Dominica, Martinique, Saint Lucia, Saint Vincent and the Grenadines, Barbados, and Grenada; and the isolated island groups of the North American continental shelf—The Bahamas and the Turks and Caicos Islands—and those of the South American shelf, including Trinidad and Tobago, Aruba, Curaçao, and Bonaire. (Bermuda, although physiographically not a part of the West Indies, has common historical and cultural ties with the other islands and is often included in definitions of the region.) (*Britannica*).

Oceania NOTE

Traditionally, Oceania has been divided into four parts: Australasia (Australia and New Zealand), Melanesia, Micronesia, and Polynesia.

Oceania is the collective name for the islands scattered throughout most of the Pacific Ocean. The term, in its widest sense, embraces the entire insular region between Asia and the Americas.

A more common definition excludes the Ryukyu, Kuril and Aleutian Islands and the Japan archipelago. The most popular usage delimits Oceania further by eliminating Indonesia, Taiwan, and the Philippines, because the peoples and cultures of those islands more closely relate historically to the Asian mainland.

Oceania then, in its most restricted meaning, includes more than 10,000 islands, with a total land area (excluding Australia, but including Papua New Guinea and New Zealand) of approximately 317,700 square miles (822,800 square km) (*Britannica*)

World Crises and Conflicts: AlertNet data

Compiled by AlertNet its latest (2010) listing of world crisis and conflict

Conflicts • Food security • Health including HIV • Sudden disasters

AFRICA
African hunger
AIDS in Africa
AIDS pandemic
Angola recovery
Bird flu

Burundi transition
Central African
Republic troubles
Chad troubles
Chikungunya
Congo (Brazzaville)
troubles
Congo (DR) conflict
Cyclone Ivan
Darfur conflict
E. African floods
2007

E. African hunger
East Sudan
insurgency
Eritrea-Ethiopia
border
Ethiopia Ogaden
crisis
Guinea unrest Indian
Ocean tsunami
Intense hurricane Igor
Intense tropical
cyclone Fanele

AMERICAS

ASIA

Aceh peace
Afghan turmoil
AIDS in Asia
AIDS pandemic
Asia extreme cold 2008
Bird flu
Cambodia recovery
Chechnya war
Chikungunya
China drought 2009/2010
China earthquake 2008
China earthquake 2010
China floods 2008
Cyclone Aila
Cyclone Sidr
East Asia typhoons 2009
East Timor nation-building
Georgia, Abkhazia, S. Ossetia
India religious violence
India's northeastern clashes
Indian Maoist violence

Indian Ocean tsunami
Indonesia earthquakes
Indonesia mudflow
Java earthquake 2006
Kashmir dispute
Kyrgyzstan violence 2010
Malaria Meningitis
Myanmar cyclone

Myanmar troubles
Nagorno-Karabakh conflict
Nepal peace
North Korea hunger
Pacific tsunami 2009

Pakistan floods 2010
Pakistan quake 2008
Pakistan violence
Pakistan/India earthquake
Papua tensions
Philippines floods 2008
Philippines-Mindanao conflict

South Asia monsoon
Severe cyclonic storm Laila
Sri Lanka conflict
Sumatra quake Sept 2009
Super cyclonic storm Phet
Super typhoon Megi
Swine flu

Thailand's southern violence
Tropical cyclone Mick
Tropical cyclone Tomas
Tropical depression Mujigae
Tropical depression One
Tropical depression Twentyseven
Tropical storm Bijli
Tropical storm Dianmu
Tropical storm Giri
Tropical storm Goni
Tropical storm Kujira
Tropical storm Lionrock
Tropical storm Mindulle
Tropical storm Namtheun
Tropical storm Nangka
Tropical storm Noul
Tropical storm Phyan
Tropical storm Soudelor
Tropical storm Three
Tropical storm Ward
Typhoon Chan-hom
Typhoon Chanthu
Typhoon Conson
Typhoon Fanapi
Typhoon Ketsana
Typhoon Kompasu

Typhoon Koppu
Typhoon Linfa
Typhoon Lupit
Typhoon Meranti
Typhoon Molave
Typhoon Morakot
Typhoon Parma
Very intense tropical
cyclone Ului

MIDDLE EAST
AIDS in Middle East
Iraq in turmoil
Israeli-Palestinian
conflict Lebanon
crisis
Swine flu
Tropical storm Bandu
Yemen clashes

EUROPE
AIDS in Eastern
Europe/Central Asia
AIDS pandemic
Bird flu
Chechnya war
Dnestr-Moldova
dispute
Georgia, Abkhazia, S.
Ossetia
Italy earthquake
2009
Kosovo future
Meningitis
Nagorno-Karabakh
conflict
Swine flu

Sources and notes

AlertNet, Alerting humanitarians to emergencies http://lite.alertnet.org/emergencies/index.htm?f=/thenews/emergency/conflicts.htm&region=

AlertNet

The Reuters Foundation, an educational and humanitarian trust, launched AlertNet in 1997. Reuters AlertNet is a humanitarian news network based around a popular website and aims to keep relief professionals and the wider public up-to-date on humanitarian crises around the globe. It has a network of 400 contributing humanitarian organizations and more than 26,000 readers receive its weekly email digest. AlertNet is a recipient of a Popular Communication award for technological innovation, a NetMedia European Online Journalism Award for its coverage of natural disasters and has been named a Millennium Product by the British Government—an award for outstanding applications of innovative technologies.

In 2004, Reuters AlertNet conducted a major analysis of humanitarian crisis reporting in collaboration with Columbia School of Journalism. The result was the Fritz Report, a major survey of relations between the media and humanitarian relief agencies. With the support of Britain's Department for International Development, Reuters AlertNet is acting on the report's recommendations in a project called MediaBridge. The project involves the creation of practical tools and services to help journalists cover difficult emergencies. These include:

- Crisis briefings—key background information on more than 70 emergencies
- Country statistics—generates graphs comparing global humanitarian facts and figures
- Who works where—directory of relief organizations and United Nations agencies working in key crises willing to help journalists
- Humanitarian heads up—an e-newsletter for journalists including early warning on looming crises
- Hotspot mapping—puts global emergencies on the map

- Interactive training—improve your humanitarian reporting with our online training modules
- World press tracker—keep tabs on global trends in crisis coverage
- MediaWatch—daily choice pickings of provocative articles on humanitarian themes from the world's media

Significant Ongoing Global Armed Conflicts to 2009-Project Ploughshares

Project Ploughshares/Information Please conflict listing
Only up to 2008-2009
Significant Ongoing Global Armed Conflicts

Main warring parties	Year began (1)
MIDDLE EAST	
U.S. and UK vs. Iraq	2003
Israel vs. Palestinians	1948
Yemen: Government forces vs. the rebel group Shabab al-Moumineen (The Youthful Believers)	2004
Turkey: Government forces vs. the Kurdish Workers' Party (PKK)	1999
ASIA	
Afghanistan: U.S., UK, and Coalition Forces vs. al-Qaeda and Taliban	2001
India vs. Kashmiri separatist groups/Pakistan	1948
India vs. Assam insurgents (various)	1979
Philippines vs. Mindanaoan separatists (MILF/ASG)	1971
Sri Lanka vs. Tamil Eelan (2)	1978
AFRICA	
Algeria vs. Armed Islamic Group (GIA)	1991
Somalia vs. rival clans and Islamist groups	1991
Sudan vs. Darfur rebel groups	2003
Uganda vs. Lord's Resistance Army (LRA)	1986
EUROPE	

Russia vs. Chechen separatists	1994
LATIN AMERICA	
Colombia vs. National Liberation Army (ELN)	1978
Colombia vs. Revolutionary Armed Forces of Colombia (FARC)	1978
Colombia vs. Autodefensas Unidas de Colombia (AUC)	1990

NOTE: As of Oct. 2009.
(1) Where multiple parties and long-standing but sporadic conflict are concerned, date of first combat deaths is given.
(2) 2002 cease-fire collapsed in 2006.
Project Ploughshares, www.ploughshares.ca and news sources
Information Please® Database © 2009 Pearson Education Inc All rights reserved, Also: Significant Ongoing Armed Conflicts, 2008—Infoplease. com http://www.infoplease.com/ipa/A0904550.html#ixzz131MyU85z
http://www.infoplease.com/ipa/A0904550.html

Global Conflicts Lists—Global Security

Global Conflicts List—World at War

The World at War
Current Conflicts

Algeria	Insurgency	1992—>
Angola	Cabinda	1975-2006 (?)
Burma	Insurgency	1950—>
China	Senkaku Islands	1968—>
China	Spratly Islands	1988—>
China	Uighur	1996—>
Colombia	Insurgencies	1970s—>
Congo (Zaire)	Congo War	1998—>
Georgia	Civil War	1991—>
India	Assam	1985—>
India	Kashmir	1970s—>

India	Naxalite Uprising	1967—>
Israel	Palestine	1967—>
Ivory Coast	Civil War	2002—>
Korea	Korean War	1953—>
Kyrgyzstan	Civil Unrest	2010—>
Laos	Hmong Insurgency	2000—>
Mexico	Drug War	2006—>
Namibia	Caprivi Strip	1966—>
Nepal	Maoists	1996-2006 (?)
Nigeria	Civil Disturbances	1997—
Pakistan	Baluchistan	2004—
Pakistan	Pashtun Jihad	2001—
Palestine	Civil War	2007—>
Peru	Shining Path	1970s—>
Philippines	Moro Uprising	1970s—>
Russia	North Caucasus Insurgency	1992—>
Somalia	Civil War	1991—>
Spain	Basque Uprising	1970s—>
Thailand	Islamic Rebels	2001—>
Turkey	Kurdistan	1984—>
United States	Afghanistan	1980—>
United States	Djibouti	2001—>
United States	Iraq	1990—>
United States	Philippines	1898—>
Uzbekistan	Civil Disturbances	2005—>
Yemen	Sheik al-Houti	2004—>

"The United Nations defines 'major wars' as military conflicts inflicting 1,000 battlefield deaths per year," Global Security, the source for these data, notes on its website.

"The new millennium began with much of the world consumed in armed conflict or cultivating an uncertain peace. As of mid-2005, there were eight Major Wars under way, with as many as two dozen 'lesser' conflicts ongoing with varying degrees of intensity. Most of these were civil or 'intrastate' wars, fueled as much by racial, ethnic, or religious animosities as by ideological fervor.

"Most victims are civilians, a feature that distinguishes modern conflicts. During World War I, civilians made up fewer than 5 percent of all casualties. Today, 75 percent or more of those killed or wounded in wars are non-combatants." The figure does not include late 2010 new and continuing conflict in North Africa and the Middle East or Southwest/ Central Asia.

"Conflict prevention, mediation, humanitarian intervention and demobilization are among the tools needed to underwrite the success of development assistance programs, Global Security advises.

"Nutrition and education programs, for example, cannot succeed in a nation at war. Billions of dollars of development assistance have been virtually wasted in war-ravaged countries." http://www.globalsecurity.org/military/world/war/index.html

Notes on torture—Optional Protocol to the United Nations Convention against Torture

Opportunity for Refugee and Migrant Rights Protection

This paper (May 2009) is an introductory briefing for human rights defenders who work with migrants, refugees and asylum seekers who have been deprived of their liberty. For more detailed information on the OPCAT, please see the APT website.
See http://www.apt.ch/content/view/40/82/lang,en/ for a complete list of State Parties and Signatories, and http://www.apt.ch/content/view/138/152/lang,en/ for a list of NPMs designated to date.

Introduction [excerpt]

The detention of refugees, asylum seekers, undocumented migrants, stateless persons and other migrants represents an ongoing challenge for human rights worldwide. Whether detained under national criminal laws, administrative laws or other dispositions, they are particularly vulnerable to ill-treatment, exploitation and deprivation of liberty in inadequate and possibly inhuman conditions. This can have serious and long-lasting consequences for their physical and mental well-being as well as a range of rights from physical integrity and judicial protection to education and health. It can also affect their access to asylum procedures and heighten the risk of additional abuse.

Work, proposals, campaigns of Optional Protocol to the United Nations Convention against Torture (OPCAT)

The Optional Protocol to the United Nations Convention against Torture (OPCAT), an innovative international treaty, creates a system that represents an important opportunity for actors who work for the protection of the rights of refugees and migrants in detention.

Torture and other cruel, inhuman or degrading treatment or punishment (TCIDT) usually occurs in institutions that are closed to public scrutiny. The experience of international and national organizations has shown that detention monitoring is an effective way to create transparency in such institutions and identify problems that were previously ignored. Monitoring not only sheds light on conditions and treatment in detention but can be instrumental in pressuring and assisting the authorities to address and improve them.

The OPCAT was adopted by the United Nations in 2002 and came into force in 2006. It aims to give States that have ratified the UN Convention against Torture a practical means by which to fulfil their existing obligations to prevent TCIDT. It creates a dual system of regular visits to places of detention in State Party jurisdictions composed of an international Sub-Committee on the Prevention of Torture (SPT), and one or several independent national institutions called National Preventive Mechanisms (NPMs). This dual system aims to serve as the basis for constructive dialogue with the authorities on improving conditions and treatment in detention. Currently, there are forty-seven State Parties to the OPCAT, twenty-four signatories and numerous other countries working toward ratification. Among the present State Parties, twenty-four have designated or created their NPM.

The SPT is made up of ten international experts, the number of whom will increase to twenty-five when there are fifty OPCAT ratifications. It conducts visits to places of detention in State

Party jurisdictions and engages in dialogue with States in order to enhance the prevention of torture. It is also mandated to advise and assist NPMs. An SPT report following an in-country visit is initially confidential but may be made public if the State Party in question so requests or itself publishes the report in full or in part. The SPT also presents a public annual report on its activities to the Committee against Torture. To date, the SPT has visited Mauritius, Maldives, Sweden, Benin, Mexico and Paraguay.

Under the OPCAT, NPMs are independent single or several institutions specifically created or designated by State Parties in accordance with the 1993 UN Paris Principles relating to the status and functioning of national human rights institutions. NPMs do not replicate existing mechanisms that investigate individual cases of torture in detention. Instead, they are mandated to carry out systematic visits to places of detention in order to analyze the treatment, conditions and administration therein. This is done with the aim of engaging the respective Government to identify and implement systemic measures to mitigate the risks of TCIDT and improve conditions generally. NPMs enjoy full powers of access to relevant installations, persons and information.

Given the broad definitions of places of detention and deprivation of liberty contained in OPCAT article 4, NPMs and the SPT have the power to visit installations specifically designed to hold refugees and migrants, including airport holding centers, camps and specialist migrant detention centers, as well as other places where migrants may be held, including prisons, police cells, military installations, psychiatric institutions and care homes.

Role for Refugee and Migrant Rights Defenders

Refugee and migrant rights defenders have a variety of roles to play with regard to the OPCAT, depending on their particular national context. They can join in national dialogue and lobbying for ratification of the OPCAT by highlighting the need to have independent mechanism(s) that specifically monitor the situation of these groups in detention and promoting the OPCAT as a practical means to this end. They can join the debate on what form the NPM should take. Upon ratification, they can also contribute to the process of implementing the OPCAT by engaging the NPM to address specifically the issue of refugees and migrants in detention in addition to more 'traditional' situations of deprivation of liberty.

The OPCAT establishes the need for NPMs to have the adequate capabilities and professional knowledge to carry out its functions. The refugee and migrant sectors should work to ensure that the NPM in each State Party is equipped with the necessary skill set in terms of membership and personnel. Finally, the refugee and migrant sector can nourish the NPM with up-to-date information, analysis and advice including by contributing to the development of migrant-specific tools and criteria to be used in monitoring and analysis.

In the case of countries that may not yet ratify the OPCAT, public debate around the need and obligation to monitor places of detention based on the OPCAT model should be generated and the migrant sector has specific experience to contribute. Promoting transparency in places of detention is in itself an essential step toward ensuring the rights of refugees and migrants.

The OPCAT represents an important opportunity for refugee and migrant rights actors and the broader human rights sector at both the national and international levels. The engagement of the refugee and migrant rights defenders will be critical in optimizing its potential.

The APT is an international NGO based in Geneva that works with Governments, independent national institutions and civil society organizations for the prevention of torture worldwide. For more information about the work of APT, the OPCAT or detention monitoring, please visit the APT website.

Convention on Cluster Munitions

U. S. non-member state

2008 Conference: Excerpt from: May 30, 2008 (Dublin), Diplomatic Conference for the Adoption of a Convention on Cluster Munitions

Concerns of States Parties to the Convention on Cluster Munitions:

- Civilian populations and individual civilians continue to bear the brunt of armed conflict
- To put an end for all time to the suffering and casualties caused by cluster munitions at the time of their use, when they fail to function as intended, or when they are abandoned,
- Cluster munition remnants
  Kill or maim civilians (including women and children)
  Obstruct economic and social development (including through the loss of livelihood) Impede post-conflict rehabilitation and reconstruction
  Delay or prevent the return of refugees and internally displaced persons
  Can negatively affect national and international peace-building and humanitarian assistance efforts
  Have other severe consequences that can persist for many years after use . . .
- Conscience— . . . Stressing the role of public conscience in furthering the principles of humanity as evidenced by the global call for an end to civilian suffering caused by cluster munitions and recognizing the efforts to that end undertaken by the United Nations, the International Committee of the Red Cross, the Cluster Munition Coalition and numerous other non-governmental organizations around the world . . .

Agreement of States Parties [excerpt]:

Article 1—General obligations and scope of application

- Each State Party undertakes never under any circumstances to:

(a) Use cluster munitions

(b) Develop, produce, otherwise acquire, stockpile, retain or transfer to anyone, directly or indirectly, cluster munitions;

(c) Assist, encourage or induce anyone to engage in any activity prohibited to a State Party under this Convention.

Article 2—Definitions

- . . . "Cluster munition" means a conventional munition designed to disperse or release explosive submunitions each weighing less than 20 kilograms, and includes those explosive submunitions. . . .

- "Explosive submunition" means a conventional munition that in order to perform its task is dispersed or released by a cluster munition and is designed to function by detonating an explosive charge prior to, on or after impact

- "Failed cluster munition" means a cluster munition that has been fired, dropped, launched, projected or otherwise delivered and which should have dispersed or released its explosive submunitions but failed to do so

- "Unexploded submunition" means an explosive submunition that has been dispersed or released by, or otherwise separated from, a cluster munition and has failed to explode as intended

- "Abandoned cluster munitions" means cluster munitions or explosive submunitions that have not been used and that have been left behind or dumped, and that are no longer under the control of the party that left them behind or dumped them. They may or may not have been prepared for use

- "Cluster munition remnants" means failed cluster munitions, abandoned cluster munitions, unexploded submunitions and unexploded bomblets

- "Transfer" involves, in addition to the physical movement of cluster munitions into or from national territory, the transfer of title to and control over cluster munitions, but does not involve the transfer of territory containing cluster munition remnants;

- "Self-destruction mechanism" means an incorporated automatically functioning mechanism which is in addition to the primary initiating mechanism of the munition and which secures the destruction of the munition into which it is incorporated;

- "Self-deactivating" means automatically rendering a munition inoperable by means of the irreversible exhaustion of a component, for example a battery, that is essential to the operation of the munition;
- "Cluster munition contaminated area" means an area known or suspected to contain cluster munition remnants;
- "Mine" means a munition designed to be placed under, on or near the ground or other surface area and to be exploded by the presence, proximity or contact of a person or a vehicle;
- "Explosive bomblet" means a conventional munition, weighing less than 20 kilograms, which is not self-propelled and which, in order to perform its task, is dispersed or released by a dispenser, and is designed to function by detonating an explosive charge prior to, on or after impact;
- "Dispenser" means a container that is designed to disperse or release explosive bomblets and which is affixed to an aircraft at the time of dispersal or release;
- "Unexploded bomblet" means an explosive bomblet that has been dispersed, released or otherwise separated from a dispenser and has failed to explode as intended.

Excluded from the meanings of Cluster munition:

- A munition or submunition designed to dispense flares, smoke, pyrotechnics or chaff; or a munition designed exclusively for an air defense role;
- (b) A munition or submunition designed to produce electrical or electronic effects;
- (c) A munition that, in order to avoid indiscriminate area effects and the risks posed by unexploded submunitions, has all of the following characteristics: Each munition contains fewer than ten explosive submunitions • Each explosive submunition weighs more than four kilograms • Each explosive submunition is designed to detect and engage a single target object • Each explosive submunition is equipped with an electronic self-destruction mechanism • Each explosive submunition is equipped with an electronic self deactivating feature . . . http://www.unog.ch/80256EDD006B8954/(httpAssets)/CE9E6C29A6941AF1C12574F7004D3A5C/$file/ccm77_english.pdf

Convention on Cluster Munitions
http://www.unog.ch/80256EE600585943/(httpPages)/F27A2B84309E
0C5AC12574F70036F176?OpenDocument

Selected News Sources of Interest

BENNETT'S STUDY: *Today's Insight News*

Bennett's Study's main feature is "Today's Insight News," a news and current affairs site (http://todaysinsightnews.blogspot.com/) centered on news and commentary on United States and international affairs and relations re-reported, compiled and edited by independent journalist, Dr. Carolyn LaDelle Bennett.

COUNTERSPIN

CounterSpin is a weekly news and current affairs program that critically examines major stories. It exposes and highlights biased and inaccurate news; censored stories; sexism, racism and homophobia in the news; the power of corporate influence; gaffes and goofs by leading TV pundits; TV news' narrow political spectrum; attacks on free speech—all combined with lively discussion and a thoughtful media critique.

Aired on more than 150 noncommercial stations across the United States and Canada (as well as being accessible online), CounterSpin is produced by Fairness and Accuracy in Reporting (FAIR) and hosted by Janine Jackson, Steve Rendall, and Peter Hart. http://www.fair.org/index.php?page=5

FAIRNESS & ACCURACY IN REPORTING, Inc. (FAIR), a registered 501(c) (3) non-profit organization, is a national media watch group that has been offering well-documented criticism of media bias and censorship since 1986. It works to invigorate the First Amendment by advocating for greater diversity in the press and by scrutinizing media practices that marginalize public interest, minority and dissenting viewpoints. As an anti-censorship organization, FAIR exposes neglected news stories and defends working journalists when they are muzzled. "As a progressive group, FAIR believes that structural reform is ultimately needed to break up the dominant media conglomerates, establish independent public broadcasting and promote strong non-profit sources of information." Along with producing CounterSpin, FAIR publishes Extra!, the hard-hitting magazine of media criticism. http://www.fair. org/index.php?page=100

DEMOCRACY NOW

> *For true democracy to work, people need easy access to independent, diverse sources of news and information. But the past two decades have seen unprecedented corporate media consolidation . . . . [S]ome fifty media conglomerates dominated all media outlets, including television, radio, newspapers, magazines, music, publishing and film. In 2000, just six corporations—corporate media outlets in the United States are legally responsible to their shareholders to maximize profits—dominated the U.S. media.*

DEMOCRACY NOW! is a national, daily, independent news and current affairs program whose "War and Peace Report" exposes audiences to people and perspectives—independent and international journalists, ordinary people from around the world who are directly affected by U.S. foreign policy, grassroots leaders and peace activists, artists, academics and independent analysts and actual debate—rarely heard via U.S. corporate-sponsored media.

Broadcast on Pacifica, NPR, community and college radio stations, public access, PBS, and satellite television including Free Speech TV (as well as being accessible online), Democracy Now! is hosted by Amy Goodman and Juan Gonzalez. http://www.democracynow.org/about

DEUTSCHE WELLE

Regulated by public law and financed by federal tax revenue, Deutsche Welle—known for its in-depth, reliable news and information in 30 languages (in Arabic and Kiswahili, Indonesian and Urdu, Russian and Spanish, German and English)—provides a full range of television, radio and online services. Classifying facts, explaining contexts and analyzing background, DW represents Germany in the international media landscape and is Germany's international broadcaster "[conveying] the country as a nation rooted in European culture and as a liberal, democratic state based on the rule of law."

As part of its statutory mission, DW worldwide works independently to present events and developments in Germany and the world (its programming reaches audiences in Africa, Asia, Australia and North America, keeping people connected to Germany and Europe); and picks up on German and other points of view on important issues. Deutsche Welle promotes exchange and understanding between the world's cultures and peoples and provides access to the German language, the daily life and the mentality of the people. In addition to regular news updates are insightful audio programs such as "Inside Europe," "Living Planet," "News Pulse," "Spectrum," "World in Progress," "WorldLink." http://www.dw.de/dw/article/0,,15703993,00.html; http://mediacenter. dw.de/english/audio/; http://mediacenter.dw.de/english/audio/

EURANET

On air since April 2008, the European Radio Network *Euranet* is an amalgamation of international, national, regional and local European broadcasters covering events in Europe from a transnational point of view. "Euranet brings a whole new dimension to reporting in Europe," aiming "set up better communication between European citizens and European Union (EU) policy-makers." Its cross-border initiative and joint programs, its multi-lingual, interactive audio offerings create a sense of togetherness and improve European communication. Among *Euranet*'s international news and analysis programs in English is "Network Europe Weekly." http://www.euranet.eu/eng/About-us

FREE SPEECH RADIO NEWS (FSRN)

Free Speech Radio News, heard daily on more than 100 community radio stations in the United States, reports national and international news as it affects real people and communities. http://fsrn.org/ http://www.facebook.com/pages/Free-Speech-Radio-News/37532461796 Free Speech Radio News [Pacifica Reporters against Censorship dba FSRN] is 'the only daily half-hour progressive radio newscast in the United States that is owned and managed by news reporters.'

Established in 2000 by 43 reporters who had worked for Pacifica Network News, FSRN is an independent news organization of hundreds of journalists reporting from dozens of states within the United States and scores of countries—including the Occupied Territories (Israel/Palestine), Iraq, Afghanistan, Argentina, Mexico, Nigeria and other African and Arab states. FSRN broadcasts over community stations (including five Pacifica Network stations) and via shortwave and the Internet. http://www.sourcewatch.org/index.php?title=Free_Speech_Radio_News

FSRN links to The Real News Network http://fsrn.org/content/real-news-network-fsrnorg/8184

Among the community stations over which FSRN airs is KPFA, the first community supported radio station (founded 1949) in the United States, broadcasting on 94.1 FM and KPFB 89.3 FM—Berkeley, and KFCF 88.1 FM-Fresno (California). KPFA's published mission: "to promote cultural diversity and pluralistic community expression; contribute to a lasting understanding among individuals of all nations, races, creeds and colors; promote freedom of the press and serve as a forum for various viewpoints; and maintain an independent funding base."

Pravda.ru

The largest news and analytical Internet-holding in Russia, Pravda.Ru attracts 4 million "Unique users" and "50 million" page views; and is the first Russian online newspaper to launch an English version. Based in Moscow, Pravda Online also offers Portuguese and Italian versions and plans Chinese and the Arabian versions. [Staraya Basmannaya Street, 16/2 Moscow, Russia, dmitry.sudakov@pravda.ru] http://english.pravda.ru/adv.html

The Internet-based news source, Pravda Online, is unaffiliated with the earlier Russian Pravda or with other newspapers using the name Pravda ("Truth"). http://en.wikipedia.org/wiki/Pravda.ru

Press TV

With global headquarters in Tehran, Iran, and staffed by outstanding Iranian and foreign media professionals and extensively networked with bureaus in "the world's most strategic cities," Press TV is the first Iranian international news network broadcasting 24 hours in English. Its vision includes—

- "Heeding often neglected voices and perspectives of a great portion of the world;
- Embracing and building bridges of cultural understanding;
- Encouraging human beings of different nationalities, races and creeds to identify with one another; and
- Bringing to light untold and overlooked stories of individuals who have experienced the vitality and versatility of political and cultural divides firsthand." http://www.presstv.com/about.html

RADIO NETHERLANDS WORLDWIDE

Via radio, television and the Internet, Dutch international public broadcaster Radio Netherlands Worldwide provides millions with 24-hour independent news, current affairs and service information. RNW works in ten languages (Dutch, English, Spanish, Portuguese, Arabic, French, Chinese, Indonesian, Papiamento and Sarnami) and from a Dutch perspective. Every day journalists, program makers, presenters, technicians, producers and others of more than 20 nationalities create distinctive and much-discussed radio program, video productions and websites. Occasionally RNW collaborates with non-profit organizations such as UNICEF, Amnesty International and Oxfam Novib; and works with Dutch government ministries, newspapers (NRC, Trouw and de Volkskrant), cultural institutions (e.g. the Royal Concertgebouw Orchestra) and public broadcasters. At an international level, RNW works intensively with local radio stations and other media partners in their target areas.

Headquartered in Hilversum, Radio Netherlands Worldwide belongs to the top five international public broadcasting organizations in the world. Some key programs: "Bridges with Africa," "Earth Beat," "South Asia Wired," "The State Were In" http://corporate.rnw.nl/english/who-are-we http://corporate.rnw.nl/english/article/mission-and-aims

"The State We're In" ("How we treat each other around the world") is a weekly radio program produced by Radio Netherlands Worldwide that features interviews and first-person stories from around the world about how we treat each other. "The State We're In" website is TSWI.org. See also http://www.facebook.com/tswi.org; http://www.rnw.nl/english/dossier/thestatewerein

Brief bios of chapter-lead quoted women

Alphabetically by last name

HANNAH ARENDT (1906-1975): German-born (1940 refugee from Nazi Germany to the United States, naturalized 1950) philosopher, political theorist, and academic who was chief editor of Schocken Books (1946-1948); and author of *Origins of Totalitarianism*, the (1951), *Human condition*, the (1958), *Eichmann in Jerusalem* (1963), *Life of the mind*, the (published posthumously, 1978).

SUSAN BROWNMILLER ([Warhaftig] 1935—): United States writer, researcher, activist whose pioneering work is the well-known book on the politics of rape (1975), *Against Our Will: Men, Women, and Rape*, selected by the New York Public Library as "one of 100 most important books of the Twentieth Century."

In 1968, Brownmiller signed the "Writers and Editors War Tax Protest" pledge, an anti-Vietnam War vow refusing to make tax payments. She also participated in 1960s equal rights movements [with CORE (Congress of Racial Equality) and SNCC (Student Nonviolent Coordinating Committee) during sit ins, with Freedom Summer (1964), on voter registration in Meridian, Mississippi, with the women's liberation in New York City]. She wrote for various print and broadcast outlets from the 1950s through the 1990s. In the 1970s came "Women speak out on rape" (1971), *Against Our Will* (1975) and the co-founding of "Women against Pornography" (1979); in the 1990s, a memoir and history of "Second Wave" radical feminism, *In Our Time: Memoir of a Revolution* (1999). The Susan Brownmiller papers are archived at the Arthur and Elizabeth Schlesinger Library on the History of Women in America. [Wikipedia, edited]

Related to Brownmiller's work Related: ANNE LLEWELLYN BARSTOW

War's Dirty Secret: Rape, Prostitution, and Other Crimes against Women (Pilgrim Press, 2001) edited by Anne Llewellyn Barstow, professor (ret.), historian, political activist. http://www.britannica.com/bps/user-profile/5881/Anne-L.-Barstow; http://www.feministpress.org/books/anne-llewellyn-barstow

Excerpt from a review[http://www.witherspoonsociety.org/dirty_secret.htm] by the Barbara Battin, Centerville, Ohio (divinity): In *War's Dirty Secret: Rape, Prostitution, and Other Crimes against Women*, Battin writes, "War-wounded women have spoken and their stories in Barstow's work impel us to speak out . . . . Barstow's work collecting and sharing the many stories of women and war

- Fulfills her intent 'to change the way (we) think about war'
- Gives us the information we need to give voice to the sexual violence that war perpetrates against women
- Inspires us to reveal the horrors of war to the world so that there may be an outcry against it."

HELEN FREMONT (1957—) United States writer, editor, academic, and attorney has authored several essays and pieces of fiction and her first book (1999), the story of her parents' survival of the Soviet and Nazi occupations and her own attempts to piece together her family's hidden identity, is the memoir *After Long Silence* https://oldmy.champlain.edu/public/community.book.program/afterlongsilence/fremontbio.php; http://www.randomhouse.ca/author/results.pperl?authorid=9328

INDIRA GANDHI (Indira Priyad Arshini Gandhi, 1917-1984): Recognized globally for her work as a leader of the developing nations, an activist on independence (1940s), politician, party leader, lawmaker (1950s-), and three-term Prime Minister of India (1966-1977); assassinated during in her fourth term (1980-1984) in office.

LORRAINE HANSBERRY (1930-1965): United States playwright and recipient of New York Drama Critics Circle Award for her 1959 play *A Raisin in the Sun*; posthumously (1970) her play *Les Blancs* voted Best American Play. She also wrote *The sign in Sidney Brustein's Window*, staged shortly before her death (1964); *To be young, gifted and black*, a dramatic self-portrait, is a selection of Hansberry's writings and letters assembled posthumously (1969).

HELEN ADAMS KELLER (1880-1968): United States writer, lecturer and educator (born blind and deaf); author of *The Story of My Life* (1903), *Optimism* (1903), *The World I Live In* (1908), *My Religion* (1927), *Helen Keller's Journal* (1938), and *The Open Door* (1957). She established a $2 million endowment fund for the American Foundation for the Blind on whose behalf she had done lecture tours that took her several times around the world.

BELVA LOCKWOOD (Belva Ann Bennett Lockwood, 1830-1917): United States lawyer and reformer, strong pacifist and member of the nominating committee for the Nobel Peace Prize, a skilled vigorous supporter of women's rights, the first woman to practice before the U.S. Supreme Court and helped promote reforms such as the Equal Pay Act for women civil servants (1872). As a member of the National Equal Rights Party, Lockwood was nominated in 1884 and 1888 for the U.S. presidency.

MAIREAD CORRIGAN MAGUIRE (1944—): Northern Irish peace activist and co-founder of the Peace People, a grassroots movement of Roman Catholic and Protestant citizens dedicated to ending the sectarian strife in Northern Ireland. Nobel Peace laureate (1976 with Betty Williams and Ciaran McKeown), joint founder (2006 with fellow Nobel Peace Prize laureates Shirin Ebadi, Jody Williams, Wangari Maathai, and Rigoberta Menchú) of the Nobel Women's Initiative.

MARGARET MEAD [Bateson] (1901-1978): United States anthropologist, researcher, writer, New York City American Museum of Natural History curator; author of *Coming of Age in Samoa* (1928/1968), *Growing Up in New Guinea* (1930/1975), *Sex and Temperament in Three Primitive Societies* (1935/reprinted 1968), *Continuities in Cultural Evolution* (1964), *Male and Female: A Study of the Sexes in a Changing World (1949/new ed. 1975)*, *Anthropology: A Human Science* (1964), *Culture and Commitment* (1970), *Ruth Benedict* (1974 biography), an autobiography of her own early years, *Blackberry Winter* (1972), *Letters from the Field* (1977). Posthumously (1979), Margaret

Mead received the United States' highest civilian honor, the Presidential Medal of Freedom.

ERIKA MUNK (1939—): Author, reporter, editor lecturer on whom biographical material is hard to find; but she appears to have been at some point associated with the Yale School of Drama and Yale Repertory Theatre and edited the journal *Up Front Theater*. She also appears on panelist lists for Socialist Scholars Conferences sponsored by the Democratic Socialists of America and the Campaign for Peace and Democracy lists her as an endorser [www.cpdweb.org/endor.shtml]. The Nation Magazine website carries this note linked into web search engines: "Erika Munk is on the faculty of the Yale University School of Drama and is editor of Theater. She reported from Bosnia and Croatia in 1993, 1994 and 1996."

ELEANOR ROOSEVELT (Anna Eleanor Roosevelt, 1884-1962): United States writer, lecturer, diplomat, humanitarian who, as delegate to the United Nations Assembly, chaired the Commission on Human Rights (1946-51) [later through 1952 U.S. representative to the UN General Assembly] and played a major role in the drafting and adoption of the *Universal Declaration of Human Rights* (1948). As United States First Lady (1933-1945) and after, she toured extensively throughout the United States reporting to the president; and traveled several times around the world visiting scores of countries, conferring with most of the world's leaders. Particularly interested in the welfare of children, reforms in housing and equal rights for women and minorities, Eleanor Roosevelt inaugurated regular White House press conferences for women correspondents, forcing wire services to hire women to ensure their wires' representation. In 1936, Eleanor Roosevelt began writing a daily syndicated newspaper column ("My Day") and continued this work into 1962. Her books include, This is my story, *This I remember*, *India and the Awakening East*, *You learn by living*, *The Lady of the White House* (1938), *The Moral basis of Democracy* (1940), *On My Own* (1958), *The Autobiography of Eleanor Roosevelt* (1937, 1949, 1958, 1960, 1961) [ER told her own story in various places: in addition to the 'My Day' columns, she published her autobiography in magazine installments, in multiple volumes, and finally in an abridged form as *Eleanor Roosevelt, Autobiography* (1961, reissued in 1992 as *The Autobiography of Eleanor Roosevelt*]. *The Eleanor Roosevelt*

Story by Archibald MacLeish published in 1965; Transcripts of ER's press conferences in Maurine Beasley (ed.): *The White House Press Conferences of Eleanor Roosevelt* (1987); by Blanche Wiesen Cook: *Eleanor Roosevelt*, 2 volumes (1992-99)

The Author

Dr. Carolyn L. Bennett is credentialed in education and print journalism and public affairs. A lifelong American writer and writer/ activist (former academic and staffer with the U.S. government in Washington), her work concerns itself with news and current affairs, historical contexts and ideas particularly related to acts and consequences of U.S. foreign relations, geopolitics, human rights, war and peace, violence and nonviolence. Bennett is an internationalist and nonpartisan progressive personally concerned with society and the common good. An educator at heart, her career began with U.S. Peace Corps teaching in Sierra Leone, West Africa. Since then, she has authored several books and numerous current affairs articles; her most recent writings are posted at *Bennett's Study*: http://todaysinsightnews.blogspot.com/. She lives in the town of Brighton at the edge of New York's Finger Lakes along the Erie Canal looking west-northwest to Niagara Falls; and can be reached at authorswork@gmail.com or cwriter85@frontiernet.net.

Works by this author

Same Ole or Something New: Uprooting Power ENTRENCHMENT
BREAKDOWN: Violence in Search of U (you)-Turn
Women's Work and Words Altering World Order
Missing News and Views in Paranoid Times
No Room for Despair: How to Hope in Troubled Times; Mary McLeod
Bethune's Cold War, Integration-era Commentary
Talking Back to Today's News
America's Human Connection

An Annotated Bibliography of Mary McLeod Bethune's Chicago Defender Columns, 1948-1955
You Can Struggle without Hating, Fight without Violence
Numerous current affairs articles, most recent ones published at Bennett's Study *Today's Insight News,* http://todaysinsightnews.blogspot.com.

Acknowledgements and Permissions

The "Fair Use" doctrine in copyright matters, as Wikipedia (http://en.wikipedia.org/wiki/Fair_use) puts it, is a limitation and exception to the exclusive right granted by copyright law to the author of a creative work. "In United States copyright law, fair use is a doctrine that permits limited use of copyrighted material without acquiring permission from the rights holders. Examples of fair use include **commentary,** criticism, **news reporting, research**, teaching, library archiving and scholarship. It provides for the legal, unlicensed citation or incorporation of copyrighted material in another author's work under a four-factor balancing test."

In determining whether the use made of a work in any particular case is a fair use the factors to be considered shall include:

(1) The purpose and character of the use, including whether such use is of a commercial nature or is for nonprofit educational purposes; **[*No Land an Island* is news reporting and re-reporting and educational though not nonprofit]**

(2) The nature of the copyrighted work;

(3) The amount and substantiality of the portion used in relation to the copyrighted work as a whole; **[the use photos and other images of others is limited, for illustration and credited throughout the book]** and

(4) The effect of the use upon the potential market for or value of the copyrighted work **[the use of images has no impact on original sources of copyrighted material]**.

Though my books are technically "commercial," money and profit have never been my driving force. I am an independent news writer and former university professor. I have never profited monetarily from my books. Their primary purposes are for reference and further study, to educate, to inform, to help fill a critical gap in clarity, perspective and understanding.

UNHCR images

United Nations High Commissioner for Refugees (The UN Refugee Agency)
Published in UNHCR's Photostream at Flickr http://www.flickr.com/photos/unhcr/
Reprinted with captions and republished by Permission of UNHCR
Seventeen images

08580.jpg

Somalia / Asylum seekers and migrants / In the cliffs of Mareero, a smuggler's departure point 14 km east of Puntland's commercial port, Bossaso, Somalis wait for the evening departure of the smuggler's boat they hope will take them to Yemen. / UNHCR / K. McKinzey / February 2006

14408.jpg

Somalia / Internally displaced people (IDPs) / / UNHCR / A. Webster / December 2006

17443.jpg

Somalia / Bosasso beach / UNHCR / A. Webster / December 2006

21730.jpg

Afghanistan / returnees / Fetching water. Members of Mr Shafi's family who are ethnic Turkmen, known for their carpet weaving skills. / Qalinbafan. / UNHCR / R. Arnold / October 2008

Qalinbafan is located in Balkh province's Nahre Shahi district, 20 km from Mazar-e-Sharif city, just beside the main road leading to Jawzjan and Herat. This is a land allocation site, and the government has allocated plots of land to Afghans who returned from Pakistan over the years, including returnees from Jalozai refugee village in 2007. About 85 ethnic Turkmen families live here. Half of them weave carpets for a living. UNHCR has provided shelter assistance, and worked with the authorities to drill a deep well in the settlement.

25722.jpg

Pakistan / Jalozai camp / Recently arrived IDPs transport a rug to their tent in Jalozai camp which hosts 47,000 people (extension of the camp - does not include previous influxes to Jalozai). As of may 27, some 2 million people had escaped the conflict in Swat, Lower Dir and Buner areas between governmental forces and Taliban groups. UNHCR / H. Caux / May 21, 2009

028205.jpg

Afghanistan / A transit camp was set up by UNHCR and aid agencies in the remote northern part of Afghanistan to host Afghan returnees from a two-decade exile in Iran. / UNHCR / W. Schellenberg / August 2009

029499.jpg

Pakistan / Yar Hussain / Women and children enjoy some more privacy behing the purdha walls (plastic sheeting and cloths provided by UNHCR). The journey to the camps and life in the camps has proved being a cultural shock for displaced women who had been living in confinement in their houses surrounded by walls in Swat and Buner districts before the conflict. Upon arrival in the camps, women were then confined to stay in the tents. "There are many men we don't know in the camp" says one of them. "In Swat, we would only leave our homes for exceptionnal circumstances, such as a wedding, a burial or a to go to the hospital. We would then be wearing a burqa and would be accompanied by a

030015.jpg

Yemen / UNHCR staff assisting IDPS after heavy rain storms destroyed a number of tents in Al Mazraq camp in haradb, northern yemen. / UNHCR Distribution of mattresses at the camp. / UNHCR / L. Chedrawi / September 2009

033402.jpg

Kenya / Somali Refugees / Dadaab / Newly arrived refugees from Somalia wait for registration at IFO camp. / UNHCR / R. Gangale / May 2010

035700.jpg

Pakistan / Floods / A couple of bed frames provide some shade and shelter from the sun for displaced people in Jacobabad / UNHCR / P. Kessler / 20 September 2010

041203.jpg

Afghanistan / The Yousef family and their Kitchen Garden Project at their home in Chamtala Returnee Settlement Nagnarhar Province. The family returned from Pakistan 3 years ago. They had spent almost 20 years as refugees in Pakistan, leaving shortly after the Soviet invasion. The family received a grant, through the shelter assistance program, to build a new home which they share with 8 other members of the family. The home was completed in 4 months, but they say they still require a boundary wall and a secure main gate. The family were also beneficiaries of a Kitchen Garden livelihood project, which now provides enough vegetables for family consumption and spare capacity for sale in the local market, generating some $30-40 per month in income. They grow, spinach, egg plant, tomatoes, broccoli and

044321.jpg

Somalia/ Mogadishu/ An internally displaced woman carries UNHCR aid supplies to her shelter at the Maajo IDP settlement in Mogadishu, Somalia on August 31, 2011 during a two days UNHCR delegation visit to drought and famine stricken southern Somalia / UNHCR/ S. Modola/ August 2011

044454.jpg

Kenya / Somali refugees / Dahira, 11 years old, holds her severely malnourished baby brother Mahad, age 2, in Dagahaley refugee camp. The family arrived in the sprawling refugee camp in June after fleeing drought and war in Baidabo, Bay region, Somalia. The journey took them 20 days. They traveled by road to Dobley and from Dobley at the Kenya border they travelled by foot and were set upon by bandits who beat the adults. Mahad was admitted to the therapeutic feeding unit at the MSF run hospital on the day these pictures were made. / UNHCR / B. Bannon / 28 July 2011

045385.jpg

Kenya / In 2011 refugees fled Somalia in such numbers that the existing camps in dadaab kenya couldn't hold them. They settled on the outskirts of Dagahaley and Ifo in self built structures. These are at the edge of Dagahaley and the refugees here are being moved to Ifo extention a tented camp that opened in august 2011 that is closer to services, schools and health centers. October 2011. Brendan Bannon/IOM/UNHCR

048676.jpg

Pakistan / A makeshift kitchen within a UNHCR emergency relief camp for flood affected communities in Zareen Khan, Sanghar District, Sindh, Pakistan on September 27, 2011. In August 2011, Heavy monsoon rains triggered flooding in lower parts of Sindh and northern parts of Punjab. To date, the Government of Pakistan reports that more than 5.3 million people have been affected. Over 300 people have lost their lives, over 4.2 million acres of land flooded and 1.59 million acres of crops destroyed. UNHCR is supplying 10,000 tents, 20,000 plastic sheets and 10,000 kits of household items as an emergency response to flood affected communities in Sindh Province. Contingent on an emergency funding appeal, UNHCR will be able to supply another 20,000 tents and relief items. / UNHCR / S. Phelps /

049610.jpg

Colombia / Recording the song "This is my territory" in the streets of Lleras, a slum in Buenaventura on Colombia's Pacific Coast. This is My Territory, a music group of 27 young Afro-Colombians, is making its first music video with help from the UN refugee agency / UNHCR / F. Fontanini / 2011

049783.jpg

Costa Rica / Costa Rican Youth Organization La Red de Jovenes sin Fronteras strives to combat xenophobia / Members of La Red de Jovenes sin Fronteras walk through downtown San Jose to raise awareness for refugees, on the occasion of World Refugee Day / UNHCR / P. Mora / 20 June 2011

050663.jpg

Yemen / Two girls stand in front of her family's classroom at 30 November school, Aden, March 13, 2012 / UNHCR / P. Rubio Larraori / March 2012
****NOT TO BE DISTRIBUTED TO THE MEDIA****

United Nations Security Council image

United Nations Photo Library, Audiovisual Services Section, News &
Media Division,
Department of Public Information, 300 East 42nd Street, New York,
Room: IN-506A (5th floor)
Phone: 212 963 0034 I Email: photolibr@un.org

Liberian President Ellen Johnson Sirleaf image

Public domain Whitehouse image

Liberian President Ellen Johnson Sirleaf waves to the audience at her
inauguration in Monrovia, Liberia, Monday, Jan. 16, 2006. President
Sirleaf is Africa's first female elected head of state. White House
'frozen in time' photo by Shealah Craighead ."This is historical
material, 'frozen in time.' The web site is no longer updated and
links to external web sites and some internal pages will not work"
http://georgewbush-whitehouse.archives.gov/news/releases/2006/01/
images/20060116-2_p011606sc-0297-1-595v.html

Map images

Worldatlas (graphic maps) images

Maps, graphics, flags, photos and original descriptions copyrighted by and created by Graphic Maps . . .
All maps, graphics, flags, photos and original descriptions copyrighted by and created by Graphic Maps; U.S. and Italy: Graphic Maps (and/or) Worldatlas.com
http://www.worldatlas.com/contact/contact.htm
U.S.A. Office: 317.550.8799; Postal Mailing Address
Graphic Maps (and/or) Worldatlas.com
2724 61st Street, Suite B, #107, Galveston, Texas 77551 USA
Rome, Italy, Office: (39) 349.728.1580
Postal Mailing Address: Woolwine-Moen Group, d/b/a Graphic Maps
Via Ludovica Albertoni 64, Interno 10, 00152 Roma, Italy

Principal Contacts:
John Moen Managing Director email
Christina Woolwine-Moen Managing Partner email
Silvano Verdat European Sales and Map Projects email
Stephanie Downing-Cantwell Website Designer and Content Manager email
Cindy Reif Research and Development email
Robin Story Research and Development email
http://www.worldatlas.com/contact/contact.htm

Drone images

U.S. Department of Defense Public domain drone images

07/15/2005

Drone Launch

A BQM-74E drone launches from the USS Boxer's flight deck in the South China Sea, July 13, 2005, during the at-sea phase of "Cooperation Afloat Readiness and Training 2005" in Malaysia. The drone can be used to simulate nearly any kind of aerial threat and gives exercise participants a live-fire threat simulation. U.S. Navy photo by Airman Paul Polach http://www.defense.gov/transformation/images/photos/2005-07/Hi-Res/050713-N-3455P-003.jpg

http://www.defense.gov/transformation/images/photos/2005-07/Hi-Res/050713-N-3455P-003.jpg

07/21/2005

Remote-Controlled Drone

A BQM-74E remote-controlled drone takes off from the flight deck of USS Samuel B. Roberts prior to starting a live-fire exercise in the Caribbean Sea, July 19, 2005. U.S. Navy photo by Petty Officer 1st Class Michael Sandberg http://www.defense.gov/transformation/images/photos/2005-07/Hi-Res/050719-N-4374S-003.jpg

http://www.defense.gov/transformation/images/photos/photo_archive/index_2005-07.html

2/22/2006

Missile Fire

This F-22A Raptor from the 27th Fighter Squadron, Langley Air Force Base, Va., fires an AIM-120 Advanced Medium Range Air-to-Air Missile at an aerial target drone over the Gulf of Mexico during a Combat Archer mission Feb. 14. This missile is one of the first fired from an F-22A Raptor. U.S. Air Force photo by Master Sgt. Michael Ammons

http://www.defense.gov/transformation/images/photos/2006-02/Hi-Res/IMG0052.jpg

NATO protest

U.S. House of Representatives Public Domain image at House Press Gallery http://housepressgallery.house.gov/

ICC façade

Other notes and credits

The book cover was designed by Xlibris graphic designer Christina Borja and based on an idea by the author and a draft by Rochester, New York, graphic designer Tina Screib. The author gratefully acknowledges overall coordination by Author Services Representative Carla Cobar; and copyediting, layout, formatting and indexing services and assistance by Xlibris staff, consultants, and contractors.

Index

The letter *t* following a page number denotes a table.
The letter *c* following a page number denotes a chart.